The Myth of Neurosis

Garth Wood was educated at Harrow and Trinity College, Cambridge, and qualified as a doctor at the Royal Free Hospital, London. He underwent training analysis with the Adlerians, and until recently he was Senior House Officer in Psychiatry at the University College Hospital, London, where he had been researching into the effects of exercise on the symptoms of anxiety and depression. This is his first book.

The Myth of Neurosis

a case for moral therapy

Dr Garth Wood

MACMILLAN

ISBN 0 333 38302 8

First published 1983 by Macmillan London Limited

Published in paperback 1984 by
PAPERMAC
a division of Macmillan Publishers Limited
4 Little Essex Street London WC2R 3LF
and Basingstoke

Associated companies in Auckland, Delhi, Dublin, Gaborone, Hamburg,
Harare, Hong Kong, Johannesburg, Kuala Lumpur, Lagos, Manzini,
Melbourne, Mexico City, Nairobi, New York, Singapore and Tokyo

Reprinted 1984

Filmset in Times by Filmtype Services Limited, Scarborough, North Yorkshire

Printed in Great Britain by The Pitman Press, Bath

Contents

To my wife Pat
and son Orlando
with all my love.

1

An Introduction to Moral Therapy

In this book I have sought to expose the clandestine conspiracy to extend indefinitely the boundaries of mental illness. For far too long people have been led to believe that the person suffering from an excess of life's problems needs 'expert' medical and psychotherapeutic intervention, thus allowing the 'patient' to qualify for 'illness', to the ultimate detriment of his mental equilibrium and often at considerable financial cost. Such a view is dangerous nonsense. If we are not ill then we are well, although we may be unhappy.

In order that we should know where we, and those dear to us, stand with regard to psychological illness, I have explained the ways in which psychiatrists make their diagnoses. It is far easier than one might think. The chapters entitled 'Are You Mentally Ill?', and 'A Layman's Guide to Psychiatric Diagnosis' demonstrate clearly the differences between real psychiatric disease such as schizophrenia and manic-depressive illness and those normal but unpleasant mental states which are an inescapable and often valuable part of everyday living. In demystifying the diagnostic process and showing the layman how to recognise disease and the lack of it, he will be prevented from employing the potentially damaging illness excuse in situations in which psychopathology does not exist, and encouraged to seek help from psychiatrists when it does.

In the redefinition of the proper boundaries of psychological illness I argue for a tougher, more rigorous and uncompromising attitude towards what does and what does not constitute disease. In particular I disavow and disallow the concept of neurosis. It is neither a useful diagnostic category, nor even an adequate

1

descriptive term. Its bogus status as a psychological condition has led to the wrongful inclusion within the illness category of millions of people whose chief deficiency is their inadequate approach to problems and their unrealistic expectations of what life should give them. A huge industry of therapists has created itself to minister to, and profit from, the plight of these 'neurotics', thus institutionalising their 'condition' whilst bolstering the prestige and self-esteem of these disciples of psychodynamism.

So, too, it serves no purpose to regard aggressive psychopaths or sociopaths as being psychologically diseased. We already have a perfectly good concept to explain and describe their moral bankruptcy. It is the notion of evil. Extreme wickedness is no surer indicator of mental illness than is extreme goodness, and we would do well not to confuse evil with disease.

In calling for a contraction of the whole field of psychiatry, for greater accuracy in the diagnosis of genuine disease, I am in conflict with those who would extend its boundaries indefinitely, thereby creating for themselves lucrative and prestigious new kingdoms at the ultimate expense of those they seek to treat. These misguided myth-makers have encouraged us to believe that the infinite mysteries of the mind are as amenable to their professed expertise as the plumbing or the motor-car engine. This is rubbish. In fact these talk therapists, practitioners of cosmetic psychiatry, have no relevant training or skills in the art of living life. It is remarkable that they have fooled us for so long. From the pages of magazines, books and newspapers, from the screens of our TV sets we are bombarded with 'clever' intellectual explanations of the reasons why we do things, why we think things. Cowed by their status as men of science, deferring to their academic titles, bewitched by the initials after their names we, the gullible, lap up their pretentious nonsense as if it was the gospel truth. We must learn to recognise them for what they are – possessors of no special knowledge of the human psyche, who have, none the less, chosen to earn their living from the dissemination of the myth that they do indeed know how the mind works, are thoroughly conversant with the 'rules' that govern human behaviour.

It has therefore been necessary to mount a two-pronged attack on the apparently opposing groups of practitioners who would force on the individual the role of patient in the absence of hard evidence of illness. On the one hand are Freud, his psychodynamic fellow travellers, and the pedlars of the talking cures who, despite the widest differences in philosophies must be considered his natural sons. To take money for mere talk, is, I would argue, in many cases, both negligent and despite the purest of motives, irresponsible. Freudian theories, and their offspring are irrelevant where they are not actually dangerous. They harm the individual in his pursuit of mental health, and by encouraging dependency and sterile introversion lower self-respect. Above all they delay interminably that brave confrontation of life's problems in which alone salvation lies. Such an approach relies for its popularity on the indubitable fact that talking about ourselves is strongly pleasurable, that we all like to be the centre of attention in situations devoid of threat, to perform before a captive and benevolent audience. In pandering to this mildly unworthy desire these people do us more than a disservice. For, to the extent that such talk therapy is pleasant, and its withdrawal difficult and traumatic, I would argue that, like valium and cocaine, it is psychologically addictive. In the short term it may make us feel better – a quick fix of confidence – but over the years we will pay a considerable price in terms of dependency and lowered self-esteem.

Apparently ranged against the Freudians and their talk therapist progeny but in fact sharing their expert/patient approach to the individual suffering a surfeit of life's problems, are the medico-biologists. Instead of intellectual insights, and exotic theories, their stock-in-trade is chemical panaceas which they dish out like sweets to individuals who are not ill. In both cases the end result is the same – a passive 'patient' prostrate at the feet of the 'healer', suffering the psychological pain of guilt as he learns to like himself less.

So talk therapy and the prescribing of valium offer no solutions in the absence of illness. They must be replaced by something of value. I offer a Moral Therapy, a philosophy based not on fantasies and pseudo-intellectual gymnastics, nor on a naive reliance on chemistry to provide the soma for a brave new world, but on common sense, on what we know in our hearts. Nobody gets paid for practising Moral Therapy. Nobody profits from solving the problems of others except in feeling that natural satisfaction we all experience when we have been of service. There are no experts, no Training Institutes, no degrees or examinations, no gurus. There is nothing but us, our experience of life, our warmth and empathy, the voice of our conscience.

In the absence of psychological illness we can practise the principles of Moral Therapy on ourselves and on others. Contentedness can only exist if self-respect is high. Only if we like ourselves can we be happy. At all times and in all situations we must obey our *own* moral codes. Only by doing what *we* ourselves consider to be right and good can we travel the royal road to self-respect. Insofar as we disregard our moral imperatives we must suffer the psychological pain of guilt. If we use the guilt mechanism properly and recoil from those actions which cause it to operate, it will serve us well. In the absence of disease, then, guilt is good for us.

It is vital that we avoid misconceptions about the nature of life, and expose as fallacy the idea that to the extent that we are unhappy and ineffective we need 'expert' intervention. Life is tough and frequently unpleasant. Our prayer, therefore, should not be for ease but for the courage to face difficulty.

The Myth of Neurosis is not a book about psychiatry. I define psychiatric illness so that it can be excluded. What remains is individuals who are responsible for their predicament, slaves to neither their environment nor their brain biochemistry, and who are therefore free, with support, to change themselves for the better.

With the right help from friends and loved ones we can all learn to like ourselves more. As concerned and forceful friends we can become the practitioners of a new Moral Therapy. Into the vacuum created by the disappearance of the paid 'expert' will step family, friends, priests, neighbours, husbands, wives and children. For too long their rightful role has been wrongfully usurped by imposters. The time has come for them to reclaim it.

In particular we should realise and encourage others to realise that self-respect is increased by searching out and achieving more difficult rather than easier objectives. By seeking difficulty and avoiding the easy way in pursuit of what we consider to be worthy ambitions we will like ourselves more.

In summary, the ideas contained in this book represent a break with the immediate past and serve as a blueprint for a more optimistic era, heralding a return to that self-sufficiency and asceticism which forms the basis of the most widely and deeply held ethical systems. I advocate the avoidance of crutches, be they pills or psychiatrists. We must learn to do without unworthy, unprofitable and transitory pleasures such as those afforded by irresponsible sex and drugs, choosing instead the tough and difficult way in order that we may experience the true contentedness which flows alone from the contemplation of a hard task well done.

2
Guilt, Morals and Self-Respect

Many of us choose to think of life's problems as unpleasant, but apparently inevitable phenomena which threaten our natural state of contentedness. We feel that we have a right to be happy and that it is only the problems of life that prevent our being so. This is a mistaken and inaccurate judgement. Man has no natural right to happiness. It is obtained only through great hardship and effort and instrumental to its attainment are the very problems of life which most of us regard with such disdain. For in overcoming difficulties and problems we increase our self-respect, and it is the central thesis of this book that self-respect and contentedness are synonymous. We cannot be happy and effective unless we like ourselves. Only if we are satisfied with our thoughts and actions can we be contented.

There is only one way to increase self-respect and that is by confronting directly the difficulties that we face. For in most situations we have a shrewd awareness of what we ought to do and ought not to do and are more or less aware of the difficulties involved in the various courses of action open to us. If we listen to our own individual moral imperatives and attempt courageously to obey them our self-respect must increase. The increase in self-respect will be directly proportional to the degree of difficulty and the amount of vigour and determination that we apply to the task. If we try hard, ultimate success is not necessary for the gain in self-respect. It is the journey and the struggle that are important, never the destination. It is apparently paradoxical that relative contentedness is achieved not by escaping our self-accepted responsibilities but by embracing them; not by indulging in what we acknowledge to be our baser

6

desires but by resisting them; not by taking the easy way but by seeking the most difficult.

Each individual has his own unique moral code, fashioned and learned from the sum of his experiences. He departs from it only at the risk of compromising his self-respect. In avoiding such a disastrous course he has an invaluable ally in the much maligned but vital psychological mechanism of guilt. In the same way that pain acts as a warning that the body is endangered, so guilt warns us that psychological equilibrium is compromised. We must listen to our guilt feelings and cease the actions that have given rise to them rather than continuing those actions whilst attempting to do away with the feelings of guilt. Thus guilt should be regarded as a valuable ally, because it will inevitably tell us when our behaviour falls short of our ideals and when self-respect is likely to be diminished. In short, in the absence of psychological illness of which it may be a symptom, guilt can be good for us if we use it correctly.

It has been the fashion in our permissive age, however, to emphasise the harmful nature of guilt feelings and to present them as unworthy, uncomfortable and unnecessarily self-limiting emotions tending to hamper self-development. The attack on guilt has come from two separate factions who on the surface would appear to have little in common. They are, however, united in their desire to alleviate the psychological pain of guilt. This is achieved by the promulgation of speculative theories whose effect is to absolve the individual from blame by denying him a large degree of responsibility for his actions.

On the one hand the psychodynamic theorists, typified by Freud, suggest that our personalities are formed at an early age in response to environmental, and particularly family influences. In later life, Freudians maintain, our dispositional tendencies to act and think in certain ways are to a very large extent determined by these early factors and can be modified only with great difficulty in the investigative process of psychoanalysis. We cannot be blamed for our current attitudes and actions since they follow inevitably from events and situations in the distant past as the result of a causal process over which we have little, if any, control. From this it must follow that it is not our fault that we are the way we are, that we do the things we do, that we think the things we think. There is no point in the psychological pain of guilt since we cannot benefit from its warning and change our attitudes and behaviour. We are blameless, but we are also impotent. We are not at fault but we are unable to help ourselves. Instead we must enlist the support of the psychoanalyst. Thus we pay a terrible price for our absolution, for how can we have self-respect if we are not responsible for what we are?

Ranged against the Freudians and neo-Freudians are those of a more biological bent who stress the speculative nature of psychoanalytic theories and point to the lack of evidence for the truth of their assertions. They prefer what they consider to be a more scientific approach. Such people tend to regard a situation in which an individual appears unhappy and sad, seems unable to cope with life's problems, is guilty and has low self-respect, in terms of an 'illness' model. The person is, or is well on the way to being, a 'patient' who 'has' a 'neurosis' or a 'personality disorder' in much the same way that he has bronchitis or a broken leg.

In support of this view they might produce evidence that both mental and physical behaviour are closely related to brain pathology and brain biochemistry. Depressive illness seems to respond to both electro-convulsive therapy as well as to tri-cyclic drugs. Schizophrenic symptoms are alleviated by phenothiazines. General paralysis of the insane (GPI) was shown in 1911 to be related to infection with the organism which causes syphilis. Thus, whilst admitting that physical treatment for 'neurosis' and 'personality disorder' are not presently available, adherents of the strictly biological approach might be expected to look to the area of pharmacology for an eventual cure.

In the meantime the person who might, for example, have been diagnosed as having a 'mild neurotic depressive illness' will be reassured and supported, possibly tranquillised if anxious, sedated at night if suffering from insomnia and above all encouraged to talk freely about his problems. The doctor might advise a holiday or a few days off work. He might attempt to explain away the patient's condition by saying, 'It's just one of those things that happens. Nobody knows what causes it. Don't worry, it will go away in time.' All the doctor's remarks will have the same purpose, namely to attempt to alleviate the *immediate* suffering of the patient, who will be encouraged not to blame himself; not to feel guilty; not to accept responsibility for his predicament. Above all, his condition will be presented as one he had little power to avoid and has less power to cure. Time, tablets, rest, support and reassurance will do the job for him.

So it can be seen that both the Freudians and their opponents, who adhere to a medico-biological approach, have very similar attitudes to the 'patient'. Both agree that he is a victim of circumstance, that his low self-respect and his guilt feelings are not his fault and that he should not be blamed for them because he is to a large extent not responsible for them. As caring people, both sets of practitioners see themselves as experts whose task it is to 'cure' the patient. The means are different but the end is the same. The patient is relatively without power and must accept a passive role in relation to the healer.

This approach, springing as it does from the very best of motives, is a profoundly pessimistic one. By removing the sense of responsibility for his actions and encouraging passivity and reliance on the healer the individual is denied the one real chance that he has to escape his unpleasant psychological feelings. For unless he can increase his self-respect by striving courageously to overcome the difficulties that he faces there is no real solution to his problem. It is essential that he must feel that he alone is responsible for his success. Only then can he reap the reward of learning to like himself. This he cannot do if he in any measure feels that he has adopted a passive role – that any change in his circumstances is due either to the pharmacological skills of the physician or the psychotherapeutic ones of the analyst.

All that Moral Therapy can offer is a life of struggle and brave confrontation of life's problems. It is not an easy way, but a hard way. Essential to the philosophy is that difficult tasks should actually be sought rather than shunned and should always be preferred to easy ones. When confronted with alternative courses of action in a certain situation the individual must choose the more difficult for its own sake in order to maximise self-respect, for in taking the easy way self-respect is unlikely to be increased and may be diminished.

It may seem paradoxical that one should eschew the easy and seek the most difficult when a consideration of human nature seems to indicate that we tend to do exactly the opposite in practice. Certainly it seems to be the commonsense view that when faced with two or more possible actions we should try to choose that which offers the least problems. It is our normal view that life is about the avoidance of problems and difficulties, which we use our considerable ingenuity to minimise.

However, it is my contention that we are seldom accurate judges of our own long-term self-interests and we pay a price for taking the easy way in terms of lessened self-respect and its constant partner the emotion of guilt. Few of us realise the source of these feelings, so accepted is it that we owe ourselves 'a good time'. What we fail to understand is that our notion of a good time is based on a misconception. For any momentary enjoyment of the easy way and the avoidance of difficulty is paid for eventually by feelings of guilt. An analogy might be made with the taking of heroin. In the specious present, few, who try it, do not enjoy the experience. In the long term, after addiction has set in, the ghastly pain of withdrawal renders any short-term enjoyment inadequate and irrelevant; whilst the physiological mechanism of tolerance ensures that larger and larger doses are required to produce the same effect.

So, too, seeking the easy way rather than the most difficult carries in it the negation of its own purpose. We must pay by suffering the psychological withdrawal symptom of guilt. For it is as useless to continue to act against our own individual moral imperatives and then attempt not to feel guilty as it is to continue to take heroin and then to attempt to deal with the withdrawal symptoms when they arise. However, in this permissive age some such course is widely advocated and guilt is considered to be something that we have the right to avoid. When we do experience it we are encouraged to perform some sort of psychological surgery on ourselves to remove it. But in the real world guilt can be removed in one way and one way alone, and that is by modifying or changing our attitudes and actions to those that increase our liking for ourselves.

3
The Value of Moral Therapy

In this book I shall offer a new way of understanding people and their problems. Further I shall show how, in a new therapeutic process, people can learn to help themselves and to help others. I have called this system Moral Therapy. It is essential to demonstrate clearly the situations in which Moral Therapy is applicable.

Firstly it is no part of my intention to suggest that this therapeutic method be used in situations where actual psychiatric illness exists. People for instance, who are suffering from schizophrenia or clinical endogenous depression, in which pathological feelings of guilt, self-blame and worthlessness are common symptoms, will not be helped and may be harmed by the therapeutic approach adopted here. To apply Moral Therapy to such people would not only be cruel and misguided but, bearing in mind the high risk of suicide in severe depressive illness, might easily be fatal. Rather it is applicable to people who are not actually psychiatrically ill, but may be in danger of becoming so. Moral Therapy therefore stands in the same relation to psychiatry as preventive medicine does to clinical medicine. It cannot be overemphasised that any factors indicative of mental illness must be recognised before one uses the Moral Therapeutic approach either on oneself or on others. Later in the book it will be explained how psychiatrists do this.

The people for whom Moral Therapy is appropriate are the many individuals who perceive life's problems as so daunting that their ability to lead a contented life is severely diminished. They are people who find it difficult to make decisions. They find it difficult to act and when they do act their actions are often not in their best long-term interests, although they may appear to themselves super-ficially to be so. Such people are seldom happy. Rarely do they enjoy themselves and they feel that life is tinged with a greyness and drabness that they suspect others do not experience. Mildly anxious and mildly depressed they stumble through life living ineffectually and dreaming of improbable and fantastical victories which will transform them magically, through no effort of their own, into the sorts of individual they feel they have a right to be. They are not actually ill and may never seek advice concerning their problems. They may hold down a job, retain a marriage and appear to an observer to be functioning relatively well. But the quality of their life is low and later they may suffer an illness of the depressive type.

Common to all of these people is a lack of self-respect. They do not like themselves and feel angry and impotent at their failure to enjoy life. From this central lack of self-respect all else stems. They resort to subterfuges and cunning schemes in an attempt to hide from themselves and from others their felt worthlessness. They blame others for their failures. Or, encouraged by psychoanalytic-type philosophies, they blame their families, their friends, their circumstances. These individuals are characterised by the 'if only' syndrome ('if only things had been different'. . . 'if only my parents had not got divorced' . . . 'if only I had been born more intelligent, with more money, taller, more attractive' etc., etc.). Constantly they shrink from challenges that they feel may put at risk their fragile self-respect. Distance is put between themselves and their objectives, as they find excuses for not tackling the tasks that they themselves acknowledge they ought to accomplish. They become static, hardly daring to move and to act, so great is their fear and expectation of failure. Obstacles are found that will either prevent them from doing what they know to be their duty or will provide a reasonable excuse should they fail. In all cases the object is to preserve their precarious self-respect. But in attempting to insure against failure by erecting obstacles to success they make failure more likely and paradoxically the effect is to reduce self-respect rather than to preserve it. Their object is to reduce self-blame by blaming others, but whatever happens the guilt mechanism is not deceived and is never effectively suppressed causing constant psychological pain.

It is unfortunate that many people, whose need to change their attitudes and behaviour is greatest, often feel that they have a strong vested interest in continuing to think and act in the way that they do. This is because in the short term such behaviour seems to prevent any serious decline in self-respect although ultimately it has the unwanted effect of preventing any increase in self-esteem. Hence they settle for second best, living vaguely unpleasant and discontented lives, whilst managing to retain some vestiges of self-respect. They do not participate fully in life because they can then, to some extent, excuse their lack of accomplishment. 'If I don't try I cannot be said to have failed' might be considered their motto. But not trying is itself a form of failure and their guilt mechanism will not be taken in by this subterfuge.

The point is that these people are very attached to their behaviour, however stultifying it may be, and they may identify any attempt to dismantle their defence mechanisms as a hostile act and view it with considerable alarm. They know that their lives are not happy but paradoxically they may resist all attempts to help them to improve their lot.

Traditional approaches in psychotherapy may unwittingly bolster this paradox and it has been said that prolonged psychotherapy of the investigative, insight type includes a tacit mutual agreement to postpone indefinitely the solution to the problem. By encouraging intellectualisation and introversion and the uncovering of postulated cause and effect mechanisms of great complexity, the individual may begin to feel that his thoughts and actions are largely psychologically determined and that he is not totally free to be other than what he is. This is an attractive concept to a person seeking to maintain a fragile self-respect.

By emphasising the 'illness' model the medico-biological approach also tends to help the individual to find an excuse, i.e. the illness, for behaving in the way that he does. Such a person may feel that it is dangerous for him to get well. So low is his opinion of himself, he feels that even if he is well he is bound to fail. He therefore feels that he is better off being ill, for at least then he has the illness to help explain away his failure.

The person who will benefit from Moral Therapy is then the person for whom life has lost its charm; for whom difficulties loom so large that he recoils from confronting them; who experiences

13

life's problems not as a stimulating challenge, but as a formidable barrier preventing action and impeding development.

At certain times in our lives all of us will fall into this category. At those times we are weak and indecisive. We become difficult to live with and blame others for our predicament. Feeling unloved we become unlovable, and a vicious circle is set up as we interpret the understandable reactions of others to our inappropriate moods and behaviour as unprovoked hostility. We become acutely aware of the breakdown of our attempts to gain satisfaction in our lives and, resenting our lack of success, our self-respect declines. We feel guilty that we are making a mess of things and bitter that the contentedness that we are encouraged to believe is our birthright seems somehow beyond our grasp. Endlessly we cast around for explanations and excuses that will hopefully relieve us of responsibility for our actions and alleviate our guilt. We hope not so much to understand our situation as to be able to explain it away, and we search out those who will collude with us in this sterile pursuit.

All of us experience periods such as this and at these times we need the help of others in order that we may be able to help ourselves. We rely during these periods on our partners, on our friends and colleagues and on our families. If they are wise and have our best interests at heart, they will not encourage us to dwell on our predicament but will rather attempt to take us out of ourselves, encouraging us to follow the path of extroversion rather than of introversion, of action rather than contemplation, of exercise and physical activity rather than sedentary intellectual ruminations. It is normal to feel like this in the same way that it is normal occasionally to be ill, and the resilience and determination that we show in extricating ourselves from our position will increase our self-respect.

For some people, though, the periods of time spent in these troughs of psychological despair are prolonged. They are not ill but they are so often unhappy that moments of satisfaction appear to them as small islands dotted on a grey sea of semi-permanent discontent. Try as they may, such people appear to be unable to deal with the problems of life. They seem hemmed in, surrounded by the high walls of their difficulties.

Hitting about them in their efforts to revenge the hurt that they feel, they may have strained the normal contracts of friendship and

14

marriage to breaking point. Moral Therapy would argue that more than any others they need the intervention of a concerned adviser who is prepared to travel with them on the difficult path ahead, the friend who will not demand love and affection in return for his involvement. Armed with the principles set out in this book we will *all* be in a position to help such a person and to help ourselves when we experience such problems. No longer will it be thought necessary for him to search out a 'mind expert' to rescue him from his predicament. The concerned and forceful friend must recapture the role that 'science' has usurped.

Moral Therapy does not attempt to solve people's problems but is rather interested in helping them solve their own. It is thus applicable to all of us but more to some than to others. For failure to deal effectively with the problems of life clearly admits of degree. Some fail seldom, others frequently, whilst for some again failure may have become a way of life. Many of us experience extended phases when things seem to go badly followed by periods of comparative success.

The continuum then spans the gap between, at one end, the person whose self-respect is high through the middle ground to the frankly unsuccessful person who views the world as an oppressive and dangerous place and may be on the verge of a mental illness. As with physical illness the severity of the situation will influence the prognosis. Those whose general ability to cope with problems is only marginally and temporarily diminished can expect to achieve the highest levels of self-respect and mental health from Moral Therapy.

At the other end of the scale are those individuals who are determined to preserve their 'illness' status, refusing to admit that they are capable of helping themselves in situations that they would prefer to believe are outside their control. For such a person the efficacy of the Moral Therapeutic approach may be more limited, though its benefits will be none the less real. Starting from a low baseline the percentage improvement in self-respect may be large despite the fact that the end result may fall short of total success. However, such a person can at least begin to learn what it means to like himself more as he listens to his individual moral imperatives and attempts to act in accordance with his own uniquely fashioned ethical code.

15

Nevertheless, a significant degree of motivation is always necessary if there is to be any worthwhile improvement, and if people do not possess it they will be unlikely to benefit from the ideas contained in this book. The person must truly want to feel better and have a genuine desire to escape his predicament. We should not connive with an individual in the maintenance of an unsatisfactory status quo whilst paying lip-service to the need to change it. This may seem obvious, but it is a fact that some people prefer to remain in their depressed and guilty states rather than face the privations and hardships that are necessary for their proper development. That they are visiting a doctor allows them to pretend to both themselves and others that they are ill, and that factors which they have no power to resist are impeding their progress and holding them captive in their present situations. Most therapies, including drug therapy and even supportive psychotherapy, help foster this unhelpful illusion. Such people will recoil from the responsibilities that Moral Therapy insists they accept, whilst the realisation that they alone are responsible for who and what they are may be profoundly disturbing to them, removing as it does their excuses and alibis. When such individuals become aware that they are going to be asked to do things which, inevitably, they will find difficult – to undertake hard work, to give up many unprofitable pleasures, and to lead a strict moral life as dictated by their own consciences – they may shrink from the situation and return to more comforting but less helpful philosophies. Nor should they be dissuaded from this course. In this 'caring society' it may seem hard that help can be given only to those who show a genuine willingness to help themselves, but in the real world it has always been thus. To pretend that there are no 'hopeless' cases is mere bravado and contradicts the commonsense view. If we are not motivated to improve our own lot, then there is little hope of our doing so, for motivation itself is an exceedingly difficult seed to implant.

The fundamental aim of Moral Therapy is to bring about a situation in which people can look at their lives with satisfaction and admiration and to give them a sense that they are worthwhile or that they have elements in them that are worthwhile. Moral Therapy cannot miraculously turn the dissatisfied into the satisfied, but its purpose is to give them some sense of achievement. It seeks also to dispel some of the more widespread misconceptions as to the nature

16

of life and to help individuals to more realistic expectations. It is to be hoped that they will come to believe that life is about problems and the solving of them; about struggle and the surmounting of difficulty; that it is essentially hard rather than easy.

This view is of course totally opposed to the general wisdom. Many of us feel that those conspicuously successful people whose self-respect is high have been dealt a superior hand, singled out for preferential treatment. Not for them the problems, insecurities and lack of opportunities which bedevil us. They, we feel, are able to bask in the calm waters of a life relatively free from difficulty and struggle. We, however, feel dispirited and unfairly treated in life's lottery, that in some way the good things have passed us by and fallen quite fortuitously elsewhere. If only the cake had been divided differently, then we would at a stroke be free of our unpleasant predicament. We daydream of how things could be made easy for us. If only we could win some money, get promoted, write that first novel, obtain a job, find someone to love us. If any or all of these things could be granted, how contented we would be. Then at last we too could live the dream and what splendid people we would feel ourselves to be.

Constantly we hope of an effortless transfer to the easier side of life as we wait for something to turn up; for our luck to change; for something to happen *to* us. We feel vaguely resentful at the unfairness of our position and insofar as we have objectives we desire more relaxation, leisure and luxury. When analysing the apparent success of others we attempt to explain it away in terms of unfair distribution of assets and situations. We tend to suggest that the successful person, whose self-esteem is high, has not suffered from our problems, has had it easier than us in terms of material benefits and environmental factors, of hereditary biological gifts such as intelligence, good looks, or of a 'strong' and attractive personality. In the allocation of qualities we feel that such a person was given tremendous advantages and as a result has found it easy to like himself. In his fortunate position we would do the same.

All this is a fundamental misconception. In reality people who like themselves and have high self-respect are people who have had many and varied problems which they have struggled extremely hard to overcome them. If they had our problems they would tend to be stimulated by them, treating them as springboards for action,

17

as fences to be jumped, rather than impassable obstacles impeding progress. Their high self-esteem springs from the Herculean nature of the tasks they have accomplished rather than from idle contemplation of advantages thrust upon them in the lottery of life.

Moral Therapy, then, will seek to show the individual how he can dispel the symptoms of non-clinical anxiety and depression. At some time or another most of us have had these feelings to a greater or lesser degree. We lack confidence and are fearful and unassertive in the presence of others. We shrink from social contact, feel unable to express ourselves and are unwilling to enter crowded rooms. Our mouth becomes dry when we have to speak and we are conscious of our heart pumping. Familiar butterflies are felt in the stomach and we may begin to sweat. Words just don't seem to come in the way that they usually do, and the whole process of rational thought seems to be an effort. We find it difficult to concentrate on any one thing and find ourselves having to read something several times before we take in its meaning. Our mood is flat and sad and everything around seems dull and boring. Above all, we lack energy. There is an emptiness and deadness within us and there seems to be little point in anything. The outside world appears grey and drab and all our senses seem blunted, so that our environment is experienced as less real and vital. Our ambition lies dormant and we feel incapable of achieving anything worthwhile. We avoid people, even close friends, as we cannot get interested in their dreams, schemes and enthusiasms. Relating to people becomes a major problem and we feel increasingly insecure and vulnerable as worries abound. A profound pessimism settles over us and all the things that we contemplate seem hedged around with dangers and difficulties. We feel strongly that if anything can go wrong it will, and we feel there is little, in our debilitated state, that we can do about it. Decision-making becomes more than usually difficult and we vacillate and postpone all decisive action. We shrink from our responsibilities. Things that we usually enjoy cease to be enjoyable and we wonder what is wrong with us that even our most reliable pleasures cease to please. We feel semi-permanently anxious about our condition, and fear, spread out thin, seems to permeate all our thoughts and activities. Sexual desire is diminished and we begin to shelve our plans for a future that looks increasingly bleak. We may eat more for comfort and our drinking increases in a futile attempt

18

to bolster our sagging confidence. It becomes difficult to get out of bed in the morning and we tend to spend more time in bed to escape from a life that seems mysteriously to have lost its charm. As all activity becomes an effort we take less exercise and, becoming flabby, we put on weight. So our deteriorating physical condition begins to contribute to our misery and we become subject to hypochondriacal preoccupations, tending to worry about our hearts, digestive systems and even our mental health as we seek explanations for our unsatisfactory predicament. We are not clinically ill, are able to carry on and others may not know of our feelings. We do not have the symptoms of severe endogenous depressive illness with sleep disturbance, early morning waking, anorexia, weight loss, thoughts of suicide and diurnal mood variation. Nor is our situation easily attributable to a set of environmental circumstances to which it might be an understandable reaction. Our anxiety, too, lacks the phobias, gross disturbances of the autonomic nervous system and panic attacks that tend to characterise clinical anxiety states. It is just that life does not feel so good any more.

Once physical and psychological illness have been excluded by a competent doctor, Moral Therapy can help. The individual will be shown that the central problem is a lack of self-respect caused by his failure to attempt to live up to his own standards, with consequent feelings of guilt manifesting themselves in a depressed and anxious mood. Once this is realised and accepted the way forward is clear. Rather than be encouraged to abandon his standards the individual will be helped to become more the person he knows he should be, and, as he learns to like himself, immerses himself in activity and hard work and abandons his futile search for excuses and scapegoats in the form of 'illness' or psychological 'determinants' in the environment, he will regain a new sense of purpose. The future once again will begin to make sense and he will know where he is going, enjoying the journey and not merely longing for the destination. His energy and ability to concentrate will return and he will regain his zest for life. Relationships will improve as, liking himself, he becomes more likeable and is able once more to relate to people as equals. In such a way will fear and anxiety diminish as confidence and self-respect grow and as difficulties are bravely confronted.

Always the self-analytic approach will be avoided and intellectual soul-searching discouraged in favour of action, commitment and involvement. No longer will the 'if . . . only' approach be employed as the individual begins to realise that the world is plastic and can be made to bend to his will. Introversion will be replaced by healthy extroversion as he seeks out the difficult rather than the easy way. Decision-making will be embraced rather than avoided and there will be an end to excuses. Sound in mind he will become sound in body too, taking regular exercise and avoiding excesses of food, drink, sleep and sex. He will lead a moral life, in tune with his own standards, in harmony with his own conscience, contented, fulfilled, brave and true, steadfast in keeping to his commitments and promises. Expecting less he will receive more as he adopts a more realistic approach to life and no longer expects something for nothing. Believing himself to be a creature of infinite possibilities he will attempt more and more in his pursuit of excellence, and as his achievements multiply and his self-respect increases so guilt, depression and anxiety will melt away.

It should be realised that there are many who will not benefit from Moral Therapy. Certainly those who are physically or psychologically ill should be referred immediately to specialists in these fields. Another significant group to whom Moral Therapy can offer nothing are those people who do not have a moral code in the accepted sense and for whom the notions of right and wrong are meaningless. In psychiatric terminology such people are often referred to as psychopaths and sociopaths. They are characterised by their seeming lack of any conscience, by their extreme emotional immaturity, low frustration tolerance and lability of mood. In many ways they are emotionally child-like although their intelligence may be high. Such people are often in conflict with society and can expect to be treated accordingly. Their lack of stability, explosive tempers and disregard for generally accepted laws make them frequent inmates of both hospitals and prisons. Moral Therapy has nothing to offer such people for if an individual has no personal morality he is a rudderless ship adrift on the sea of life. Guilt as a compass is meaningless for him, and as he has no idea of where he is going or of what he is trying to achieve, he has no yardstick against which he can assess his performance. Thus he can never respect himself and can only enjoy transient pleasures snatched from others and invariably at their expense, for which they will insist on retribution. The possession of a moral code is then a necessary prerequisite if the individual is to benefit from the principles of Moral Therapy. If no such code exists it cannot be created *de novo* and forced on an individual who would be, by definition, both unwilling and ill-equipped to receive it.

In general the person who can benefit from therapy will already be functioning in the outside world. His problem will be that he is not functioning particularly well and is not gaining satisfaction from his life. He is sane but discontented; he is in touch with reality but finds no comfort in it; he is 'well' but he does not feel good. To benefit he need not possess the high intelligence and verbal ability considered so desirable in those undergoing psychoanalysis or therapies of the investigative, insight type, for in Moral Therapy the emphasis will be on action rather than on talk and on doing rather than on thinking. He should be motivated, and be genuinely prepared to try to change. These, then, are the people who are ripe for Moral Therapy.

4

Are You Mentally Ill?

At some time or another most of us have wondered if we might not be a little mad. At times, too, we wonder if our friends or loved ones might actually be 'ill' in the psychiatric sense. Despite widespread public knowledge of subjects medical and surgical little is known about psychiatry and, more specifically, about the art of psychiatric diagnosis. Nobody really seems to know what psychiatrists do when they attempt to decide whether or not the person who confronts them is mentally unwell. Certainly it would be generally agreed that it is a difficult and mysterious process, requiring long training, high intelligence and perhaps almost supernatural powers of insight and intuition. Popularly it is believed that psychiatrists have the ability to 'see into our minds', to understand the workings of the psyche, and possibly even to predict our future behaviour. In reality of course they possess no such skills.

In this chapter I shall explain how psychiatrists recognise the symptoms and signs of mental illness, the sorts of things they look for, the methods they use in making their diagnosis. I shall also define those areas of thought, emotion and behaviour which are rightly the province of psychiatry and, perhaps more important, those that are not. The purpose of this is to correct misapprehensions about the nature of psychological illness, to prevent the misguided application of Moral Therapy to the mentally ill and to alert people to the warning signs of psychological disease, so that they can ask for professional help in the early stages of the process when intervention may be more effective. Another important aim of this section is to undermine the illness excuse. If we are not ill, then we are well – and responsible for our predicament. And if, despite the absence of illness we are unhappy, depressed and anxious then we can use the principles of Moral Therapy to improve our condition.

Psychiatry is not a difficult subject. On the whole it is rather an easy one. The workings of the minds of others being largely inaccessible to us, and most knowledge of them being derived via analogy with our own mental processes, psychiatry contents itself with the recognition and treatment of various syndromes usually on the empirical basis of what 'works'. Lithium 'works' in cases of manic-depressive illness, electro-convulsive therapy (E.C.T.) in cases of severe retarded depression of delusional intensity, and phenothiazine tranquillisers undoubtedly help to relieve schizophrenic symptoms. Why these treatments work is the subject of much speculation and research, but as yet hard causal mechanisms have not been found.

In truth there are very few illnesses in psychiatry, and even fewer successful treatments, although certain treatments which do exist are often startlingly successful. In the large majority of cases the recognition of psychiatric disease is not at all complicated, and in nine out of ten cases psychiatrists will agree on the diagnosis. Certainly there are small areas in psychiatry where difficult decisions do have to be made and in which experienced doctors are often in disagreement. The difficulty for example in differentiating between an emotion-laden schizophrenia and manic-depressive illness, or between a genuine psychosis and a severe 'hysterical personality disorder' is genuine, and such cases take up a disproportionate amount of time, and give rise to much stimulating argument at psychiatric case conferences and ward rounds. Intelligent minds have a natural tendency to stretch themselves by concentrating on difficult matters. It is right that they should do so – a potent source of increased self-respect – but an unfortunate by-product has been that in concentrating on the small print of the subject, in the pinpointing of esoteric diagnostic categories, in the postulating of hypothetical psychological and biochemical causative processes, psychiatrists have tended to lay a smokescreen over the indubitable fact that in the real world it is not hard either to recognise or to treat the large majority of psychiatric illnesses. *It would take the intelligent layman a long weekend to learn how to do it.* There are parallels with general medicine here although medicine is a vastly more complicated subject. The GP deals mainly with coughs and colds, aches and pains, worries and depressions, pregnancies and their complications. Perhaps 80 per cent of his medical training is of little use to him. He gets 'qualified', but he learns the job as he goes along. So in psychiatry the time has come to avoid the death by a thousand qualifications, and to get to the heart of the matter. Let pedants and perfectionists carp and purists dissent, the fact is that we can all learn to recognise psychiatric illness, and come to know about the most effective and appropriate treatments.

In those cases where doubt exists the true professional may not be of much help as often other experts will be found to disagree. Certainly in the field of forensic psychiatry, when psychiatrists are asked to determine whether or not a person committing a crime was genuinely responsible for his actions – because of illness did not know the difference between right and wrong at the time of his offence – the warring experts in the courtroom often achieve little except to show clearly that the grey areas of psychiatric diagnosis are a no man's land in which victory is usually awarded to the best orator, to the most charismatic personality or to the man with the most initials after his name. Putting for one moment these disputed hinterlands aside, we are left with well-trodden territory, its signposts in place and well marked. The diagnostic action is in the psychiatric out-patients' departments of the hospitals and in the accident and emergency departments where the sheep, metaphorically speaking, are sorted from the goats; where the decision is made whether or not genuine psychological illness exists.

It will be the purpose of this chapter to allow the person who worries and wonders about his or another's mental health or psychiatric status to do the sort of thing that psychiatrists do, to look at the world through their eyes so that he can reach the kind of conclusions which they reach, 'know' the type of things that they 'know'. Basically what psychiatrists do is something called the Mental State Exam (M.S.E.). They do it again and again. It is the fundamental tool of their trade, the equivalent of the surgeon's physical examination. Initially it is a diagnostic aid. Later it becomes the instrument by which progress or the lack of it in response to treatment is measured. The M.S.E. is relatively easy to perform and takes about twenty minutes.

At the end of the M.S.E. the psychiatrist is reasonably sure whether or not he is dealing with somebody who has a psychiatric illness and what that illness is. He makes his diagnosis on the basis of the M.S.E. and that diagnosis has implications for treatment and prognosis. I am not saying that he always knows, is always correct, but rather that the index of probability is high that he is correct. In the appendix (A Layman's Guide to Psychiatric Diagnosis) the form and content of the M.S.E., remarkably similar throughout the hospitals and clinics of Britain and North America, will be outlined. The idea is that by the end of the chapter the reader will be well prepared for the recognition of psychological illness in others, although lack of insight, itself a symptom of many forms of disease, may mean that he is less equipped for self-diagnosis. However, with regard to the extremely common disturbances of the emotions, he will get a reasonably good idea of whether or not a psychiatrist might allocate him to the illness category.

In addition to the M.S.E. the psychiatrist does four other things, which enable him to 'flesh' out his findings, to confirm, refute or refine his diagnosis, to illuminate possibilities for treatment and to provide a framework for the assessment of likely outcome. Firstly, and before he performs the M.S.E., he takes a Psychiatric History (P.H.), which includes the reason for referral, an account of the patient's complaints, the history of his present condition, and comprehensive details of his personal and family history including past medical and psychiatric history, use of drugs or medicines and present life situation. During the P.H. the psychiatrist will attempt to assess the patient's personality, and the extent to which it has changed since the onset of symptoms and signs. Secondly, if at all possible, he obtains corroborating evidence or otherwise from an informant, somebody who knows the patient well and has seen the problems complained of develop. Thirdly he performs a physical examination to exclude physical illness as a cause of psychiatric symptoms. Fourthly he performs various pathological and other investigations to exclude certain physical conditions which may not have revealed themselves at the physical examination.

Before embarking on a description of the psychiatrist's diagnostic armature we should know what we are looking for. What are the illnesses in psychiatry? What are the treatments? I maintain that they can be adequately explained and enumerated in a chapter (see appendix). Intellectuals might recoil in horror at the enormity of such a project, theoreticians throw up their hands at the heresies involved, at the injustice done to the complexity of the subject in the name of simplicity. Books have been written on the subject of psychiatric diagnosis, careers dedicated to the elaboration of techniques and panels of learned men, involved for years in the standardisation of diagnostic procedures, dreaming up along the way such exotic 'illnesses' as 'Tobacco Use Disorder', 'Social Phobia', 'Academic Underachievement Disorder' and 'Specific Academic or Work Inhibition'. Anti-psychiatrists criticise the whole concept of 'mental illness', the talk therapists pour scorn on those who look to biology for their classification of disease, the scientists ridicule the metapsychologists. Is psychiatric diagnosis political? Is psychiatry merely an authoritarian branch of the establishment? Does psychiatric diagnosis do little more than hand down tautological edicts in which the labels 'mad' or 'crazy' merely mirror the view of society on what consitutes 'mad' or 'crazy' behaviour? Or is it an exact science and, if so, why is there so much disagreement over what it describes, about the usefulness of its descriptions?

All such speculations are very stimulating, pleasant to indulge in, possibly even 'useful' although their ability to produce workable conclusions is suspect. However, they do not help people to answer the question, 'Do I have a psychological illness?' and that is a question to which people would like an answer, whether or not it is an appropriate theoretical question. The fact remains that there is a rough and ready consensus, broad agreement within the psychiatric profession, on what constitutes illness despite the fact that we recognise that all classifications are to some extent inventions, ways of looking at the world, which make effective intervention possible.

The classification that I have outlined below and the methods of applying that classification in diagnosis are widely used in psychiatry, although individuals might take exception to parts of them. In general, however, this is the method that psychiatrists use, the one that the consumer consumes. Nevertheless, although any psychiatrist would readily agree that the diseases mentioned below undoubtedly represent psychological illness, most would maintain that there are startling, indeed glaring omissions. The fact that whole categories of what are generally regarded as *bona fide* psychological conditions have been removed from the classification of illness is no oversight. I argue that the time has come to reduce the province of psychiatry drastically, to redefine its borders, to redistribute its territory.

Here then is my classification:—

GROUP ONE

The following are genuine psychiatric illnesses.

Psychiatric Illness	Treatment	Effectiveness of Treatment
1. *Schizophrenia*	Anti-psychotic medication e.g. Chlorpromazine	Effective in relieving symptoms. May need Anti-Parkinsonian drugs for side effects
2. *Disorders of Mood and Emotion*		
a. *Manic-Depressive Illness* (Bi-polar)	Long term Lithium treatment for prevention of repeated attacks. Major tranquilliser for control of acute manic phase. As below for depressive phase	Lithium is very effective, but potentially toxic. Requires careful monitoring
b. *Depressive Illness* (inc. Uni-polar, Endogenous, Involutional, and Reactive)	Anti-depressant medication e.g. Amitriptyline, Imipramine	Not very effective, but significantly superior to placebo. Dangerous in overdose
	Electroconvulsive Therapy	Extremely effective in severe retarded or psychotic depression. Insignificant side effects
c. *Clinical Anxiety*, (including phobic anxiety states and panic disorders)	Minor Tranquillisers e.g. Diazepam	Mild symptomatic relief, but addictive

27

c. *Clinical Anxiety* (cont.)	Anti-depressant medication, if, as often, there is concurrent depression	See above
	Behaviour Therapy	Not very effective. Of some use for phobias
	Beta-blockers e.g. Propranolol	Very limited symptomatic relief
3. *Obsessive/ Compulsive States*	Behaviour Therapy	Not very effective
	Anti-depressant medication if, as often, there is concurrent depression	See above
4. *Eating Disorders* e.g. *Anorexia Nervosa*	Strict re-feeding regime with bed rest in hospital for Anorexia Nervosa	In Anorexia Nervosa 30–35 per cent recover fully with treatment. 5 per cent die.

Group Two

The following are conditions treated as well, if not better, by physicians as by psychiatrists.

Illness	Treatment	Effectiveness of Treatment
1. *Dementia*	Investigate thoroughly to exclude treatable cause	In large majority of cases no effective treatment
2. *Delirium*	Investigate thoroughly to discover organic cause	Depends on response to treatment of underlying cause of delirious mental state
3. *Subnormality and Severe Subnormality*	Care rather than treatment	No effective treatment

28

GROUP THREE

The following are conditions considered today within the rightful province of psychiatry. I argue that they do not represent true psychological illness.

'Illness'

1. Abnormal Personality or Personality Disorder
2. Abnormal Personality Reactions
3. Psychopathy/Sociopathy
4. Hysteria and Hysterical Reactions
5. Drug Abuse and Alcoholism
6. Sexual Dysfunction and Sexual Deviation

Some psychiatrists may approve of this drastic reduction of their territory – if not perhaps on a theoretical basis, then at least because it would remove from their terrain the great majority of cases for which they feel the least sympathy, with which they have the least inclination to deal. They know, too, that they possess no relevant treatment skills which are applicable to such people. In short their psychiatric training gives them no clue as to how they should react and so they have to improvise, to make it up as they go along, using their common sense or drawing from the mothy collection of psychodynamic theories to which most psychiatric text-books half-heartedly refer. At the back of their minds they might recognise that their intrinsic distaste for the personality disorders, the sociopaths, and the drug abusers is based on the sneaking suspicion that their unsatisfactory behaviour and lives are in reality nothing but self-inflicted wounds, not illnesses at all, and therefore not worthy of the considerable time and effort they demand, energy which could be far better spent on more deserving causes. That psychiatry has become the dustbin for society's misfits is not to the taste of all psychiatrists. However, no group of people, professional or other-wise, is keen to lose control over areas which have previously been widely considered their sovereign territory. That is human nature. There is the implication that their usefulness may be somewhat reduced in the process, indispensability compromised, and at the end of the day job-security threatened. And so those who emotionally might have little objection to a more rigorous, a tougher and more uncompromising attitude towards psychiatric diagnosis may find themselves disinclined to turn away from their 'care' those with the most tenuous claim to 'illness'.

These attitudes are, of course, the product of the liberal times in which we find ourselves. If somebody presents himself for 'help', throws himself on our mercy, then we feel we should bend over backwards to provide it. It makes us feel better if we do, worse if we don't. Psychiatry after all prides itself that, of the various medical disciplines, it is the most 'caring'. Thus the sufferers from the problems of life, served up to the psychiatrists by the impotent GPs, are often taken on in the out-patients' department for periodic sessions of reassurance and support, given trial courses of various pills or, very occasionally, if considered especially interesting and verbal, recommended for psychotherapy. In this way does the unsuccessful individual latch on to the illness excuse, win the illness treatment, when in fact he is not ill, merely a failure at life. Gratefully he embraces it with all its implied promise of a quick fix for his troubles, often at heavy long-term cost to himself. The psychiatrist unwittingly colludes with him in the expert/layman relationship because that is what he knows how to do, although he has little idea, perhaps, of what should be done in terms of treatment if indeed treatment is thought to be required.

In fact what is needed is that such people learn how to treat themselves, and they are hindered from doing so by being told, at least by implication, that they are ill. Once illness is excluded they should be turned away, referred perhaps in the case of drug abusers to specialised units with a heavy emphasis on discipline or, in the case of alcoholics, to the very excellent Alcoholics Anonymous with its emphasis on moral commitment. To turn someone away from treatment is perhaps the hardest and most responsible decision that a psychiatrist makes, with all its attendant risks and implications. It is so much easier to 'take the patient on' as an insurance policy against disaster, for inevitably there will be tragic events which could in theory and with the benefit of hindsight, have been avoided. Such is often the case with the threat of suicide. Many people threaten psychiatrists with such action, often in a demonstrably manipulative way, especially when the courageous psychiatrist refuses their demands for treatment which he feels is not needed. But, in the absence of illness, we are responsible for our own lives, and that includes the taking of them. You are not of necessity mentally ill, although frequently it is a symptom of psychological illness, to attempt to take your own life.

In the section entitled 'A Layman's Guide to Psychiatric Diagnosis', which should be read in conjunction with this chapter, we will consider the first two groups of my classification. Group One contains the genuine psychiatric illnesses. Group Two consists of those conditions which produce primarily psychiatric symptoms and signs, but are the result of clear-cut organic impairment. These, I suggest, are perhaps best treated by physicians, geriatricians and neurologists.

A classification provides no new knowledge, rather it is an arrangement of existing knowledge. In drawing the lines between categories one does little justice to the grey areas. That classifications are not perfect does not diminish their usefulness, or does so only marginally. Certainly the classification that I have made has implications for life and the living of it. If it was generally accepted, it would make a big difference and would free many from the seductive protective cloak of invalidism and subject them once again to the bracing winds of life with all the potential for increased self-respect that this implies. Some may not survive the rigours of the mountainside, but without the opportunity to demonstrate bravery and courage there is little else. Without trying we can only fail. Some may develop a psychological illness, in which case psychiatry can help; others will cling to their inadequate, depressing and anxiety-producing attitudes and behaviour, failing miserably but in effect choosing to do so having discovered some perverted masochistic satisfaction in their choice. We cannot, must not, regard them as being determined in their behaviour, enslaved, not free to change, at the mercy of 'neurosis'. Instead we must emphasise the possibilities for change, the methods by which it can be brought about, through which at least some improvement can be made. In the practice of a Moral Therapy – their own Moral Therapy – such people hold the key to an escape from their predicament. They must be shown that they possess it.

The first two Groups in my classification, containing the genuine illnesses, are discussed separately (see appendix). I will now discuss the conditions which are widely considered to be within the province of psychiatry, but which I argue are not really illnesses at all.

Psychopathy/sociopathy: Evil Posing as Illness

Psychiatrists describe sociopaths (a name preferred by many to the term psychopath) as those people whose disregard for society, inability to learn from experience, and low frustration tolerance tend to bring them into conflict with others. They may end up in prison, and are frequently to be found in mental hospitals. Often they are shuttled between the two. They are occasionally aggressive, sometimes merely inadequate.

The aggressive psychopath starts early and is often sexually precocious and promiscuous, showing explosive behaviour and a characteristic callous disregard for the rights and well-being of others. He gets into fights, steals, plays truant from school and abuses his teachers. At work he is incapable of taking criticism and tends to get the sack. In his social relationships he is manipulative, often a pathological liar and incapable of forming deep and steady relationships. He seeks out those of a similar personality to his own who share his irresponsibility and disregard for society's rules. When he gets married he is unfaithful, and soon he is divorced. Despite his wanton immorality he is not necessarily unintelligent, and can be charming even though his charm may be used to profit from others. Above all he is deeply and single-mindedly selfish.

Alcoholism and drug abuse are commonly associated with sociopathy, as are so-called 'conversion symptoms' (unexplained neurological symptoms). A disturbed family environment seems to predispose people towards this type of personality and there is some suggestion from studies of twins that there might be a genetic predisposition as well. Most realistic psychiatrists would agree that there is no cure for sociopathy although such people do best in a rather strictly controlled environment where they receive the discipline which they are unable or unwilling to provide for themselves.

The view is taken here that such people are bad rather than mad, and should be treated as such, being far better off in prison than in hospital if they have broken the law. It is not enough to say that they are ill merely because they behave badly, and wrong to maintain that bad behaviour, even of the most extreme sort, is an infallible pointer to illness. For if we are to define mental illness in terms of what society finds acceptable or unacceptable behaviour, then we will have to change our definitions of illness as society's attitudes change.

The deficiency in sociopathy is a moral deficiency. The individual exhibits no conscience, cannot hear, or chooses to ignore, its dictates. He chooses to be bad in exactly the same way as others choose consistently to be good. He represents the inferior end of the good-bad continuum. It is no more logical to include such a person in the illness category than it is the unusual and abnormal paragon of virtue whose personality is the exact mirror image of the psychopath's.

In the absence of genuine psychological illness then, we should leave the sociopath to those whose task it is to preserve society from unacceptable behaviour. Psychopathic/Sociopathic Personality Disorder is not a psychiatric illness. It is, in my view, a description of badness and should be considered no adequate defence against conviction for crime against society, or reason why the perpetrator of offences against others should escape the consequences of his actions.

It has become the fashion of late to consider that the development of an unsatisfactory personality should carry with it no implications of blame, should not occasion feelings of guilt. Further it is considered that if the personality is sufficiently unacceptable, then there may well be grounds for insinuating that responsibility for action is in some way diminished. Those who hold such attitudes stress the importance of environmental and constitutional factors in the development of personality, preferring to see us as victims of such phenomena, with little ability to rise above them, to overcome them. The pressures are so great, they might argue, that our personalities, our way of looking at the world, are conditioned and determined and that in some fundamental way we are not free to be otherwise – that we are slaves to our genes and our environments.

These attitudes are more easily acquired when considering the personalities which manifest themselves at the lower end of the good/bad continuum. Certainly it is not often argued that those who are abnormal and remarkable for the balance and equilibrium of their characters are similarly shaped by forces outside their control. This, of course, is part and parcel of the great movement of liberal paternalism which has for so long controlled the intellectual high ground of the 'caring' society. Thus the bad are 'sick', the inadequate and unpleasant are 'deprived', the habitual and violent criminal 'ill' rather than evil. Hospital rather than prison, it is argued, is the rightful destination of this latter category, the couch and the prescription pad the best method of dealing with the former.

But if our personalities are not our own creative act, the most fundamental reflection of our essence, of our hopes and ambitions, what are we but machines? If it is true that belief in the freedom of the spirit is misconceived, then we would be far wiser to pretend that it were not so. For if we are not allowed to blame the psychopath for his actions, then we are not free to praise and admire his antithesis, are divested of the hope that through our own efforts we can rise above disadvantageous circumstances and inherited weakness, are precluded from aspiring to goodness and greatness, are not to be praised for our failure to succumb to temptation, wickedness and evil. This is the depressing legacy of such outwardly loving and caring attitudes.

Schizoid, cyclothymic, paranoid, obsessional, vulnerable, and hysterical personality disorders

Psychiatrists are fond of classifying the various personality disorders in their quest for a more complete understanding of their patients. Yet most realise this is an inexact and unrewarding art. Methods of objective measurement are generally unsatisfactory, and attempts at categorisation tend to obscure the reality that there is endless overlap between personality types and that at different times, with different people and in different situations, we show widely varying personality reactions. Our propensities to think and act are in the end as many and varied as the complexities of each individual and attempts at classification are crude, whilst efforts to draw meaningful conclusions from the labelling process are often misleading. However, the illusion still exists that if you can put a word to something then you have to some extent explained it and so most psychiatric text-books include a chapter explaining the different types of disordered personalities.

There is a certain usefulness in identifying some personality traits in that it may help in the diagnosis and prognosis of certain conditions. The schizoid personality – shy, aloof, withdrawn, dreamy, suspicious, introverted, bizarre, preoccupied with mystical thoughts – seems particularly liable to schizophrenia of the bad prognosis type. Similarly the cyclothymic personality, prone to cyclical mood swings both above and below the normal, has a tendency to develop manic-depressive illness.

The hysterical personality – shallow, histrionic, manipulative, prone to exaggeration, attention-seeking, role-playing, untruthful, unreliable, outwardly seductive and yet fundamentally uninterested in sex, incapable of deep relationships – is a widely described 'personality disorder' as is the paranoid personality – mistrusting, suspicious, over-sensitive and prickly. Other personalities are described as vulnerable or inadequate, meaning that these people have a history of failing to cope, of 'breaking down'.

To 'have' any of these personalities, or a combination of them, is not to be ill. However, it is not surprising that when genuine psychiatric illness manifests itself the previous personality will be reflected in the symptoms. Thus the paranoid personality might be expected to experience paranoid delusions in psychosis, while the rigid, obsessional, neat and perfectionistic person might fall prey to cleaning and tidying rituals in obsessive/compulsive illness. But the fact remains that although specific personalities might be susceptible to illness in the same way that smoking may predispose people to lung cancer or relatively high alcohol intake to cirrhosis, there is no need for *medical* intervention in the absence of hard psychopathology. Our personalities may well be the cause of much unhappiness, both to ourselves and others, and act as a barrier to our enjoyment of life, but they do not need 'treatment' from 'experts'. If we feel that they do us a disservice, then we can strive to modify them. Nothing prevents us but our own disinclination to change. No mysterious force stands in our way. It is up to us. That is both the good and the bad news.

Sexual Problems

In general the so-called anomalies and perversions such as homosexuality, sadism/masochism, fetishism, transvestism, transsexualism, and even bestiality are not evidence of mental illness, although, of course, mental illness can and does often co-exist with these phenomena. Thus an unwanted tendency towards homosexuality might be a potent source of stress tending to precipitate an illness of the affective type. However, even the most outlandish sexual behaviour is in the end merely an expression of preference, which, although possibly abnormal and illegal is not of necessity and in isolation a symptom of psychological illness.

Where sexual behaviour leads to offences against the law and in the absence of other psychopathology the offender should be denied the illness excuse for his behaviour and dealt with by society, rather than 'treated' by psychiatrists. Whether or not particular sexual behaviour is deviant is then a matter for social and legal rather than medical judgement.

It may be that an individual, unhappy with his own sexual preferences, goes to a doctor for help. Certainly there are methods, most of them of strictly limited efficacy, by which he can be encouraged to change the direction of his sexual urges or at least curtail his unwanted sexual behaviour. The same is true of cigarette smoking. However, in no way does this intervention imply the existence of an illness.

Much the same can be said for the sexual dysfunctions such as impotence, failure of ejaculation, premature ejaculation, frigidity and vaginismus. Of course, these may, in a minority of cases, be caused by genuine physical illness and this should always be suspected in cases where sexual desire is maintained and where previous sexual function has been unimpaired. Causes can vary from diabetes, heart disease, drugs such as alcohol, tri-cyclic antidepressants and methyldopa, and various neurological and vascular disorders. These should be excluded by a physician, not necessarily a psychiatrist.

One is then left, in the large majority of cases, with what is in effect a problem of living analogous to having difficulty in meeting the mortgage payments or finding a job. The problem is that sex is no longer satisfying, or the sexual partner is complaining that *they* no longer find it satisfying. The question, as with all life's problems, is 'What can be done about it?' For those of a rather clinical and cold-blooded frame of mind there are the behavioural techniques of Masters and Johnson – available from any bookshop and widely regarded as being effective.

There is another solution from which the opinion makers of the liberal era will recoil in speechless horror. If sex is no longer satisfying, a potent source of pleasure, why not merely give it up? Is it so vitally important and if so, why? Or is it rather that we have all been brainwashed into believing that we have a divine right to this, the ultimate pleasure, and in so far as we do not experience its joys we are inferior, inadequate – perhaps even ill, stunted human beings, leading sad, attenuated lives, victims of the most formidable disability? The truth of the matter is that many of us do not subscribe to the mores of the permissive age in which sexual expression has become an overvalued activity as a result of the preposterous theories of the psychoanalysts which have swept away common sense. It is difficult to swim against the tide of 'scientific' opinion, to ignore the wisdom of the 'experts', to realise that the Emperor is naked, but that is what we must do if we are to restore a sense of proportion in our attitudes towards sexual problems.

Alcoholism and drug dependence

In general alcoholism is a social and medical problem rather than a psychiatric one, unless it is complicated, as is frequently the case, by co-existent psychological illness. After the initial withdrawal from alcohol, which should be supervised by doctors but not necessarily psychiatrists, organisations such as Alcoholics Anonymous, which apply a strict, no-nonsense, commonsense approach, are probably the best people to deal with the problem.

Traditionally it has been considered the job of psychiatrists to discover *why* a person has turned to drink, as if such behaviour must of necessity be indicative of some malfunction, the sign perhaps of a 'disordered personality'. In truth people drink because alcohol is available, because drinking is pleasurable and socially condoned, because in certain jobs there is pressure to drink, because it provides short-term relief from stress, and because alcohol possesses the property of causing both psychological and physiological dependence.

Hysterical disorder

There is little agreement in psychiatry on the classification of hysterical disorders, but it is maintained here that they do not and should not constitute an illness category of their own. In England the salient features of hysterical conditions are thought to be the presence of some degree of dissociation, with or without conversion symptoms (some unexplained neurological physical deficit in the absence of any demonstrable pathology e.g. amnesia, paralysis, mutism) and the existence of some real, imagined and usually unrecognised *gain* for the individual in the demonstration of these symptoms. The gain may be the attention and interest that the inexplicable symptoms arouse and the usually female perpetrator of the behaviour may be totally unaware of, have successfully dissociated herself from, the purpose of her actions. In reality, of course, such behaviour has no advantage for the individual as the price paid in pain or disability is out of all proportion to the significance of any reward. In America psychiatrists tend to prefer a narrower definition known as Briquet's Syndrome. In this a woman demonstrates from early life a bewildering array of physical symptoms often involving many body systems especially the gastro-intestinal, the central nervous and the reproductive systems. Characteristically these are described in a dramatic and histrionic way and lead to many hospitalisations, operations, investigations and treatments. The disorder is chronic.

Not all sufferers from hysterical symptoms demonstrate the hysterical personality described in the section on personality disorders, but there appears to be a definite link with sociopathic/psychopathic mechanisms. The fact that hysterical symptoms tend to be confined to women whilst sociopathic ones are more typically male has led some to speculate that these men and women have the same underlying approach to life, which may merely be manifesting itself in a different way, determined perhaps by sexual and cultural factors.

Certainly the phenomenon of gain in hysterical symptoms seems to indicate that semi-purposive motivation is at work in a way, for instance, that it is not in the genuine illnesses such as schizophrenia.

The sufferer in effect chooses to ignore what she is doing, refuses to recognise the processes at work as she dissociates herself from responsibility for, and the consequences of, her actions. As the practised hysteric becomes more accomplished in the perpetration of her dissociative techniques, the mechanism begins to take on a life of its own and there is a sense in which she is actually unaware of what she is doing. But it is a weak sense of 'unawareness' akin perhaps to the 'unawareness' of the drunkard who kills people in his motor car. He cannot remember the disaster and was totally incapable at the time, but his behaviour was a self-inflicted wound and, when he started out on his evening, his drinking perhaps had a functional gain for him in the provision of relaxation and the avoidance of stress. At the other end of the scale hysterical symptoms may shade by degree into frank malingering, the individual either elaborating a genuine physical symptom for gain, or perhaps harming herself by cutting or scratching herself to manipulate herself into some position of fancied advantage.

Long-term follow-up of those suffering from hysterical symptoms reveals that very frequently they develop either physical or psychological illness of a genuine kind, and in nearly all cases the diagnosis has to be revised to that of schizophrenia, affective illness, epilepsy or other organic disease whilst in other cases the hysterical symptoms are seen with the benefit of hindsight to be explicable in terms of histrionic, 'acting out', manipulative behaviour.

Having read this chapter in conjunction with the section 'A Layman's Guide to Psychiatric Diagnosis', we will be in a position to know whether or not we or our friends are ill. If we are we should immediately consult a doctor and tell him of our suspicions. If our friend is ill we should persuade him to do the same, or in the absence of his having insight, we should alert the medical profession to his predicament.

If on the other hand we are not ill and yet our lives are miserable, then we must learn to practise the principles of Moral Therapy, to escape from our failures through our own efforts – guided by guilt, listening to the voice of conscience. In admitting that we are fundamentally well and in abandoning the illness excuse we shed a mighty burden in our journey towards self-respect.

The Role of the Doctor

Where illness exists there is no place for Moral Therapy. In its absence, however, the doctor may have no role to play in helping us to deal with the problems of life. Apart from his vital function of excluding psychological illness, and the psychological manifestations of physical illness, in other respects a medical training may not necessarily be the best grounding for the successful practice of Moral Therapy.

This is partly due to a tendency in medical education to emphasise the scientific method, which results in many doctors being ill at ease with, and therefore inclined to disregard, that which cannot easily be measured or inferred from measurement. More importantly the selection procedure for those embarking on a career in medicine discriminates in favour of a certain personality type whose past history and present attitude denote them as being the sort of people who will be good at passing medical exams and can be relied upon to behave in a way deemed appropriate for members of the medical profession. Well grounded in science rather than arts subjects they will have worked hard at school and tended to relate well to those in authority. In general they are conservative, conformist people who tend to believe in scientific solutions to the problems of the people who approach them. The medico-biological attitude is second nature to them, and because they may have little first-hand experience, in their own well-ordered lives, of the type of life problem that is frequently brought to them, they may have much sympathy for it, but little understanding of it.

Doctors, too, are not well placed for the easy functioning of the therapeutic friendship so necessary in the practice of Moral Therapy. Professional ethics seem to demand that they stand well back from their 'patients' whilst dispensing knowledge and expertise in an attempt to cure them. They are encouraged to feel for them but not with them; to care for them in a dispassionate rather than a passionate way; to have sympathy rather than empathy. Above all, most subscribe to the desirability of a hierarchical relationship in which, at least in the consultative situation, the doctor assumes a superior position and the patient an inferior one. The patient invests his trust and faith in the other's greater knowledge and skill. The effective prostration and passivity of the patient is felt to be positively therapeutic, as it is thought to ensure that his frame of mind is more receptive to the doctor's reassurance. It increases the patient's suggestibility and allows the doctor to do things to and for him, rather than with him. This satisfies the doctor's need for action and reduces his feelings of impotence in situations with which he may feel ill equipped to deal. However, this is an approach that is unlikely to have as its end effect a lasting increase in the individual's self-respect.

Doctors have much to lose by showing their human face and tend to hide behind their professionalism for reasons that are not always concerned with the benefit of their patients. They may feel that if they give up their position of authority they will have little to offer the patient on a human level. Others may favour a more brave and helpful approach. As concerned and forceful friends we may find that we are better equipped to perform Moral Therapy than any man of science. In the field of helping others to help themselves there is no substitute for firm but caring involvement on a personal level, and no room at all for intellectual posturing and the affecting of a spurious expertise.

The doctor's role then is largely a screening one. It is up to him to exclude both psychological and also, importantly, physical illness. For it must never be forgotten that in many cases actual physical illness can have symptoms and signs that manifest themselves chiefly in disturbances of mood, thought, intelligence and behaviour.

41

5
The Myth of Neurosis and the Validity of Blame

Deep and important misconceptions regarding our moral imperatives are rare although our desire to pretend, and skill in pretending, confusion and ignorance as to what we ought to do is usually highly developed. Deep in our hearts we invariably know the right way forward, but we recoil from its difficulty, from the hardships that it will entail, from the disappointments that we feel will follow from failure in what we tell ourselves is an over-ambitious project. So it may be that we prefer to hide from our friends the true nature of our real ambitions. If taken in by our subterfuges our friends may urge courses of action on us that are actually inimical to our best interests. They may also make the mistake of attempting to impose their own value-systems upon us, advising behaviour that whilst in tune with their own moral attitudes is not necessarily in harmony with ours. Or again they might make the mistake of urging us to obey laws and rules of society which contravene the dictates of our own conscience. But there can be no blueprint for the building of self-respect unless it is our blueprint. A plan cannot successfully or usefully be imposed upon us unless we ourselves will it and recognise that it is appropriate for us. It is our own decision to act on our own internal commands that is of value to our mental health. Anything that tends or conspires to remove our right and ability to self-determination, however well meaning, is doomed to failure and is liable to harm us psychologically by limiting our potential to increase our self-respect by our own efforts.

42

Our discipline must be self-discipline, our respect must be self-respect, our restraint must be self-restraint.

The individual must take the central role. It is up to him faithfully to acknowledge and to report his innermost feelings, desires and ambitions so that he can be encouraged to actualise them. Where they are obscure, which will be rare, they may be clarified in discussions with friends – but where they are deficient or of inferior quality then new and superior values must not be, and indeed cannot be, externally imposed. It is not our job to question the value systems of others once we are satisfied as to their nature. That they exist is enough. Our task will be to help ensure that in all cases an individual's behaviour obeys his own conscience whatever that conscience may be. We may disapprove of and dislike a person's ethics and abhor the behaviour that results from a faithful observance of the commands of that moral system, but we cannot deny that such a person is mentally healthy. For if a man is at peace with himself it matters not to him that he is at war with others.

In attempting to help another person, therefore, we should not set ourselves up as judges of what is good or bad, right or wrong. Instead we should be interested alone in what the individual feels is good or bad, right or wrong and in how he can be helped to act in accordance with these deeply held beliefs. Moral Therapy is not about knowing what is good for other people but is about the drawing out and examination of their own self-knowledge, of their own self-interest and encouraging them to behave in a way congruous with their own ethical systems. In the deepest sense, then, the wise friend and practitioner of Moral Therapy will eschew the directive approach in that he will not choose the directions but rather will encourage us to follow our own directions. The forceful, concerned and enlightened friend who truly has our best interests at heart, should, however, be prepared to take on the responsibility of applying pressure on us to behave in the way that we know in our hearts to be right for us. Such a person has no special power over, or expert knowledge of, our lives. But his common sense tells him we are in trouble and that he can provide that initial thrust which will eventually enable us to escape our predicament. He will show us how to make the best use of our resources; urge us on when we falter; prop us up when we are in danger of falling; encourage us when our spirits are low and our will is weak; help us to become doers rather than thinkers; discourage passivity, inactivity and introspection; have faith in us when we have none in ourselves. He should always remain optimistic, secure in the knowledge that all of us have a potential for liking ourselves and that this ultimate objective is beyond the reach of none. He will not be afraid to inject his energy into us, to get us going – but it is we who must decide where we are going. He may force us to act but we will choose the actions. He may suggest the methods but the credit for the awakening of our self-esteem will be ours alone.

So we should encourage the troubled individual to describe the sort of person that in a 'perfect world' he feels he would like to be, to talk of what he knows he ought to do and what he should leave undone. The truth and the relevance of these assertions must be discussed freely.

'Is that what you *really* want from life?'

'Or are you merely paying lip-service to what you feel is a socially acceptable or fashionable ambition?'

'Do you really crave only to be liked and respected by others or is your deeper and more fundamental desire to know that you are *worthy* of that liking and respect?'

'Do you want, above all, to escape loneliness or would you prefer to be the sort of person whose self-sufficiency and self-esteem were so high that loneliness would become tolerable, even pleasant?'

Always the desires must be separated from the basic needs as the two are seldom synonymous. The individual may know in his heart what sort of things he should do but may fall a victim to the St Augustine syndrome, 'Oh Lord make me good, but not yet'! He knows that he should do something or cease to do it but his desires are at war with his moral imperatives. 'I know that I ought to do X, but I don't want to' is so often an expression of 'X is hard and I tend to avoid hardship'.

Moral Therapy insists that we always *need* to do what we feel we ought to do, even though often we don't *want* to do it. It is the purpose of Moral Therapy to teach the individual to want what he needs by demonstrating to him the psychological benefits that must surely follow from a strict observance of the dictates of his own conscience.

Together with friends the aims, objectives and destinations will be planned, the milestones along the way mapped, the oases charted. Such a discussion will not be a particularly normal one because in this age it is not fashionable to encourage people to talk freely of their morals, their guilt, their self-respect.

This is the sort of thing that we tend to associate with earlier eras in which, some hold, they lacked the expertise at living that we now possess. In today's climate discussions would be more likely to centre on childhood experiences, or a factual analysis of the individual's past or present environment and relationships, than on his hopes and dreams for the future. Unfortunately the object today is to explain and quantify the effects of such phenomena on the moulding and shaping of the patient, who is then presented as a pawn on the chessboard of life manipulated by a mysterious, unknown and all-powerful player, with little or no influence of his own in the shaping of his destiny. But if by implication we disavow the individual's ability to control his present and his future, what hope can he be offered for ever improving his lot?

So Moral Therapy will be rather uninterested in the past. It is unchangeable; the damage done. Its effect on the present and the future is as difficult to analyse as it is to predict. The future is the place; 'What are we going to do about it?' is the question; to strive for the agreed objectives is the task. To concentrate on the 'here and now' is not superficial, as the psychodynamists might suggest, or counterproductive, to be played down in the medico-biologists' act of reassurance. In Moral Therapy present attitudes are used and analysed not for intellectual satisfaction in the elucidation of postulated causes, nor because the act of analysis itself has any beneficial curative qualities, but because the information provided can be used as a prelude to action. Analysis of the moral code, the guilt, the self-respect is useful because it points a way forward. It tells us what to do and how to do it.

Obviously strenuous attempts are made to get it right and in this the tendency of individuals with a shared culture freely to choose codes of a fundamental similarity may be helpful. Thus in the absence of psychopathy we might regard with some suspicion the protestations of someone who professed to seeing no value in keeping promises, being kind to others, being loyal, not stealing, etc. However, although it is useful to be correct in the analysis of the underlying moral code it is not absolutely essential.

Indeed, the practitioner of Moral Therapy is not so interested in 'objective truth', at best an uncertain concept when one is dealing with such an obscure and plastic entity as the human mind. Moral Therapy recognises that our thoughts, feelings and intentions are not immutable but rather exhibit a constantly changing pattern, showing certain recurring themes that allow them to possess some sort of semi-permanent identity. In the absence of hard, permanent, unalterable purposes we should encourage the individual to settle for 'useful fictions' whereby he attaches himself to a more or less finalised ambition which is basically in tune with his moral heritage. He must behave as if he has a firm goal whether it is a realistic one or not.

In contrast to psychodynamic dogma in which each piece of information is given equal importance as an expression of the personality's internal economy the concerned friend should be interested only in material that is useful; which can be used in a positive way. That he has a sense of direction is more important than his arrival at a 'correct' destination. Any other 'facts' about his personality or predispositional tendencies will be ignored wherever they might conjure up that pessimism which is so often described as realism but whose only function is to surround the individual with a wall of disbelief in his abilities and potential for success which can only impede his development and lower his self-respect.

In Moral Therapy all movement and action has a tendency to be good, all stasis and passivity a tendency to be bad. Insofar as this is true it is far from fatal that an individual should embark on a journey in the wrong direction, for the decision to move at all will itself have positive implications for self-respect. Few of us regret our decisions to act. It is our failures to act for which we tend to be sorry. Moral Therapy agrees with John Donne that 'Change is the nursery of music, joy, life, and eternity'. It is more important to have the courage to make changes, to take decisions than to shrink from doing so. This is the way to increased self-respect provided that the hand of conscience is on the rudder of the boat.

In Moral Therapy, then, information gathering and analysis do not have the importance or emphasis that they are given in both the psychodynamic or medico-biological approaches because the person who follows its principles is more interested in results than in being right; in common sense than in obscure intellectualising; in optimism than in pessimism; in motion than in inertia.

At this stage it is important to emphasise a basic attitude of Moral Therapy that is directly at variance with the views of the psychodynamists, the medico-biologists and much of popular wisdom. Perhaps the most important tenet of the doctrine of Moral Therapy is that only by doing what we believe to be right can we be contented. It follows from this that if we behave in a way that we ourselves acknowledge to be bad, then discontent must inevitably follow. The Moral Therapist will investigate discontent in terms of individual ethical codes contravened, of personal moral commands disobeyed. In taking this position Moral Therapy lends support to a theory that has wide acceptance amongst those laymen and others who do not follow to views of a liberal and permissive type, but instead subscribe to a more robust and conservative philosophy. Certainly both the psychodynamists and the medico-biologists would strive to discredit the inescapable conclusion of Moral Therapy that it must follow that if our discontent has its foundation in our wrong-doing we are correct to blame ourselves for our shortcomings. Furthermore because in most cases our moral codes will be similar to those of our national, racial and socio-economic peers with whom we share a common environment and educational process, they may be right to blame us too. Thus it may be more correct and even valuable that our failures should be regarded with rather less pity and understanding and with rather more hostility or uninterest. Few would maintain that it is good to fail but many would have us believe that we are blameless when we do so. Moral Therapy seeks to redress the balance of a pendulum that has swung too far towards a state of affairs in which all 'neurosis' is excused, all guilt discouraged, all blame avoided and all responsibility removed. In taking this stance Moral Therapy signals a return to more traditional attitudes which the psychodynamists and psychoactive drug advocates have done so much and with so little reason to undermine. By their insistence that we are largely controlled by respectively our past environments and our brain biochemistry they have rendered us at once blameless yet irresponsible; innocent but helpless; in theory without guilt but emasculated.

It may seem odd that the accumulated wisdom of generations could be pushed aside so easily when no irrefutable concrete evidence has been produced to discredit it. Certainly there is no conclusive proof that the metapsychological posturings of the psychodynamists have any relevance to the understanding of how we live our lives or have contributed towards increasing their quality. Similarly the biochemists have produced no substances that add in any worthwhile way to the psychological well-being of those who are not suffering from actual psychiatric illness. And yet these two groups from their separate vantage-points have contributed to the malaise and sense of impotence which we tend to experience when our problems get on top of us. Moral Therapy seeks to rectify this and encourages people to accept blame so that they may act to divert it; to embrace guilt so that by modifying their behaviour they can diminish it; to take responsibility for their actions so that they can experience the fruits of success.

Thus paradoxically it is the acceptance of blame that is the optimistic attitude and its denial the pessimistic one, and what appears the harder line is the more kind, the softer the more cruel.

Against those who would say that Moral Therapy is attempting to put back the clock it can be argued with force that there existed no reason to put it 'forward' in the first place. Freud and his followers must always be credited with the fact that they made mental illness itself respectable in the sense that the misguided treatments of the nineteenth century such as the straitjackets and incarceration became unfashionable and irrelevant once it was realised that the mind was as amenable to disease as the body. This change of prevailing climate was in no small measure due to the exertions of Freud and his colleagues.

On the debit side of the balance sheet Freud and the psychodynamists were responsible, in opening the door to new and more enlightened attitudes towards psychopathology, for the creation of a whole new 'science', one of the achievements of which was to produce a whole new illness category – namely that of neurosis. Moral Therapy argues that for many thousands of years the human race has done without this concept of neurosis and must and will learn to do so again. That we have a word for it does not explain what it is, if it exists or what, if it truly exists, is the best thing to do about it. The concept of 'neurosis' has not helped the plight of 'neurotics'. For in truth neurosis is the word we use in an attempt to explain the condition of those who have chosen for some reason scarcely perceived even by themselves to make a mess of their lives, to live unsuccessfully and to experience semi-permanent psychological pain.

In dignifying the failure to lead a satisfactory life with the descriptive term 'neurosis', a new disease category is created with its own natural history, signs, symptoms and prognosis. This old philosophical mistake of the hypostasisation of an abstraction, in which the existence of a word is mistakenly taken to imply the existence of a real entity which that word describes, leads to the idea that there exist neuroses in the same way that there exist broken legs and heart murmurs. As soon as an illness has been promulgated, then practitioners must be found to administer cures and alleviate symptoms of a condition which it is believed descends upon patients like rheumatism or the 'flu'. Such people maintain that if the patient *has* a 'neurosis' it is no fault of his own. Insofar as blame is relevant at all in disease they might single out the family unit or the environment for the accusing finger, in the same way as cigarettes are implicated (in this case correctly) in the pathogenesis of lung cancer, or air pollution in bronchitis.

In reality, of course, to behave in a 'neurotic' way is not a disease but a misguided decision and such behaviour is a function of our basic freedom to choose, of our self-determination, of our responsibility for our own lives. Perhaps in some perfect world of the psychodynamists in which all were exposed to their teachings and methods, such freedoms would be superfluous and there would remain only well-adjusted people, their psyches working smoothly in close accordance with the blueprint for some mental machine dreamed up by metaphysical conceptualists who were longer on theory than they were on common sense.

It is an old religious concept that if we are to be free to do well we must conversely be free to do badly. If there is good that can be freely chosen, then there must of necessity exist the possibility of choosing evil. In religious terminology blame accrues to the person who chooses wrongly, praise to he who makes the correct choice. Forgiveness is always available to the sinner if, in recanting, he is sincere. It is not part of the doctrine of Moral Therapy to espouse the cause of any particular religion, although the individual who freely chooses and truly believes in the tenets of one of the great religious faiths with their comprehensive and all-embracing ethical codes has a tremendous advantage in the struggle for self-respect over those whose decision it is to hold no such institutionalised beliefs. The religious analogy is made because it can be extended into the area of mental health. Moral Therapy maintains that it is inefficient, irresponsible and even bad to live our lives unsuccessfully, experiencing constant psychological pain, and that the individual should be encouraged to accept responsibility for this, and even blame. Here again it cannot be emphasised strongly enough that this only holds where actual psychological illness of the affective type has been categorically excluded.

The unsuccessful person with his low self-esteem can, like the sinner, return at any time to the correct path and can be helped to do so. But he will not be helped by a denial of his problem or by reassurances that he does not really have one, or again that if he does have a problem it is through no fault of his own. All these attitudes merely serve to reinforce a status quo that, if the individual is to benefit, must be changed forthwith. Traditional wisdom since Freud maintains that it is harsh, unkind and insensitive to confront the unsuccessful person with his responsibility for his own shortcomings, and further that it is ineffective and cruel because he is not to blame for his situation. Instead, it is argued, we should try to understand him, to unravel the causal processes that determined his unhappy position, hoping piously that this investigation will in some magical way 'make him better'. Others will argue that the thing to do is to obliterate his unpleasant feelings, along with most others as well, with blunderbuss tranquillising drug therapy. Above all we should avoid any censorious tone, any intimation that we do not approve of his behaviour and should rely on psychological 'knowledge and expertise' to solve his problems for him.

Luckily in everyday life friends and loved ones seldom fall into the trap into which the so-called experts have so readily fallen. We do not tend to over-indulge those of our friends who make a career out of being in a psychological mess. Instead we employ a more rough and ready, a more stimulating and in the end more successful approach. We are not manipulated as are so many of the talk therapists into entering that impenetrable jungle of psychological cause and effect in which introversion and intellectualising are at a premium whilst activity, extroversion and common sense are discounted. We are not afraid to employ a carrot-and-stick approach because we realise that ultimately the person who makes a lifetime's career out of being in trouble has chosen that path because of the 'benefits' that it brings him. That those benefits are a sham, false, not really benefits at all, is something that we recognise and we suspect that he does too. So we may threaten withdrawal of our friendship or other more minor sanctions if he continues with his tiresome behaviour whilst rewarding his return to more reasonable activities and attitudes with increased interest, greater contact, etc. We are not afraid to tell him what he is up to and blame him for it.

The more liberal approach using, as it prefers to do, the illness model of the 'neurosis' or 'personality disorder' is profoundly unhelpful and soon the patient *has* a 'neurosis' and an analyst to prove it. He becomes at a stroke a card-carrying fully paid-up member of the psychological walking wounded. He has a role to play and fellow actors with which to play it, in that he can keep in touch with the activities and emotions of those who share his 'diagnosis' by a diligent reading of psychodynamic texts, a careful digestion of cocktail-party psychobabble, a studied observation of psychodramatic plays and films, a casual perusal of glossy magazines and women's journals.

In truth we can do without the concept of neurosis. For there is no actual illness that exists as a tangible entity to which the term refers and the diagnosis has no valuable implications for prognosis or treatment. The 'neurotic' is the person who has taken the wrong path to the detriment of himself and others. He has freely chosen to do so and is therefore responsible for his choice. He could have behaved differently, and in similar circumstances others have done so. He has decided to be his own worst enemy and to view others as hostile and aggressive. He lives in the real world but realism fails to characterise his hopes and aspirations. He has made his own bed and now he must sleep in it. He has nobody but himself to blame and we must not shrink from telling him so. This approach is not a matter of chastisement, of punishment. Its purpose is purely therapeutic – to return to the individual that sense of control over his own destiny, that responsibility for his own actions which the psychodynamists and the medico-biologists are so keen to deny him. In doing so the decks are cleared for the positive action that alone will do him good.

That there is a risk in this approach cannot be denied, but life is risky. Risks must always be taken when the circumstances demand them. It is as risky, although superficially it may appear not to be, to create a passive, dependent 'patient', with an institutionalised 'neurosis' psychologically addicted to talk therapy, as it is to produce a tranquillised automaton dependent on pills for the avoidance of psychological pain. Moral Therapy suggests that both these alternatives are more dangerous for the patient than firmly confronting him with his own responsibility for his own actions. However, although more dangerous for the patient, in the current climate of professional attitudes, pills and talk therapy are far less dangerous for the doctor. For these are the panaceas that the patient expects and wants, although they are seldom what he needs.

The ostensibly more brutal, but ultimately more kind, approach in which the individual is held to be both responsible and therefore blameworthy lays the doctor open to complaints of callousness and hard-heartedness. Further the sufferer may attempt to punish the doctor who has refused to collude with him in maintaining his 'illness' status by harming himself or threatening so to do. 'You said it was all my fault so I might as well kill myself,' could be a response.

Moral Therapy admits that there is some risk to the individual here but maintains that it is an acceptable risk, a calculated gamble whose potential benefits far outweigh the possible harm that might ensue.

Surely the more cowardly approach is to conspire with the patient to preserve his status of 'neurotic' paying lip-service to his 'psychological disability'. Thus the doctor may talk around the problem in a knowing way, as if a few fine adjustments are all that are required before the machine is again working efficiently. Reassurance and a tranquilliser will do the rest as the hard-worked doctor moves towards his objective of getting the patient out of his office with a marginally and temporarily improved mood, so that he cannot be held responsible for any increase in his patient's psychological pain and can gain a spurious 'ersatz' gratification from the visible but transient effects of his efforts.

So it can be seen that reassurance, pills and sympathy are the low-risk/high-risk approach – that is to say low for the doctor but ultimately high for the patient. Moral Therapy seeks to be more heroic. Like the surgeon who is unafraid of amputating the gangrenous leg of the elderly patient with cardio-vascular disease despite the risks of major surgery, the practitioner of Moral Therapy will be prepared to tell the individual the truth with regard to his failings and be prepared to load on to him the responsibility for them. For until he comes to terms with his potential for choosing a more efficient way of leading his life he will be condemned indefinitely to live in the twilight world of psychological discomfort, blaming others for a predicament that is, in reality, of his own making. And so as the surgeon risks the death of his patient in order to remove the diseased and life-threatening leg, we should not be afraid in the absence of psychopathology to agree with the individual that his behaviour is indeed unsatisfactory.

For Moral Therapy recognises that, in many significant ways, the individual who presents himself for help is indeed inferior. With regard to the fact that he is unhappy, guilty, behaving in a way of which he himself does not approve, he is less good than many people at the successful practice of the art of life. He is not *intrinsically* inferior, in that he has the power and capability to be better than average at living with a greater than normal self-respect if he chooses to make the effort so to be. His failure is not constitutional. It is a failure of choice, showing a weakness of will, a lack of determination and perseverance, and above all a failure of direction and approach. As such it can be rectified but only after a complete recognition that his failure is his own fault; that at this point of time he is inferior; that he made himself unhappy and so can now make himself less so; that nobody is to blame for his predicament but himself.

Some people pay lip-service to their own responsibility for their unsatisfactory condition but argue at the same time that they cannot get themselves out of it. These people use their own inadequacies as a stick to beat themselves with. 'Look at me,' they might say, 'I made this mess. I destroyed myself and now I hate myself for having done so!' 'What a terrible person I must be to be so self-destructive!' 'Surely there can be no hope,' they argue, 'for somebody who has so freely chosen such an unhelpful path!' Thus do they attempt to disarm the person who would return to them the responsibility for their own actions. In their desperation to hang on to their 'illness' they are even prepared to tolerate guilt and the pain of low self-respect. Admitting their responsibility they then advance such wanton and apparently capricious self-destruction as evidence for the fact that they are clearly sick. 'What possible advantage,' they ask, 'can I be gaining from this misery?' That they choose so badly, so disastrously is for them evidence of a disability so great that they consider themselves diseased and they tend to find little difficulty in persuading doctors to agree with their self-diagnosis. They admit that they chose their actions and behaviour but at the same time maintain that their unfortunate choice was determined by their 'neurosis' or their 'disordered personality'.

Such people effectively maintain two contradictory positions. On the one hand they admit that they are free to choose their unsatisfactory attitudes and behaviour in that they were not externally coerced or environmentally influenced to behave in that way – that in theory they *could* have chosen differently. At the same time they use their unsatisfactory life history as evidence that in some sense their actions *are* determined. They have such a strong dispositional tendency to act and think in this unhelpful way that in point of fact they have always done so and presumably will continue so to do. They feel that although in theory they could have acted differently and therefore are prepared to accept the guilt and blame for their situation, in *fact* they have seldom or never acted positively and therefore some mysterious evil force must be responsible for their continuing to choose disastrous actions and negative thoughts. Their energy and that of their 'expert' advisers is then spent in the identification and explanation of this force in the hope that in the act of being identified it will in some way disappear or become more amenable to being made to do so. Once the treasure hunt for this shadowy entity has been embarked upon all hope is lost, for by this stage both doctor and patient will have effectively denied the individual's ultimate and meaningful responsibility for his attitudes and actions.

Thus do psychodynamists of the traditional school employ methods which tend to sap the self-esteem of those they would try to help. For their patients the regular visit, frequently over a long time-span, is analogous to the valium tablet of the medico-biologist. The weekly, or, in psychoanalysis daily, visit builds dependence on the psychiatrist as the patient's confidence declines. 'I don't know what I would do without my analyst' is a statement that is all too often heard. In this case, too, the individual is sheltered from facing up to his responsibility for his own failure for now he can point proudly to his 'neurosis', the existence of which is implied by the 'necessity' for his frequent visits to his analyst. As long as he has an analyst he has a neurosis. As long as he has a valium prescription he has an illness. If he has neither and is turned away from both analyst and doctor he has no excuses and only himself to blame. Then at last he will be free to set about confronting the problems that only he can solve.

6
Freudian Fantasies: Inventing the Illness Excuse

Let us for a few pages shine the light of common sense upon the theories of Freud. They can be divided into two parts. Firstly there is the philosophy, the metapsychology of psychoanalysis, revealed apparently to Freud from a consideration of his patients. Secondly there is the use of psychoanalysis as a therapeutic tool, a process that is in some way supposed to benefit the person on whom it is used. So lacking is the evidence for any specific beneficial effect of psychoanalysis as a therapy that many of its practitioners have ceased to claim too much for it in this respect, although, of course, continuing to earn their living from its practice. As a metapsychology, as a religion perhaps, they remain publicly convinced of its truth. What exactly are we asked to believe? Certainly it is a fantastical story.

All of us remain fundamentally unaware, unless steeped in psychoanalytic dogma, that two basic instincts provide the force, the underlying energy, for all our thoughts and actions. These two instincts are, unfortunately, in direct opposition to one another. Eros, the life instinct, consists of the instinct for self-preservation. One need not be an Einstein, or even a Freud, to see that such an instinct is primary and vital in all of us. Common sense tells us that it is so. However, if we are to believe Freud there is an instinct towards self-destruction, too – described by him as Thanatos, the death instinct. But if we strive for life is it intrinsically likely that we should all at the same time be struggling towards its opposite? Do

56

we really want to die, have the basic urge to return to that disorganised state from which we were originally constituted? Certainly entropy, the universal tendency towards disintegration, is a useful physical principle and nothing is more certain than that we will die, but surely there is no sense in which we *want* to cease to exist.

Freud came to his belief in the death instinct through his consideration of such phenomena as aggression, masochism, suicide and such apparently self-destructive behaviour as alcoholism and drug addiction. From such things he *deduced* the existence of the death instinct. But they can be explained quite satisfactorily in other and more plausible ways, in terms of the desire for momentary gratification, of shortsightedness, of feeling threatened, of being threatened, of inability to withstand pain and misery, etc. One might think it a mighty leap in the dark from an observance of aggression and suicide to the absolute certainty of the existence in *all* of us, whether or not we exhibit aggression or suicidal ideas, of an instinct for self-destruction. Indeed the theory of the death instinct provides a marvellous example of how Freud, professing himself a scientist practising the scientific method, actually plucked his theories from thin air and then set about using his considerable intelligence and powers of persuasion to increase their plausibility and make them acceptable to his disciples. The death instinct's existence is proved beyond doubt from a consideration of the 'evidence', we are told. It is a scientific 'fact'. The argument runs something like this. Human behaviour provides examples which do not seem to fit a theory in which Eros alone provides the sole instinctual drive. People are often gratuitously aggressive and occasionally seek to harm themselves. Some seem to gain pleasure from pain inflicted on them by others. It would seem that we need another concept which will make such behaviour 'explicable' in terms of Freudian theory. A death instinct would to some extent make sense of it. Therefore there is a death instinct. Q.E.D.

In such a way are the Freudian myths built. But is there not an intrinsic ridiculousness in assuming the universal existence of a death instinct, and if common sense and the scientific method both tell us that the method by which it is 'known' is to say the least suspect, might we not retain a healthy suspicion with regard to the more plausible tenets of Freudian philosophy?

Before the discovery, dare we say invention, of the death instinct Freud's theory of the instincts tended to concentrate on Eros. Contained within the instinct for self-preservation, or co-existing with it, is that typically Freudian fantasy animal, the libido. This is the instinct towards physical gratification of the senses, which, in its purest and most unadulterated form, is manifested as the desire for sexual pleasure. The libidinal energy – bubbling, primeval – provides a powerful force to our instinctual drive towards physical satisfaction – the pleasure principle that governs so much of conscious thought. Now Eros, with its component instincts for self-preservation and the pursuit of pleasure, together with Thanatos, the death instinct, inhabit an ancient, shadowy and mystical realm known to Freudians as the 'id'. The id, in which the instincts repose, makes us do things, think things, want things and need things. We want to stay alive and extract pleasure from ourselves and our environment. At the same time we are apparently thrusting ourselves towards death. Of course, before Freud we were in blissful ignorance of the fact that we all possessed an id because we none of us had ever experienced this ghostly province. This is understandable because, according to Freud, the id remains of necessity permanently inaccessible, unconscious, literally not experienced in consciousness, unknown directly.

How, one might ask, did Freud get to know of its existence, if by definition it cannot be experienced? His answer would have to be that the existence of this psychical apparatus is inferred from a study of the development of human beings, intuited from an observance of the behaviour and reported thoughts of others, or from a consideration of his own introspected, conscious thought-processes. But the id, like so much else in psychoanalysis, requires the eye of the believer before it can be 'seen'. Others in *their* consideration of human thought and action, and despite having been alerted by Freud to its supposed existence, have found no signs or indicators of the mythical entity. In truth the concept of the id is something we can do without, have done without before, and will do without again. Certainly, in view of the fact that the id is one of the most vital foundation stones on which the whole shaky edifice of psychoanalytic philosophy is built, one would have hoped that its existence and nature could have been more clearly demonstrated. One might even be forgiven for thinking that firm and unshakeable belief in an undemonstrable and quintessentially unconscious entity might have the logical status of a religious belief rather than of a 'scientific discovery', and it may indeed be no coincidence that it was the Roman Catholic church which Freud regarded as the most substantial enemy of psychoanalysis. Happily, however, if throughout history we have believed in Gods, it is only in the last few decades that we have been asked to believe in the id and one cannot help but wonder how it is that such an important entity, literally the fount of all motivation and desire, should for so long have remained unrecognised and unknown. Could it just be that what was required was not somebody to recognise but rather to invent it and, having done so, to flog it as a concept for the consumption of the gullible?

Lest it be thought that one is unfair to Freud in suggesting that he thought of the id as an actual entity, rather than as merely a figurative term for describing something with no real existence over and above the idea that encapsulates it, one can refer to his view that in the fullness of time, as science advanced in its understanding of the human brain, it would be possible to define the exact location and borders of the psychical provinces or agencies such as the ego and the id in terms of anatomical neuronal areas, or, perhaps, of facilitated neuronal pathways. Further he believed that the determined thoughts and actions which he used the blunt instrument of psychoanalysis to predict and to explain causally would eventually be predictable and explicable in terms of physico-chemical or other physical causal laws. The fact remains that if the id was an analogy then the physical counterpart to which it supposedly refers was not demonstrated by him, and has not been demonstrated by science since. The form and content of the id have remained speculative metaphysics to all but the psychoanalytic faithful.

In the intellectual climate of today it is difficult to see how the concept of the id and of the drive towards sensual pleasure once seemed so plausible. Certainly if tomorrow the theory were to make its debut *de novo* it might be regarded with very considerable scepticism, not to say ridicule. It is not as if the theory itself is intrinsically plausible, even believable, although one can see how Freud, steeped in the atmosphere of turn-of-the-century scientific principles and influenced by the great strides that were being made in physics, chemistry and biology, might have been attracted to the idea of a fundamental and dynamic energy force providing the stimulus to thought and action. It is also likely that as a good philosopher, and an even better populariser of his philosophy, he would realise the advantage of keeping such dynamic forces to as manageably a small number as would 'fit' the 'facts'. That the idea caught on was the result of the happy coincidence that it fell on the receptive ears of a society ripe for its message, ready for a sexual permissiveness which its tenets have indubitably done much to advance, willing the reaction against the severity of the puritan ethic which in those times held sway. A society which tended to discourage overt sexual expression and its discussion was bound to take notice of a theory which suggested that the pursuit of physical gratification was one of our most fundamental instincts.

Let us continue with the survey of Freudian theory. If left to its own devices, we are asked to believe, the untrammelled, uncontrolled libidinous instincts and other drives of the id would bring us into conflict with our fellow men in the 'real' world. Therefore, Freud maintains, one part of the id undergoes a special development for the purpose of mediating between the potentially antisocial id and the external world. This psychical entity is concerned with self-preservation and the principle of reality. It is called the ego. The id remains wholly unconscious, whilst the ego rules within the narrower confines of consciousness. The super-ego is the name given to a portion of the ego which has become detached and consists of the learned morality, the sum total of the moral imperatives gleaned from the environment and especially from the parents. It exercises its powers throughout the arena of the conscious mind and also within the realms of the pre-conscious, the latter being defined as that reservoir of potentially voluntarily recallable material that is not actually conscious but at any moment could easily be so. The ego acts as a kind of ringmaster attempting to reconcile the often conflicting demands of the id's instinctual drives, the super-ego's various strictures, and the demands of reality which spring from the real world. The ego strives hard to minimise the tensions that continually arise from these ceaseless conflicts of interest, and in so doing employs a wide variety of defence mechanisms in its endless quest for harmony between the warring elements of the personality. Such defensive weaponry includes the well-known phenomena of repression and sublimation, regression, projection and displacement. The ego works hard as it acts to channel the drives and thrusts of the instincts in a way that will not result in disaster for the individual, and its general purpose is to keep tension and excitation to a bare minimum. It strives to keep the energy level within the system at a constant and acceptably low level. This it does by forcing out of consciousness those ideas which would, if the individual became aware of them, tend to increase excitation to an unacceptable height. Thus does the ego control the personality by expending its own energy to neutralise the tensions of dangerous impulses and ideas.

In so far as the ego, without the expenditure of too much of its own energy in the process, tends towards success in establishing a tenuous equilibrium, we veer towards mental health. To the extent that it fails to maintain the balance, or is forced to mount too costly a defence against the threatening unconscious impulses, we tend towards 'neurosis', even psychosis. No ego is ever one hundred per cent successful and therefore, the theory maintains, we can all do with a bit of psychoanalysis. What's more, the 'beneficial effects' of a few years of psychoanalysis are limited and so, in an ideal world, the analytic process should be constantly repeated. This is of course a useful philosophy if your income, status and prestige depend on your practice of this particular 'profession'.

Such is the 'meat' of Freudian theory – namely, the account of the psychical apparatus and the theory of instincts. Now the true purpose of our lives is revealed to us. We live, apparently, to satisfy our fundamental needs – to survive, to destroy and be destroyed, to experience physical gratification, which, in its purest form is to be found in sexual activity. We know, too, as a result of Freud's careful study of his Viennese patients that our mental apparatus is divided into ego, id and super-ego, into conscious, unconscious and preconscious. Is this really how we see ourselves? Is the evidence at all convincing? Is the theory plausible, or is it a lot of nonsense – meaningless verbiage, unverifiable rubbish, merely a magical way of thinking about things with no application to the real world, nothing more than fantasy and therefore ultimately of no value at all?

Let us take a quotation from Freud and look at it closely – 'The power of the id expresses the true purpose of the individual organism's life'. Certainly the structure of the sentence is grammatically correct, and it would appear to be expressing a meaningful proposition, one which might be either true or false. The concept expressed is a theoretical one. Like quarks, quasars, and black holes, ids do not appear directly to the senses but must be inferred from sense data which we do experience. So if remarks about ids are to be of more use and importance than remarks about abracadabras, we need to be aware of the sort of facts that would point unequivocally to the existence of, and illuminate the nature and attributes of ids, and of nothing else. Thus if a set of evidence demands the existence of ids, their presence in all of us, that they contain the instincts, that their content is unconscious of necessity, that 'they express the true purpose of the individual's life' etc, then the evidence must not be capable of a different interpretation, used for example to define another concept altogether. Also the evidence must be capable of being validated or invalidated and we must be clear about the sort of things that would prove or disprove the existence and nature of the id even if those things are not immediately to hand.

If psychoanalytic theory was advanced merely as a metapsychology such questions would be academic, of little immediate use except to the philosophers who would earn their living by discussing them. But psychoanalysis is a multi-billion dollar industry, a therapeutic method which presumes to treat those with genuine psychological illness as well as 'neurotics', a theory apparently based on a consideration of evidence and on nothing else. If it is philosophically unsound we ought to know about it.

How, then, does Freud's remark about the id stand up in the light of the above criteria? Not very well. For in truth there is nothing in human thought or behaviour which points specifically and indubitably to the existence and nature of ids, to the fact that they express the true purpose of an individual's life, or anything else for that matter. Further, one can conceive of no set of experiences which would be generally agreed to either validate or invalidate Freud's proposition. Negative findings don't invalidate it nor positive ones prove its truth. The concept of the id is just too vague, intangible, mysterious, woolly to be proved or disproved by anything at all. For the Freudian all behaviour and thought lead inescapably to the 'fact' of the id, but the non-believer, considering the same phenomena, does not find it. It would appear to be a question of belief, an article of faith, akin to the religious way of knowing.

Freud, it seems, dreamed up what was for him a plausible entity, and then set about finding mental phenomena which for him, but not for others, tended to support it. This mistake runs throughout the whole of psychoanalytic theory. In fact psychoanalysis is not only scientifically invalid, it is, in my view, implausible too. It fails to do justice to our notions of the true meaning of life, the finer elements of humanity. Instead it reduces us to the level of psychically determined machines, all thought and action being held to follow of necessity from anterior events in a way fundamentally beyond our control and for which we must ultimately be irresponsible, beyond blame, beyond praise. Freud's grubby robot man, controlled by mean urges, groping for sexual gratification, drifting through a desired life towards a desired death, gripped by varying degrees of 'neurosis' is indeed an unappetising phenomenon. Luckily it is one we can easily do without – there being no reason to believe that his ids, his death wishes, his libidos and his ego-defence mechanisms are anything but the product of an active, fertile but wholly misdirected mind.

Even if, by some remarkable conceptual 'hit', Freud had by chance arrived at an ultimate truth, provable and testable at a future date to the satisfaction of all, then in the interim we would be wise to ignore it, to act as if it wasn't so, preferring to believe in a more uplifting and efficacious philosophy in which our motives and instincts are not necessarily base and selfish, in which thought and action are not determined but instead represent our own creative response to life.

Having arrived at an 'understanding' of the very nature of the mind itself from a consideration of the superficial utterances and reported behaviour of his patients, hardly a group representative of humanity at the time and less so now, and having constructed his ambitious and exotic metapsychology Freud moves from the general to the more particular. How do we get to know what is going on in the mysterious world of the unexperienced unconscious, the place where the action is? As a substitute for the reading of the entrails we are offered a world of dreams whose interpretation, according to Freud, provides the royal road to knowledge of the unconscious mind. Dreams, of course, like hands and handwriting, had been 'read' before. For Freud they are, rather than fodder for the fair-ground booth or an open sesame to Joseph's political

63

career, 'the securest foundation of psychoanalysis'. They are, together with Galton's discovery, free-association, and an analysis of 'Freudian slips', the means by which he not only discovered the secrets of the mind, but sought to 'explain' human behaviour, render 'understandable' the processes of human thought.

In many ways this desire to explain and understand human thought and behaviour is the root problem of psychoanalysis and the other psychodynamic doctrines. For why should it be explicable? Is the mind really accessible to mere minds? Can the mind know itself, comprehend and make sense of its own essence? Is it not a fundamentally different thing to use the mind to study the external world, including our own bodies, and to attempt to employ it ontologically? Nothing daunted, determined to succeed in the daunting task of explaining the inexplicable, the psychoanalysts in the end persuade few of their ability besides themselves, and, hopefully for them, their patients.

Despite their protestations to the contrary psychoanalysts do not explain behaviour and thought in terms of its sufficient and necessary causality, do not elucidate actual causal mechanisms which exist in the real world. Instead what they do is offer an explanation of events in terms of their own theory. In that way they 'make sense' of actions and thoughts from the standpoint of their own prejudices. When a psychoanalyst listens to an account of behaviour he interprets it psychoanalytically. A Jungian or an Adlerian would interpret the same behaviour according to his philosophy. The behaviour, the facts are the same. Only the interpretation is different. And when the understanding differs according to the philosophical viewpoint of the observer can there be any true explanation at all? Surely we are then in the realm of opinion and beliefs rather than in an area of scientific fact. Nor would one find much uniformity of explanation, universality of understanding, within the psychoanalytic profession itself. The same dream is interpreted differently by different analysts, and careful recourse to the undisputed 'facts' of the dream's content and form do not appear to reduce the confusion. Thus do the schisms which periodically rend the profession arise, casting doubts on the scientific nature of its procedures. For it is not enough to 'make sense' of human behaviour by making it fit a particular conceptual framework. The sense that is made must have some relationship to reality, and be generally recognised to do so.

Let us look briefly at Freud's theories with regard to dream interpretation. The argument goes like this. Everything that happens in a dream has a meaning, although that meaning is often obscure. Not only does it have a meaning, it has a purpose too, the purpose of wish fulfilment in which the desires of the unconscious mind are satisfied. Frequently these wishes cause excess excitation. Now it will be remembered that one of the functions of the ego is to dampen excitement and tension, keeping its level within what is in effect a self-regulating control system relatively constant. These potentially threatening and anxiety-producing unconscious wishes must be heavily disguised in the dreams if they are not to wreak havoc with the delicate arrangement of controls and balances which characterise the Freudian personality structure. So, for Freud, the manifest content of the dream is not all that it seems – and it is for the hidden meaning, the latent content that he searches, ferreting out and identifying the various mechanisms, such as condensation and displacement, dramatisation, symbolism and secondary elaboration, which the ego uses in the dream as it works to prevent the raw and unacceptable wishes of the unconscious presenting themselves in their damaging and unadulterated form to consciousness. Prominent amongst such unwelcome mental phenomena are the sinister wishes for sexual gratification powered by the libidinous urges. Penises and vaginas and the appalling juxtaposition of the twain are particularly to be guarded against in view of their potentially disastrous effect on the precarious id/ego/super-ego relationships of the worthy burghers of Vienna who frequented Freud's consulting rooms. So unacceptable to the psyche is, apparently, the contemplation of such anatomical appendages and receptacles that they must be disguised by symbols whenever they occur. Thus things long and pointed such as cigarettes and church towers and things that go off like guns or eject like hose pipes represent in symbolic fashion the dreaded phallus. Tunnels, holes, caves, anything hollow, represent the consciously unacceptable vagina. Motor-bikes, cars and trains, especially when they drive through tunnels, symbolise sexual intercourse. It is not difficult to improvise on the theme.

Several thoughts occur immediately. Is conscious contemplation of sexual activity, of penises and vaginas, really so threatening that we can't dream of them directly – and if so then why do we so frequently *have* overtly sexual dreams, and in glorious technicolour? Were dreams of sexual intercourse so rare in the Vienna of Freudian times? Possibly it was just 'not done' to talk about them, not even to the creator of psychoanalysis, perhaps especially not to him. The result might have been that Freud, who maintained steadfastly that all his theories were constructed and modified on the basis of what he learned from his patients, may have been misled by their socially conditioned unwillingness to discuss dream material which was all the time perfectly amenable to being experienced by consciousness and without untoward effects. Determined to discover latent sexuality to satisfy his theory of the instincts, he was forced to 'find' it when it didn't exist. In this way do innocent dreams come to bubble with subterranean hidden meanings of a sexual nature. And so now, at least for the psychoanalytic faithful, surrogate penises and vaginas are condemned forever to stalk the sidewalks and thoroughfares of our nocturnal thought processes. At the last count there were well over two hundred such symbols. Why, one might ask, are so many necessary?

There are few aspects of Freudian theory which appear so fundamentally ridiculous as his insistence that our dreams are riddled with disguised sexuality. For if our dreams are pregnant with latent meanings usually of a sexual nature, what becomes of the innocent dreams of childhood? A child learns to ride a bicycle. That night, tired but happy, he dreams of riding it beneath the railway bridge past the field of cows a few hundred yards from his home. Symbolic of the wish for intercourse, possibly with his mother, says the psychoanalyst. 'Rubbish,' I suspect we would wish to chorus in reply. This example is typical of the psychoanalytic 'scientific' method. Once you have made the leap of faith, have swallowed the Freudian myth, then everything can be interpreted in the light of the theory. If you remain a disbeliever, then you sit back amazed, and possibly appalled at the distortions of reality in which the Freudians indulge. When the Freudian sees vaginas and the wish for sex we see bicycles and bridges, and sleepy but contented children. It is a question of choice.

One can't help feeling that if Freud were alive today, basking in the tradition of permissive liberalism which his work has done so much to foster, he might well have wanted to modify his theory of the interpretation of dreams and possibly much else besides. For he was, as we all are, a creature of the times, living in an age when matters sexual were scarcely discussed, seldom referred to openly, hardly the approved topic for dinner-party conversations, TV chat shows, the endless preoccupation of newspapers and magazines. Certainly there are taboo topics today, death and class for example, but sex is certainly no longer one of them. So for Freud sex was a clandestine activity, prevalent and central, but hidden and disguised, to be rooted out and exposed verbally on his consulting-room couch. Today the seeker after sexual soul-searching need go no further than the corner news-stand and the agony columns of the glossy magazines, which are, in many ways, his legacy. The well-heeled, verbal, middle-class 'neurotics' of early twentieth-century Vienna tended to keep their sexual cards closer to their chests than the psychological breast beaters of the 1980s, and Freud's approach both reflected and profited from that situation.

It is perhaps in a consideration of Freud's theories of dream interpretation that one is confronted most vividly by his preoccupation with things sexual, but it is in his notorious theory of child development that the importance of sex to psychoanalysis is most clearly demonstrated. According to Freud sexuality starts soon after birth and the sexual pleasure flows in turn from different pleasure areas, the so-called erogenous zones of mouth, anus and genitals. Later on the sexual desire of the little boy for his mother gives rise to jealousy of the father and the repressed fear that the father, learning of his erotic wishes, will castrate him. Women provide an ever-present example of what it might be like to have no penis. At the same developmental stage the little girl comes to the realisation that she has no penis, a sorry state of affairs for which she blames her mother. Her father, however, *is* equipped with this strangely important piece of equipment and she begins to envy his possession of it. So she begins to identify and relate to the father, considering herself in competition with her mother for his interest.

After the turmoils of this seminal Oedipal period the child enters, from the age of about five, into a period of sexual inertia known as

67

the latency period, before exploding once again during the stage of adolescence into a second phase of active sexual interest.

The idea that sexual life begins at the very earliest age and that the search for sexual gratification characterises all of us from just after birth to the age of about five is one of Freud's most controversial. The theory is central to the explanations of later 'neurotic' behaviour and it is maintained that the vast majority of emotional and behavioural maladaptations in later life can be traced to unresolved problems during early development and especially at the Oedipal stage.

Many of us have much experience of the bringing up of children, and in general our observation of their behaviour is keen and acute. Do our own findings point irrevocably to the truth of Freud's theories? After all, it was from a consideration of the 'evidence' that the theories were apparently constructed. The truth seems to be that the theories go far beyond anything that can actually be observed. Freud lets his imagination run free with the 'facts' and then constructs his theory as if it was a logical deduction, as if the 'facts' had given rise to it. From then on the 'facts' are always interpreted in the light of the theory and thus tend always to appear to 'confirm' it.

Take for example the indubitable fact that the baby appears to gain satisfaction from sucking the breast. That in itself is not very remarkable. It is the only way that he can get food, can survive. He is born with a suck reflex and is genetically programmed to gain satisfaction from feeding at the breast. From such small beginnings can mighty theories grow. Firstly the pleasure derived from this activity is described as sexual, with all the implications of the word. But to do so only makes sense if one has decided to believe that all pleasure is in a sense sexual, an assumption that tends to be made in psychoanalysis but which is by no means a common assumption. Next we are told that the child becomes 'angry' with the mother when she delays for one reason or another in satisfying his oral 'sexual' pleasures. His attitude towards the mother becomes 'ambivalent' and his 'aggression' is expressed in a tendency to bite at her breast. This biting behaviour has the double purpose of 'introjecting' a part of the mother into himself, of consuming a part of her so that she cannot leave him. At a primitive level he experiences 'fears' of the consequences of his 'ambivalence' etc, etc.

It is all very imaginative, but is it likely? Is this really what happens, or are words being used in a specialised and unusual way? What can it mean to say that one so young is ambivalent about his mother, that he fears the consequences of his ambivalence? What possible evidence can point to the truth of this remarkable assertion, this wild shot in the dark. Are we really to believe that a five-year-old 'fears castration', whether the fear is 'repressed' or not? Does he have an innate concept of what it might be like to lose his penis? Does he really want to make love to his mother? The ship of Freudian theory founders on the mighty rocks of common sense when these questions are seriously considered, but unshakeable in their faith the Freudians refuse to admit that the ship is no longer afloat. They point to the 'evidence' of the case histories, to that of Little Hans, for example.

Let us look at this nasty little example of dialogue in which the father, a disciple of Freud's and a firm believer in psychoanalytic dogma, questions his five-year-old son. Little Hans' supposedly spontaneous answers are thought by the cognoscenti to be perhaps the clearest objective evidence in the Freudian literature of the existence of the Oedipus complex. Freud, incidentally, saw Little Hans on one occasion alone.

Father: It seems to me that, all the same, you do wish Mummy would have a baby.

Hans: But I don't want it to happen.

Father: But you do wish for it?

Hans: Oh, yes, wish.

Father: Do you know why you wish for it? It's because you'd like to be Daddy.

Hans: Yes. How does it work?

Father: You'd like to be Daddy and married to Mummy; you'd like to be as big as me and have a moustache; and you'd like Mummy to have a baby.

Hans: And Daddy, when I'm married I'll have only one if I want to, when I'm married to Mummy, and if I don't want a baby, God won't want it either when I'm married.

Father: Would you like to be married to Mummy?

Hans: Oh yes.

If this took place in a court of law you can imagine counsel for the defence leaping forward constantly with the shout 'Objection, counsel is leading the witness' and hear the judge's weary reply 'Objection sustained'. Under this sort of inquisition from a persistent and authoritarian figure of whom he was naturally fond and whom he wanted to please, poor Little Hans might have admitted to very nearly anything. It is just as well that the father at least seems to have had a clear idea of the Oedipus complex, otherwise he would have almost certainly failed to extract any part of it from his unfortunate son. Even so, many would argue that despite his determination to do so he did not in fact succeed.

So here we have the psychoanalytic method, a small but revealing example of the 'evidence' from the couch that supposedly meant so much to Freud. Of what does it consist? Merely, I would argue, of the determination of prejudiced, bigoted men, exposed for too long to a ridiculous creed rich in mumbo-jumbo, to see what they want to see, and hear what they want to hear whether or not it bears any relation to reality.

Their approach and methodology are selective and self-confirming, narrow and inflexible, rigid and unyielding in their refusal to admit anything that is not explicable in terms of the philosophy they dare not question. Peering at the world through their distorting spectacles it is not surprising that theirs is a distorted vision. Uncritical generally of their master's voice they reserve their bile for those who fail to share their dogma, interpreting antipathy as the signs and symptoms of personality deficiency or disequilibrium for which a course of psychoanalysis might, with benefit, be prescribed. Thus can critics' brains be washed clear of heresy, and their arguments neutralised by the ascription of psychopathology, by the suggestion that some ego defence mechanism is at work in the attempt to dissipate anxiety to which some aspect of psychoanalytic theory has given rise. In attacking psychoanalysis it is not one's ideas that are scorned, but oneself. One's arguments are not contradicted but devalued by being described as evidence of 'neurosis'. So much for the scientific method of Freud, the strict disciplinarian who would brook no criticism.

For Freud upheld that no unanalysed person could be expected fully to understand the truth of psychoanalytic doctrine, thus disarming his critics in advance. Only when you are one of us, the argument runs, only when you have been subjected to the full indoctrination process, will we take seriously your criticisms. Even then, if you do not fully accept the theories, we will wonder about the success of your analysis rather than take note of what you say. But if indeed the undergoing of a classical analysis is so essential to a proper understanding of the philosophy, might one not wonder why it was that Freud himself never underwent this process, whilst insisting that all his followers were analysed. Does this mean that Freud was cynical or wrong in maintaining that to experience the truth of psychoanalysis one had to be analysed by another? It is surely true that he never experienced the 'truth' of it himself. The great man would trust none of his acolytes with *his* psyche. Was he worried what they might find, scurrying beneath the upturned stone in the unaccustomed light? Whatever the reason, he preferred self-analysis in the investigation of his own personality, of the mental processes from which the whole extraordinary theory sprung, and this despite his statement that 'Self-analysis is really impossible'.

Of course, Freud cannot be judged by the same rules by which both he and his disciples would want to judge the latter category. There must be *droit du seigneur*, privileges of the inventor. But in fact there was a difference in interest between the founder of psychoanalysis and its practitioners. What Freud did, and what he was primarily interested in doing, was to construct a psychological theory that would explain thought and action. The tool which he maintains he used to do this was the 'scientific' method of psychoanalysis. This is to say that psychoanalysis was primarily an instrument of discovery through which great and important truths could be arrived at. For Freud, that was perhaps the most important function of psychoanalysis, to unravel the causal mechanisms, to gain insight and self-knowledge, to allow one most truly to be oneself.

The disciples emphasised a somewhat different aspect of psychoanalysis. The fundamental 'discoveries' had already been made and extensively described by the master. It was an article of faith if they were to ply their trade as psychoanalysts that they accept the thrust, the hard core of Freud's teachings. For them psychoanalysis is of incidental interest as an experimental method,

as an illuminator of the mysterious mechanisms of the psychic substance. Instead they are primarily interested in the *therapeutic*
possibilities of psychoanalysis as a talking cure by which 'neurotic'
mechanisms are recognised, accepted into consciousness, and, in
that acceptance, to some extent attenuated if not abolished.

So we come to the question: Does psychoanalysis work? and the
subsidiary question, Does it work in the way that it purports to
work? There is another and possibly graver question, seldom asked
or even hinted at: Is psychoanalysis harmful, or potentially harmful
in a way that transcends the acceptable risk/reward ratio implied in
any therapeutic process? I argue that there is no proof that
psychoanalysis benefits humanity and furthermore that in many
cases and many situations it is both dangerous and destructive.

When asking whether or not psychoanalysis works, one should be
clear about what it sets out to do and what is involved in the process.
Firstly it is expensive, time-consuming and labour intensive. Going
rates in New York City for private classical analysis are
approximately $50 for the traditional 50-minute hour, four to five
times a week with a holiday in August, for a period of six to eight
years. This involves an outlay per patient of approximately $60,000,
not allowing for inflation. Clearly on this basis each analyst does not
see very many patients, although many do not complete the analysis
usually because they have moved away, can no longer afford it, or
can no longer stand it.

During the fifty-minute session the patient lies on the couch with
the analyst sitting unseen behind his head, and says whatever occurs
to him, holding nothing back. The analyst is supposed to listen, to
reveal nothing of himself and his personality but instead to act as a
sounding board, a mirror, bouncing back the thoughts and utterances of the patient who apparently gains in the process insight
into the causal mechanisms within his psyche which enslave and
control him. As he free associates, recounts his dreams and tells of
his apparently faulty or haphazard actions (the Freudian slips or
parapraxes, apparently chance but in fact unconsciously predetermined), the analyst listens with the knowing ear, allowing
himself the occasional interpretation as he coaxes the inferred and
threatening unconscious thoughts into the patient's awareness. The
analogy which Freud himself liked is with surgery, as the analyst
carves away at the layers of superficial tissue until he has exposed

72

the cancerous growth to the sharp knife of psychoanalytic technique. Pain is unavoidable, even desirable, as the patient is led, slowly and inexorably, to a recognition of the infantile urges that govern his behaviour and cause his symptoms. Gradually he comes to realise that all his problems, his angst, stem from those distant events, dimly and inadequately remembered, which took place between the ages of three and six when Oedipal considerations ruled his life.

During the often stormy, and as often grotesquely dull relationship both patient and analyst will have to handle the transference as the patient invests in the analyst the strong feelings that he has felt for important and authoritarian figures in the past. Thus hate and more classically love are often demonstrated by the patient for the analyst, these feelings occasionally being returned amplified in the counter-transference in which the poorly analysed analyst indulges in the same emotions *vis à vis* his patient.

Everything that happens in the psychoanalytic situation is regarded as being important, especially the transference. All is important for the giving and receiving of insight. At no time is the aim to make the patient feel better or to 'cure' him. Instead the task is to help him to an awareness of his 'real' self, to the realisation that infantile urges and primitive desires are at work in the shaping of his personality.

Let us suppose we believed that we are little more than butterflies pinned to the board of life by the sharp needle of the Oedipus complex which reaches out from our childhoods into adult life to impale us. How can it possibly benefit us to recognise this fact, and how, in the recognition, can we escape our predicament? The psychoanalyst would say that in the expression of our true desires and impulses, by talking about them and recognising them, we are less likely to act them out and translate them into movement. But is this really the case? Supposing I come to the realisation that my anxiety and inability to function with and relate to authoritarian figures are the result of a poorly resolved Oedipal complex, in which my fear and hatred of my father and my frustration at being prevented from satisfying my sexual urges for my mother have spilled over into adult life to incapacitate me. I am no better off in knowing that my self-acknowledged unsatisfactory behaviour is the determined result of this depressing little causal mechanism. Certainly the next time I am confronted by authority and the juices begin to flow I may parade my 'insight' and behave in a more reasonable way, refusing to act on the conjured-up emotions. But the insight is not necessary for me to modify my behaviour if I decide truly that my attitude towards authority is unworthy, self-limiting and productive of guilt feelings. I can decide not to act on emotions which are at variance with how I feel I should behave and tend to reduce self-respect. My reasons for doing so are straightforward and uncomplicated, and I am unburdened by theoretical beliefs that my behaviour is constrained by the past. Why I had those emotions in the first place is both speculative and irrelevant, the process of discovery expensive and time-consuming. For Freud, the pioneering 'scientist' interested only in the 'truth', there was doubtless something intrinsically pleasing in the very process of the search for knowledge and understanding. It was thought to be good in itself. It was enough for Freud to 'transform hysterical misery into common unhappiness', in the interests of greater clarity, but is it enough for psychoanalytic patients? Most psychoanalysts assume (and have a vested interest in doing so) that one benefits from psychoanalysis, but if 'common unhappiness' is the destination, has the $60,000 been well spent? They admit, however, that failures are legion, dramatic improvements few and far between, that progress is slow and difficult to measure. Yet despite their less than extravagant claims about the efficacy of psychoanalysis they, like the 'neurotics' they treat, seem doomed endlessly to repeat their esoteric behaviour, priests of a secular religion, locked in procedural rituals, questioning not, but obedient to the dictates of their mentor whose words live on in the text of the Standard Edition of Freud's works, bible to the true believers, prayer book to the faithful.

To prove beyond doubt that psychoanalysis either does or does not have any beneficial effect on its recipients is no easy task. The human mind and the totality of human behaviour defy accurate measurement and we should be thankful for this. So, especially in the category of 'healthy neurotics' with whom psychoanalysis prefers to deal, it is often impossible to isolate and measure 'improvement' in the same way that it can be evaluated by noting the reduction in the symptoms of psychosis after a course of largactil. It is difficult, too, to judge the specificity of the effect of the psychoanalytic intervention as no one psychoanalysis resembles another. If there is improvement, is it due to the technique of analysis, the individual analyst's personal interpretation of the technique, the personality and charisma of the analyst, the chemistry between his personality and that of the patient, the patient's suggestibility, the placebo effect, etc? If it is difficult to isolate cause and effect within a particular analysis, it is even more difficult to compare one analysis with another, or large groups of analysed patients with those who have had no treatment at all or some other type of therapeutic intervention. The unique complexity of individuals and the extraordinarily intangible global experience of psychoanalysis render all such investigations suspect.

Nonetheless, studies have been attempted. Those which tend to demonstrate the efficacy of psychoanalysis suffer from the fact that in most cases improvement is defined by either analyst, patient or both. This is an obvious deficiency in view of the time and money invested by each in the process. All such studies suffer from considerable methodological difficulties. The selection of patients, the construction and treatment of comparable control groups, the assessment of outcome and the pinpointing of phenomena bearing a causal relationship to that outcome, are all factors which pose enormous problems. Some studies, too, have indicated that 'neurosis', whatever it is, is a self-limiting condition, and that time rather than analysis is the great healer.

What appears certain is that if psychoanalysis does have any specific beneficial effect on people, then it has never been clearly and conclusively demonstrated, nor indeed adequately defined.

But psychoanalysis is not harmless. It may be rubbish, but it is dangerous and demeaning rubbish, tending to rob us of our natural belief that we are in control of our mental and physical behaviour, fostering the illusion of our lack of responsibility, of our passivity. This is the fundamental crime of psychodynamism, of which Freudian psychoanalysis is the cornerstone. As the tentacles of this pernicious doctrine reach out to embrace the arts, politics and education nothing remains untouched by the poison of its determinism as it degrades creativity, debases ambition and reduces the value of human aspiration. Human nature can be understood, reduced, explained away by Freudian theories in terms of the pathetic supposed lusts of our no longer innocent childhoods, the mystery gone, the splendour eclipsed. All around us and within us we are encouraged to look and to find evidence of conditioned psychological malaise, the legacy of our childhood from which, according to Freud, none of us emerges unscathed. We are asked to dwell on the 'psychopathology of everyday life', finding illness to excuse us wherever we turn. Believing ourselves puppets dancing on the string of our libidinal urges, we lose our self-respect, our admiration for ourselves, our pride in our achievements, our satisfaction in the surmounting of difficulty, gravitating instead towards that anxious dependency, that vulnerable passivity, which provide the cannon fodder and the income for those who peddle a talking cure.

Of course, psychoanalysis today, except in the hierarchies of the psychiatric profession, where the psychodynamic way of thinking has tended to live on, is a movement in disrepute – its self-confidence lost, leaderless, fragmented and like the Church itself rent asunder by schisms, distressed by heresies. Psychoanalysis is discredited as a method of scientific investigation, doubted as a psychology, scorned for its lack of effect as a therapy. The climate of opinion has turned against the once fashionable but pessimistic vision of human nature, against its rigidity and its doctrinaire approach, its trades-union type closed shop, and above all against the time it takes to do whatever it is supposed to do. Instant cures and panaceas are what today's consumer of therapies desires. Perhaps even more vitally, he desires methods that are easy, pleasurable and which involve the minimum expenditure of effort and energy. Psychoanalysis – hard, unyielding, uncompromising in its practice of painful surgery by a distant, unempathetic analyst, promising little and costing much – has made only struggling efforts to catch up. Such has been the brainwashing power of the psychoanalytic experience that the majority of psychoanalytic revolutionaries are little more than fellow travellers, bending Freud a little here and there and incidentally incurring the wrath of the founder and his high priests, but hanging on to the basic principles such as the seminal importance of the emotional life of early childhood and the revealing nature of dreams. In particular they believe in 'neurosis' and the efficacy of their particular therapies to alleviate its symptoms.

So in Adler's Individual Psychology the dynamic principle of life is seen as the individual's attempts to compensate for the natural feelings of inferiority felt as a helpless child, which are manifested in the life style. Modifying this theme marginally, Karen Horney considered the anxious child's search for security as paramount and saw it as her task to understand the individual's adjustment to this anxiety in the process of character analysis. For Fromm the prime consideration was the study of the personality's relationship with the culture of the society in which it found itself. Sullivan, like Horney, saw the need for security in a social context as fundamental and, influenced by Meyer, saw the personality of man as a synthesis of his biological inheritance and the effect of the environment on that heredity. Jung's Analytical Psychology, with its mystical theories of the collective unconscious and his perceptive descriptions of personality types, represents a rather more exotic chip off the Freudian block. More recently the emphasis has been on changes of *style* in the therapeutic relationship, especially since the work of the Chicago school. Nowadays analysts are less distant, more friendly, more flexible, more prepared to 'relate' and perhaps even to compromise on the once sacred principle of *time* in, for example, the short-term therapies of Sifneos, Malan, Bellak and Balint.

These, in brief, are a sample of the psychodynamic psychotherapies, cerebral, intellectual, long on words and explanations, on philosophy and interpretations based on that philosophy. In general the variations that they represent when compared with classical psychoanalysis amount to attempts to humanise the process, to dilute the austerity of the Freudian approach. They all, however, represent systems in which 'experts' cure 'patients' – in which specific 'skills' are used to disseminate 'knowledge', in which founding fathers (or mothers) have arrived at 'new' insights into human nature, in which disciples follow masters, and in which money changes hands with respect to services whose efficacy remains suspect. In all this their effect is to popularise and institutionalise a wider category of illness, that of 'neurosis', whose existence is mistakenly implied by the existence of so many intelligent, articulate, vocal and charismatic 'professionals'. As they push their philosophy, the recognised boundaries of mental illness expand remorselessly until we are all to some extent 'not well', and are thus free to take the illness option. Whether it is done unashamedly, without apology in the name of the doctrines of classical analysis, or masked and camouflaged, wearing the persona of humanism, warmth and hope, we are all encouraged to slip passively into the illness mode in the face of difficulty, to acquiesce in the patient role, to learn the helpless reliance on the healer that will best foster the illusion of 'cure'. Thus when well we take on the mantle of illness, when merely unhappy, anxious and ineffective we cling to the leaky raft of 'neurosis' and paddle it furiously towards the prison ship of psychodynamism where the shackles of dependence and determinism await us. In our headlong flight from freedom and responsibility we do ourselves a terrible disservice, and those who collude with us in our attempted escape take our money as they compound our error.

Freud's cardinal sin is that he has given a spurious validity to the illness excuse, has spawned a vast industry of talk therapists who ply their trade in areas where genuine mental illness does not exist, and occasionally and more dangerously, when it does. He is the grandfather of the talking cure and, although the therapies of today have strayed far from his path, the lines of communication between psychoanalysis and the mental flatulence of the California experientialist movement are clear. And so now the therapy industry is big business, with an estimated annual turnover in the USA alone of $17 billion and an estimated 100,000 practitioners, catering for the 'needs' of the approximately 25 million Americans who seek help for psychological problems each year.

Freud started the process when he maintained that even the psychologically healthy, if indeed such a rare animal existed, would benefit from psychoanalysis. Now in the self-actualisation programmes of the Human Potential Movement the logical conclusion of that philosophy can be seen. Apparently we are all 'in need', in need of gurus, in need of leaders, in need of philosophical psychologies that explain human nature, in need of greater 'awareness' of ourselves and of how we 'grow', in need of more 'experience', in need of love, in need of meaning. And so as we strive towards the perfection that is supposedly our natural birthright we are helped on our way by the talking cure, encouraged to let it all hang out. A good talk has, since Freud, become the panacea for all ills. If we can but bend the ear of a caring listener all our troubles will melt away. In the very act of verbalisation we exorcise the devils of our disability. A new and perhaps naive optimism characterises the therapies of today, replacing the austere pessimism of psychoanalysis, but in both it is words more than anything else that are thought to provide the passport to salvation. But there are no easy transports to delight, no short cuts signposted by 'experts'. Instead there is toil and sacrifice, hard work and struggle, self-discipline and denial – that is the only road towards satisfaction. The hardships are necessary and valuable, providing the obstacles in the overcoming of which we learn to like ourselves more. Never should we underestimate the importance of difficulty.

7

The Mind Sweets:
Bitter Pills for Anxiety

In contrast to the reaction of the talk therapists when confronted by a person weighted down by the problems of life is that of the doctor who puts his trust in pills. Mood-altering drugs (psychoactive medication) are prescribed in very large quantities. It has been estimated that the number of prescriptions for psychoactive drugs per year in the USA far exceeds the total population, excluding those issued in hospitals and clinics.

Apart from drugs that stimulate the central nervous system, such as amphetamines which were widely prescribed at one time as appetite suppressants, the large majority of these prescriptions are for C.N.S. depressants with sedating qualities. These include the sleep-inducing barbiturates prescribed to counteract insomnia. Over recent years, however, there has been a dramatic increase in the prescribing of the minor tranquillisers of the benzo-diazepine group such as diazepam (valium, atensine); chlordiazepoxide (librium, calmoden); oxazepam (serenid-D, serax); lorazepam (ativan); medazepam (nobrium); and clobazam (frisium).

These drugs are known as anxiolytics and are prescribed in the overwhelming majority of cases for general anxiety, tension, apprehension, and agitation. On a short-term basis they are undoubtedly effective in relieving the symptoms of stress.

This calming effect is probably the main reason that they are effective in the promotion of sleep, and other drugs of this group are marketed primarily as anti-insomnia agents. These include the popular nitrazepam (mogadon, nitrados, remnos, somnased, somnite); flurazepam (dalmane); and temazepam (euphynos, normison).

By far the most common reason for the prescribing of these drugs is to bring about some change in the individual's psychological state, and it is worthwhile to quote from the literature of the Hoffman-La Roche company, the manufacturers of the widely used 'valium' tablets. They state that 'Valium is indicated for the symptomatic relief of anxiety and tension associated with anxiety disorders, transient situational disturbances and functional or organic disorders. It is useful in psychoneurotic states manifested by tension, anxiety, apprehension, fatigue, depressive symptoms or agitation.'

So wide is this decription that it is immediately apparent that one could make a case for prescribing valium in very nearly any situation in which difficulties temporarily arise and unfortunately many doctors do just that. But there are times when all of us are tense and anxious, tired and worried, fed up, sad and agitated. It is often an extremely appropriate response to trying circumstances, a natural reaction to the problems that we face. We are short of money and there are bills to be paid. We worry about the health of those we love. We have problems at work and difficulties in our personal relationships. At times everything seems to go wrong for us. We may experience dreadful grief at the death of a loved one, and occasionally it seems as if life is hardly worth living.

This is not unnatural. It is totally normal occasionally to feel this way. It is always unpleasant, but it is not without a use. For such problems exist to try us and to test us and in successfully overcoming them our self-respect must increase. Our bravery and tenacity in such unfavourable circumstances will give us the self-confidence to face other trials. We may rely on our friends and those we love to help us through, but we need to know that in the end we did it all ourselves.

We can and must learn to regard our feelings of anxiety and worry in a positive way. Very often our body's hormones prepare us physiologically for action in response to external threatening stimuli. An example of this is the fight, fright or flight adrenaline response in which blood is pumped preferentially to the muscles, the pupils dilate, and the heart beats faster as the body is made ready for an appropriate response to danger. So the psychological feelings of anxiety, worry and tension can be used to prepare us for positive action. For if we don't worry about our problems to a certain extent how can we summon up the necessary energy to solve them? If they don't make us anxious, can they be said to be problems? And if we have no problems, how can we respect ourselves by solving them? If at the first sign of psychological tension we condition ourselves to obliterate such feelings chemically, we will be tending towards that passive, spectator role that Moral Therapy is so keen to discourage.

In most cases, therefore, we should not be afraid of anxiety, nor should we consider it abnormal nor without use. Instead we should regard it as a spur to action, an unpleasant experience whose job is to get us moving. Our anxiety should lead us to a brave confrontation of our problems and an increase in our self-respect. Having performed its function, it will then disappear with the net result that we like ourselves more.

Always we must avoid the mistake of concentrating on the anxiety itself and turning *that* into our problem. Encouraged by the constant expressions of the introverted psychobabble of the mind pundits, many of us end up worrying more about our anxiety than about getting on with our lives and behaving as we believe that we should. 'I can't do anything to get rid of my anxiety because I am so incapacitated by it' is often the attitude.

It may be of course that such a diagnosis is the correct one and that an actual *'anxiety state'* does exist, a genuine pathological condition that requires psychiatric intervention. This will be discussed later. More often, however, such sentiments, encouraged if not actually expressed by the patient's doctor, will be used as excuses to avoid difficult but worthwhile courses of action to the ultimate detriment of the individual. The tranquilliser tablet gives substance to the excuse, since surely no doctor would prescribe medicine unless there was an actual condition that needed to be treated. 'If I can just get rid of this anxiety for a few days I will be able to get on with my life' runs the argument.

The doctor, knowing all too well that he has little chance to confront adequately the complex life problems of his patient, both because he doesn't know how to and because he has neither the time nor the inclination, colludes with his patient in the valium solution. In thirty seconds the drugs are prescribed. The doctor is secure in the knowledge that they can do little harm and will bring him the gratitude of the patient for the immediate relief that they provide. He knows that their side effects are minor, that they are of low toxicity and therefore unlikely to be used in any successful suicide attempt, and that they are one of the most widely prescribed of the psychoactive medicines. The patients are soon on their way with the doctor's reassurance ringing in their ears. He has done his bit.

Rather than admitting that he has no solution to the life problems of another individual short of making a commitment to him as a friend, an action that his medical ethical code, his natural predilections and his lack of time tend to exclude, he hides behind his prescription pad. Instead he reduces the problem of the wife's extra-marital affair or the husband's alcohol abuse, or the high mortgage repayments and the children's erratic behaviour, and considers them as if they had some relation to an area in which he does have some expertise. He has after all been trained in brain anatomy, physiology and chemistry, and so, wearing his medico-biologist's hat, he explains all these little upsets in terms of momentarily disturbed brain function, and reaches for his prescription pad realising all the time that he is playing the role that society has cast for him.

It is not difficult for the doctor sometimes to confuse his job as healer with his task of relieving pain and discomfort. When confronted by a patient experiencing mental anguish he has a strong desire to abolish it in the quickest, least dangerous and most effective way possible. He is a compassionate man and sees it as his job to relieve suffering whenever it occurs. Thus he dispenses the mind drugs like sweets, treating the symptoms rather than the underlying situation of which they are the outward manifestation. Symptomatic treatment in the absence of the ability to cure is acceptable in medicine, but not when the particular treatment used itself exacerbates the basic problem and when more effective methods are available. This is the case with the prescribing of tranquillising drugs when the individual trades temporary relief for more lasting diminution of self-respect. The physician would not be so lax in the prescribing of analgesic drugs for the alleviation of pain. He may prescribe them but he would want to spend some time investigating and obliterating the pathology of which the physical pain is only the symptom. He would not expect analgesics to cure the basic pathology in a physical condition, and so he has no reason to believe that anxiolytics (anxiety-easing drugs) can have any long-term relevance to a psychological one. The fact that his behaviour is understandable does not make it any the less blameworthy. The motive is good but

83

in failing to perceive the final results of his action the prescriber of the tranquillisers can do real harm.

'Can I give you a little something for your nerves?' many doctors will ask to cover up the impotence they feel as they confront their patient's misery. Feeling that the doctor knows best and needing little persuasion to escape his predicament the patient concurs, although he may know deep within him that he is doing the wrong thing.

The patient may make it easier for the doctor to behave like this. He may well arrive at the consulting rooms demanding the little yellow pills that had done so much good for his neighbour when he had been feeling that he could not cope. If he doesn't get them he may go elsewhere. The doctor, knowing what is expected of him and that an alternative source of supply will be found if he doesn't play the game, may feel that it is better to give in so that at least he will be able to exert some monitoring effect on the patient's use of the drug.

The good doctor, who recognises the dangers of the misuse of tranquillisers and who refuses to prescribe them incorrectly, will have to be prepared to replace them with something of greater value. He will have to suggest alternative courses of action for the solution of the problems that the patient faces, and should realise that this will consume large quantitites both of his time and his emotional energies. It is the vague awareness of this open-ended commitment that encourages so many doctors to opt for the easier solution. So often the complaints are heard 'He wouldn't listen', 'He just gave me pills', 'I wasn't in there for more than two or three mintues', 'He said if I took these tablets it would all be OK'. Too many doctors are extremely uncomfortable with patients who try to discuss their psychological and life problems. Trained as scientists, they are only at ease when discussing the body as a malfunctioning machine and thus many of them attempt to cut short all discussion and head immediately for the biochemical solution.

Doctors, too, tend to believe in the printed word. Through their letter boxes each day pour streams of literature from the big drug companies in which the virtues of various psycho-tropic medications are extolled. In the hospitals the drug-company representatives give elaborate lunches in exchange for the watching of films and the listening to talks at which that company's products are advertised. The doctor is the target for an extremely efficient and well-mounted advertising campaign in which the advantages of psycho-tropic drugs are emphasised and their disadvantages minimised. Unfortunately, drug companies and to some extent doctors tend to be interested only in what can be measured, or inferred from measurement. Such notions as self-respect, guilt and individual moral codes cannot be tested in double-blind clinical trials and are therefore ignored. And so these drugs march on, sapping self-esteem and draining the individual's will, until he is so conditioned that he is unable to face the day without his tablet.

Surely we must come to terms with the fact that life was not designed to be easy or even pleasant, and that happiness and contentedness must be earned. How different is the generally accepted theory that we have a natural right to a life free of psychological pain, a view that leads us to consult the 'experts' whenever we experience it. It is this erroneous and harmful attitude to life that leads us to seek chemical panaceas that cost us our self-respect. Who, one wonders, was responsible for the propagation of the myth that life should be good most of the time whether we work hard at it or not? Was it ever thus? Did the manual labourers of long ago feel that they had a natural right to unearned happiness? Do those in the underprivileged areas of the world today expect contentedness irrespective of what they do and how they behave? Of course they don't. For the truth is that somewhere along the line, those of us who live in affluent societies have been exposed to the insidious intellectual myths of the psychodynamists and have come to believe that lack of happiness, discontent and psychological discomfort are not natural and are manifestations of some malfunction in our mental processes. Further, they are responsible for the idea that such malfunctions can be isolated, examined and understood and that eventually they can be abolished and 'proper' psychological function restored by making us aware of the causal processes that have conspired to create them. Heavily influenced by the metapsychological posturings of these talk therapists, the medico-biologists, although overtly out of sympathy with their methods, agree that psychological distress, however appropriate and beneficial it may be, is a sign of biochemical disturbance to be abolished whenever and wherever it occurs. They prefer to talk of electro-chemical brain events. The currency of the psychodynamists is ideas. Both agree that there is a problem that requires their 'expert' intervention.

Science has provided the medico-biologists with a perfect tool, in the form of the mind sweets, to mount their onslaught against those mechanisms which alone provide the early warning system telling the individual he is behaving in a way which contravenes his moral system, and that he should cease and desist from such actions. In doing so they place him in the same position of danger as the person who experiences no pain. So keen is the doctor to abolish the symptoms, he effectively masks the awareness of their cause. As a result the individual struggles forward in the wrong direction, dimly aware he is doing so until such behaviour is so entrenched it can only be eradicated with the greatest difficulty. In exactly the same way, the person who feels no pain will persevere in actions that are actually harmful to his body because he possesses no warning system to guide him. So with the tranquillising drugs, guilt is dulled and a vicious circle is set up whereby inappropriate actions continue, thus giving rise to increasing lack of self-respect the effects of which require even greater doses of tranquillisers to minimise.

This circle must be broken and the idea disseminated that bad times are normal, and that although unpleasant they have a value. They alone can make us strong, and the psychological distress that we experience in the contemplation of perceived inadequacies is vital if we are to mend our ways and improve our lives. In the taking of tranquillising drugs we do not solve our own problems but rather those of the doctor who saves time and energy by prescribing them and of the manufacturers who derive profit from their sale.

It might be worthwhile to ask ourselves whether in terms of happiness, contentedness and mental health the world is in fact a better place since we have apparently acquired such expertise in the manipulation, and insight into the workings, of the mind. Have the prevalence of cunning psychological theories in which the mysterious mechanisms of the psyche are purported to be 'understood' resulted in widespread alleviation of mental suffering and a more balanced and saner world? Or have they merely resulted in the growth of a lucrative industry that panders to the weakness in humans and to their potentially self-destructive desire for dependence and attention? Is analysis, one might ask, psychologically addictive? It seems to me that in societies in which such psychologists do not exist to satisfy the desires, which are not the needs, of the populace there is no noticeable diminution in psychological health. Similarly, have mind drugs of the minor tranquillising type, in the few years since their discovery, increased the mental well-being of the population?

The fact that they have failed to do so is not because they have been insufficiently used. I suspect that few people really believe that these drugs do anything but put off the day when we ourselves will have to confront our own problems. Surely we are all aware that insofar as they are a crutch, an easy way out, an admission of failures they are not good for us and that it demonstrates a weakness of will regularly to use them. It may be that the general public know the truth of this better than the medical profession itself as they are the ultimate consumers and therefore the people who have to live with their effects. The doctor effectively treats his own feelings of anxiety and impotence by prescribing tablets to others and because, quite rightly, he is loath to project his own feelings of right and wrong on to his patient he makes the mistake of ignoring the moral issue *in toto* and fails to consider his patient's self-respect. What he fails to understand is the vital importance of the moral issue for the patient himself in terms of the patient's *own* personal morality. If the doctor were able to take the time and trouble to investigate that patient's own view of the consequences for his self-respect of the mind-altering drugs he might avoid his mistake. But because doctors are taught not to judge their patients they forget that patients constantly judge themselves. The effects of this oversight are often profound.

There is a major point that has as yet to be given the recognition it requires by both the medical profession and the public at large. The manufacturers of valium hint at the problem when they state that 'Particularly addiction-prone individuals such as drug addicts and alcoholics should be under careful surveillance when receiving diazepam ... because of the predisposition of such patients to habituation and dependence'. Here they are referring to the possibility of psychological addiction, in which the individual shows a continual pre-occupation with his drug and its source of supply, and has a strong psychological compulsion to acquire it and to use it regularly. Characteristically, such people show a high relapse rate after withdrawal. They also state that 'Although infrequently seen, milder withdrawal symptoms have also been reported following abrupt discontinuation of benzodiazepines taken continuously, generally at higher therapeutic levels, for at least several months.' This hints at the presence of a withdrawal syndrome that would indicate that valium can cause physiological dependence or addiction (NB dependence and addiction are terms that can be used interchangeably). This situation is said to occur when withdrawal of the drug precipitates a recognised withdrawal syndrome specific to the particular drug. The alcoholic withdrawal syndrome in its mildest form is the well-known hangover and in its most severe the state of delirium tremens. Sudden withdrawal from heroin ('cold turkey') results after a few hours in an extremely unpleasant withdrawal state characterised by increased salivation and runny nose, vomiting, diarrhoea, colicky abdominal pains, generalised cramps, chills, increased sweating and a tendency to yawn – all coupled with exquisite mental anguish and an overwhelming and desperate desire to obtain the drug. So, too, precipitous withdrawal of high-dose long-term valium treatment can result in fits, whilst considerable psychological malaise, inertia and severe sleep disturbance may also be experienced. Although not mentioned by the makers the American Food and Drug Administration (F.D.A.), the watchdog organisation that monitors and controls the manufacture and distribution of drugs in the USA, has stated that the other condition for *physical dependence,* namely *tolerance,* is also a characteristic of these drugs. (Tolerance refers to the situation in which increasingly large quantities of the drug are required to produce the same effect.)

There is now evidence that diazepam tranquillisers are extremely psychologically addictive and can often produce physical dependence as well. Very recent estimates have suggested that as many as 100,000 people in the UK alone are to some extent addicted to tranquillising drugs. Although it may be true to say that some people are more prone to addiction than others, that is *not* to say it is safe to prescribe these drugs to anyone who has not shown addictive behaviour with other substances. By definition the person who is felt to require diazepam is experiencing some kind of psychological angst. For a short period the drug can alleviate the symptoms of this distress. Thus for the immediate short-term relief that they provide the using of these drugs is strongly pleasurable, and to this extent all of us, who feel we need them, are at risk of becoming psychologically dependent on them and not just those who have demonstrated previous addictive behaviour. Nor is it fair to put all the blame for the drug's addictive properties on the inadequacies of the people who use them. Whilst there would be no addicts if we were all strong, it is also true to say that there would be no addicts if we were all weak but had no drugs. Other drugs such as aspirin which have a powerful ability to remove unpleasantness in the form of the pains of headaches seldom if ever become psychologically addictive. We must therefore conclude that, as with the drugs alcohol and nicotine, there is a quality of the benzodiazepines that tends to produce a strong compulsion in those that use them regularly to continue their use. Clearly this craving admits of degree. There is a continuum between mild habituation at one end of the scale and full-blown psychological addiction at the other. Thus a predispositional tendency to take a valium when the going gets tough may progress slowly and imperceptibly towards that state when one feels an inability to lead one's life without the tablets. The point is that it is a slippery slope and all those who embark on the journey down the hill run the terrible risk of a precipitous descent to the bottom. The doctor by his action in dispensing these potentially dangerous tablets may not just be contributing to a mild decrease in his patient's self-respect. He may be taking the initial step in a fast-moving sequence of events that can result in his patient becoming a full-scale drug addict completely dependent on the tablets, with incalculable effects on his self-esteem and psychological health. And so, what started out as an ersatz way of dealing with problems, an occasional quick trip to instant pleasure and relief, expands into a vast problem as we become enslaved and debased by the mind sweets.

The possibilities for psychological dependence on the benzodiazepine tranquillisers are just beginning to be realised, but as yet they are only hinted at in the psychiatric text books which tend to emphasise the safety of these drugs whilst of course avoiding all reference to the implications for the user's self-respect. Drug company literature is also remiss in failing adequately to warn of their possibilities for abuse. Those enlightened doctors who have realised that diazepam and the other benzodiazepines are intensely habit-forming have contributed to some reduction in their use since 1975, but the vast scale of the problem still to be solved is shown by the fact that in 1978 the F.D.A. estimates, five billion of these tablets were swallowed in the USA alone. So worried have the F.D.A. become that in July 1980 they felt it necessary to circularise all physicians in the USA instructing them not to prescribe these drugs for 'everyday stress', and in future the manufacturers will include in their information to doctors a statement reading 'anxiety or tension associated with the stress of everyday life usually does not require treatment with an anxiolytic drug'.

Of course, it remains up to the individual doctor to decide whether or not the patient is suffering from everyday stress or more unusual anxiety and tension. Moral Therapy feels that there is no place for these drugs in the case even of unusual anxiety and tension where that stress is not thought to represent actual psychopathology. It may be that severe financial problems have arisen or possibly a divorce. Such stresses would not necessarily be described as everyday, but in the view of Moral Therapy they should not provide sufficient reason for the prescribing of these tranquillisers for the reasons given above.

However, so high is the consumption of these drugs it is more than clear that their use extends widely into that category of normal, natural anxiety that all of us do and should experience if we are living our lives to the fullest extent. Such anxiety is good, not bad; it is valuable not harmful; it is a sure indication that we are striving to accomplish difficult objectives, testing ourselves, being courageous rather than timid, being active rather than passive, living our lives rather than merely enduring them. Anxiety is the emotion that tells us we have selected an objective or course of action that will be difficult for us, and it is in the attempting or achieving of such objectives that we alone can increase our self-respect. The absence of anxiety, on the other hand, indicates that our objectives are easily within our capabilities, that we are not stretching ourselves but merely coasting along, doing little or nothing that will give us cause to like ourselves more.

Moral Therapy will seek to instil in the individual this positive view of anxiety, and will emphasise that not all things that are unpleasant are bad for us in the same way that not all things that are pleasant are good for us – that what we need is not often what we want or desire. For lasting self-respect is assured only by facing and confronting anxiety and never by seeking to hide from it or attempting to abolish it artificially.

Apart from its function of demonstrating to us that we are engaged in activities that are worthy of us, that provide a suitable test of our courage, ability and resolve, anxiety can also occur as an accompaniment to feelings of guilt, as an early warning system that we are not behaving as we think we should. As with guilt feelings we should take note of our anxieties and learn from them. We should try to act or cease to act in a way that removes the necessity for feeling anxious rather than attempt to obliterate the anxiety itself. We are worried about money so we should economise, work harder, try to take an evening job. We are anxious that we are not loved so we should attempt to become more lovable. We fear that we may lose our jobs, so we should strive to make ourselves indispensable. The important thing about anxiety is that we take up the correct attitude towards it and instead of wasting time, energy and effort in attempting to deal with the emotion itself we should concentrate on action to deal with the problems that have given rise to it. We have nothing to fear unless we begin to worry about anxiety itself.

And this is the mistake that the valium 'solution' encourages us to make. We begin to focus on the anxiety itself as the cause of all our problems, arguing that if it was not for the anxiety all would be well. Our problem becomes that we are anxious and that anxiety becomes institutionalised as the stumbling block that impedes our progress. Those inadequacies and failures that are the root cause of the emotion rather than its result are ignored as we attempt to escape responsibility for our predicament. For the emotion of anxiety can be thought of conveniently as an entity in itself that has sprung from nowhere to plague us. After all, anxious people have low exercise tolerance, low thresholds of pain and high levels of blood lactic acid after exercise stress – so perhaps anxiety is caused by an imbalance in physiology. Or is it passed on in the genes, as the fact that anxiety tends to run in families might suggest to some? Such comforting theories reinforce the fundamentally unhelpful idea that anxiety be treated as an unfortunate impediment thrust upon us through no fault of our own, to be obliterated by any means available to science. So we are encouraged to swallow the benzo-diazepine tranquillisers and risk addiction in order to rid ourselves of an extremely useful if uncomfortable mechanism for preserving mental health. It is not the anxiety, but our attitude towards it that is at fault. If we react towards it in a positive way it will serve us well.

By dampening anxiety and slowing down the individual these drugs help to ensure that he is less capable of the intense activity that is usually required for the solution of the problems that he faces. Paradoxically, by removing the symptom they help to prevent or delay any effective cure. Tired and sleepy, passive and tranquillised we are in no shape to do the things that need to be done. We have to some extent shifted our responsibility to the doctor who has prescribed the pills and is now in charge of our 'condition' – is seeking to 'cure' our 'nerves' with his biochemical skills. But deep down we know that we have opted out; have sought a temporary truce in a war that has still to be fought; have tried to walk way from life rather than participate in it; have paid the price of diminished self-respect for a transient respite.

It seems difficult to imagine how continual recourse to these pills can fail to be a potent source of guilt and self-dislike, and this alone should provide a powerful reason for avoiding them. It is no surprise to the practitioner of Moral Therapy that those people of an ex-trovert nature who are highly active, the doers rather than the thinkers, often respond to the benzodiazepines by becoming in-creasingly anxious. This is because the most effective way of dealing with anxiety is by that very intense and carefully directed activity and physical movement that these drugs are so efficient at reducing. No wonder such people may react in a panicky way to being cut off from their normal, correct and efficient methods of dealing with anxiety. On the other hand the passive, introverted dreamers and thinkers may find valium very much to their liking. Eschewing hard physical activity they may have found that all attempts to defeat anxiety by intellectual means alone have been a dismal failure. Much used to the role of spectator, of dispassionate observer of life, they are well suited to the type of mental and physical state that tranquillising drugs tend to produce. They do not mind being less capable of action, as where possible they have avoided it. They tend to be eager for a synthetic reduction of anxiety as they have never learned how to benefit from it. However, they *do* remain powerfully aware that they had no solution before and they have not found it in the use of drugs. Their anxiety may have been dampened but their overall mental condition has deteriorated.

Avoiding such an unhelpful approach, our task must be to install confidence and self-respect in the individual *himself*, and to avoid the elaboration of complicated and virtually meaningless manoeuvres, be they biochemical or metapsychological, whose purpose is to build faith in the skills of the expert healer. For this is the politics of dependence and dependence is the mortal enemy of self-respect without which mental health cannot exist.

Many of the medico-biologists fail to recognise this, and their patients too are unaware of the pitfalls involved in prostration before and subservience to the professional who owes his position to the exams he has passed, to the conventional wisdom to which he perhaps unthinkingly adheres. The patient trusts the doctor because he believes in the myth of the doctor's superior expertise in an area in which he possesses none. In reality the doctor's specialised skills are confined to what he has learned during his medical training and in his subsequent practice of traditional medicine. He is qualified to recognise mental and physical illness, but he is not necessarily any better than the man in the street at living his life or advising others how to live theirs. Life is not learned from books. It is something we all have to make up as we go along, helped by the voice of our own conscience and relying on moral imperatives that we alone have freely developed, in response to our environment and heredity, to keep us on the straight and narrow path. We should rely on our conscience for advice – not on some well-meaning but ultimately uninterested stranger, and where we need support in the difficult courses of action dictated to us by our moral codes it should be to friends and loved ones that we turn. Those doctors who pose as experts in the art of living, whilst dispensing the 'valium' solution in the absence of proper indications for it, are as irresponsible as they are inept, lowering self-respect, manufacturing illness, peddling excuses, increasing guilt, undermining our ability to withstand and benefit from stress. Unwittingly they help to create a situation in which their patient is misguided and misled, investing his confidence in his doctor rather than in himself. The widespread over-prescribing of the Mind Sweets is its own accusation, evidence that the patient's confidence is doubly misplaced.

Any success that the patient achieves whilst taking such drugs is invalidated by the very fact of their presence in his bloodstream, as all failures are excused by the 'illness' that the 'necessity' for the prescription of these medicines implies. The very 'requirement' for this treatment reinforces the patient's own low opinion of himself and, at the same time, he becomes increasingly dependent upon the drugs for the small degree of alleviation they afford from the pain of low self-respect.

He is then in a vicious double bind. He feels guilty that he has to rely on the tablets, and yet in the very short term the tablets help to lessen the feelings of guilt. The doctor, seeing no improvement, may feel it necessary to increase the dose and frequency, thus exacerbating the situation further. The end result is a patient who can function but who can never experience high self-respect and who can never wholeheartedly like himself. Stuck permanently on the edge of the 'illness mode' he struggles on, incompetent and unsuccessful, resenting the achievements of others, obsessed by his own failure. Taking the lead from his doctor he pretends to the outside world that his predicament is no fault of his own, but rather of imbalances in his brain biochemistry, which drugs alone can alleviate.

It is necessary, however, to distinguish between that normal anxiety which is appropriate to the situation that causes it, however severe it may be, and the type of anxiety experience that is completely out of all proportion to the stimulus that gives rise to it, or exists in the apparent absence of any cause at all. The first, as we have discussed, is useful to us in the same way that pain is useful.

The second type of anxiety, although similar as an experience may have characteristics that, to the person trained in their recognition, may indicate that psychological illness exists. This second type we will call pathological anxiety. The difference between normal, healthy, valuable anxiety and its pathological counterpart is not easy to define, but in the pathological variety the cause is often more obscure. Pathological anxiety can occur as a secondary phenomenon in a wide variety of physical and psychological illnesses. Insofar as we are unable in these situations to cure ourselves, the anxiety we feel has no useful function for us. It does not exist as a spur to effective action but is the result of processes over which we have no control. Thus we may experience anxiety as part of the symptoms of genuine disease like a depressive illness, schizophrenia, obsessive/compulsive states, delirium and dementia. Physical illness, too, especially hyperthyroidism and heart disease, often cause considerable anxiety.

Having excluded physical and psychological illnesses that might be causes of secondary anxiety, or treated them if they exist, the physician must satisfy himself that the symptoms of anxiety with which he is confronted are not evidence of the existence of that psychiatric diagnostic category the primary anxiety state. In its most classic form this refers to a chronic illness during which the individual suffers from clearly defined entities known as panic attacks. These may occur out of the blue or be precipitated by minor stress. In such an attack the victim will feel a sudden and overwhelming sense of fear, apprehension and panic often associated with intense feelings of impending doom. He may feel that things around him appear strange (derealisation) or that in some way his body is unreal (depersonalisation). He shows the bodily signs of increased sympathetic nervous system stimulation with increased heart rate, sweating, palpitations, dilated pupils and dry mouth. He trembles and breathes faster as he experiences a sensation of being smothered. By washing out carbon dioxide from his lungs he begins to suffer from the hyperventilation syndrome which exacerbates his feelings of anxiety. He becomes pale and light-headed and feels that he is going to faint and he may feel tingling sensations in his extremities. Such attacks finish as dramatically and spontaneously as they begin. In the absence of any physical or other psychological condition they are regarded as diagnostic of an anxiety state.

The situation is somewhat complicated by the fact that anxiety, itself a psychological subjective state well described as 'fear spread out thin', is almost invariably accompanied by physical sensations that we know collectively as the experience of tension. This intimate relationship between the mental component of apprehension and the accompanying bodily one of tension has led some to question the commonly held Cartesian 'ghost in the machine' explanation in which mental events are held to antecede and to cause physical ones. They have speculated that our experience of anxiety may be nothing more than the contemplation of the physical events occurring within our bodies – that anxiety is an awareness of our physiological processes rather than a cause of them. Whatever the philosophical truths are the fact remains that in feelings of anxiety the psyche and the soma are more than usually closely interrelated. This leads us to the understandable phenomenon that gross hypochondriacal preoccupations are one of the most characteristic features of a pathological anxiety state. Because the body feels odd the pathologically anxious person comes to believe that it is indeed odd and so complains to the doctor of symptoms in those systems most affected by the release of catecholamine hormones that, according to your viewpoint, either cause, accompany or constitute the anxiety process itself.

The most common symptoms are those of palpitations of the heart, whilst tiredness, breathlessness and chest pain are frequently experienced. The anxious person may feel dizzy and faint and complain of difficulty in breathing. All these symptoms occur against a continuing background of nervousness and apprehension, the so-called free-floating anxiety, for which it is often difficult to pin-point a sufficient and appropriate cause. Since many of the symptoms are the same as those of cardio-vascular disease and because the individual is searching for explanations for his psychological and physical discomfort it is understandable that he begins to worry that something is wrong with his heart. The doctor, too, may share his concern and will have to satisfy himself in the physical examination and, if thought necessary, by performing chest X-rays, an E.C.G. (E.K.G.), full blood count and cardiac enzyme assays, that it is psychopathology and not physical disease with which he is dealing.

The gastro-intestinal system is also much affected by the sympathomimetic amines released during anxiety states. The individual may complain of loss of appetite, of a sinking feeling in the stomach, and of nausea. He may vomit and have diarrhoea. In the central nervous system headaches, parasthesias, trembling and shakiness are the most complained of symptoms and signs. The feeling of tension often manifests itself as generalised or localised muscular aches and pains and in particular chronic backache can probably be caused by, and is certainly exacerbated by, pathological anxiety.

In summary so far, the existence of panic attacks should alert the physician to the near certainty that pathological anxiety exists whilst gross hypochondriacal preoccupations that severely hamper the individual's normal functioning with or without marked physical disturbances should also be regarded as an important indication of pathological anxiety.

The existence of phobias, intense unreasonable fears of entities and situations that the vast majority of people would find unworthy of provoking such emotions and which lead to a considerable interference with the ability to lead everyday normal life, is always indicative of psychopathology. Such phobias may be directed towards specific items such as cats or dogs or be more generalised such as fear of enclosed spaces (claustrophobia) or of large, public places (agoraphobia). This latter phobia, in which, usually, women experience acute attacks of panic on leaving their homes and entering such places as supermarkets, may lead them to a situation in which they are effectively housebound and unwilling to go out at all. Such a debilitating phobia requires immediate psychiatric intervention. In other instances the borderline between idiosyncratic dislike of heights, of spiders, of flying in aeroplanes etc., and pathological phobic anxiety states may not be so clear, but in each case the appropriateness of the reaction, gauged by the extent to which it is generally experienced and can be explained as a relatively reasoned response to a genuinely threatening stimulus, together with the extent to which it hampers and hinders our ability to lead normal and satisfactory lives, should provide sufficient information to enable the doctor to identify psychopathology where it exists.

In these cases, then, of primary or secondary anxiety it might well be necessary for the physician to prescribe some type of anti-anxiety drug, such as the benzodiazepine tranquillisers. Such anxiety has no value for the individual, since it does not signify any contravention of his own moral code. It is through no fault of his own that he knows the pain of such anxiety and there is little he can do to remove it. It is intolerable, impeding rather than encouraging action, and reducing ability to function. Its biochemical removal will carry no negative implications for self-respect, and it would be misguided to allow the sufferer to struggle on in a battle he has little hope of winning or of acquitting himself with honour.

8
The Therapeutic Friendship

In this chapter I shall argue that in the field of helping others to help themselves there are no experts. In the absence of illness we all can, and should, be practitioners of Moral Therapy. We can practise it on ourselves and on others. We need possess no formal skills or qualifications except our common sense and our experience of life, and our capacity for empathy will be of infinitely more importance than a superior intelligence or a knowledge of psychology. We must all prepare ourselves to take back the role that the talk therapists have so recently hi-jacked, that doctors are so unwilling and often poorly qualified to fulfil.

In our efforts to help others we should always avoid the hierarchical approach, refusing to pose as an expert who is in a position to dispense wisdom and 'know-how' to somebody who does not possess it. Instead we should never attempt to hide the persona of our private lives and should reject any spurious authority that the role of 'helper' might seem to imply. We should react naturally as a person rather than as a professional, when being approached by someone in trouble. A doctor, for example, should be keenly aware that he has no superior knowledge of how life should be lived by virtue of his position. He cannot lay down the law and pretend that in some way he is more qualified to understand the complexities of human thought and behaviour than anyone else. Certainly in the medical training no secret boxes are unlocked in this respect, otherwise we might expect doctors, psychiatrists, psychotherapists and others of that ilk to be conspicuously more successful at life than others, whereas there is, of course, no evidence to suggest that this is so. Instead when we are approached by someone in trouble we should remember that at another time, in another place, we may experience similar difficulties and our attitudes and reactions should reflect this possibility.

In contrast to the well-meaning questions of the doctor concerning the mood and spirits of his patient, the practitioner of the principles of Moral Therapy will seek to deduce them from more general conversation and empathetic observation of behaviour in situations unconfined to the unpromising atmosphere of consulting rooms and surgeries. Unlike the psychoanalyst, whose approach to the patient's emotional life is through such pseudo-scientific methods as the interpretation of dreams and word association games, we should rely on the institution of friendship to provide us with knowledge about the individual we wish to help. For that is the natural way to get to know somebody. We must be prepared to reveal our own personalities, to give as well as to take. The 'experts' and the 'professionals', as one might expect, shrink from such an approach, preferring to hide behind the mask of their expertise. But why should we expose our innermost feelings to an aloof 'professional', who has given us no concrete indications that he really cares about us?

So we should emphasise the equality of our relationship with an individual in trouble, while recognising that in terms of contentedness our present position may be in contrast to his. If we wish to draw him out it may well be that we should start by admitting our own insecurities and weaknesses. By equalising the level of our interaction, we increase his confidence in us and restore to some extent his compromised self-respect by showing him that his problems may be not dissimilar to our own.

If we are to help another person we must know his problems, and understand his felt shortcomings. We must discover the person he truly feels he should be, lay bare his moral code. To do that we need to gather information about him, and to ignore the disinformation that it may be part of his unhappy predicament constantly to provide. To get that accurate information we must above all gain his confidence. There is no quicker way to do this than to exhibit a genuine willingness to act as a human being rather than an expert. With our friends we are not afraid to express our own views, to disagree, to praise, to give advice and to receive it, to gather information and to dispense it. So it must be in any therapeutic relationship that can have any lasting results in terms of increased self-respect. If we are to expect reciprocity we must be prepared to talk of our own self-image, guilt and moral imperatives. We must not be afraid to express opinions about ourselves, our own ideas, hopes and aspirations, although such revelations may not be enjoyable for us. To do otherwise would be to impose on the relationship an artificiality which Moral Therapy seeks to destroy.

Nor should it be thought that the process of learning about another's problems and attitudes need of necessity be a harrowing experience, and laughter and jokes should be more usual than tantrums and tears. This is because the wise friend does not concentrate on the analysis of problems to the exclusion of a wider interest in all aspects of the individual's life. By searching for another's strengths and emphasising them we will contribute to the rehabilitation of the other's self-respect. When gathering information we should not concentrate on the negative aspects of the case to the exclusion of the positive ones, and in the search for the firm foundations on which self-respect can be rebuilt and guilt diminished the individual's virtues must never be overlooked.

Many of the medico-biologists and the more rigid of the psychodynamists would shrink from this friendship model, preferring to believe that the job of helping others to lead more fruitful lives is an exact science rather than an uncertain art. The here and now is of interest to them chiefly insofar as it can provide information about antecedent causal processes in which they believe the key to successful treatment lies.

The psychodynamist takes the immediate information and uses it to sketch fantastical scenarios stretching back deep into the past which have the advantage that, if false, they can never be proved to be so.

The medico-biologist attempts to explain the same state of affairs by referring to partially understood theories in the field of brain biochemistry, whose one constant feature is the rapidity and frequency with which they are continually disproved or revised in the face of a steady and unrelenting flow of new information.

The Moral Therapist shares none of these preoccupations, preferring to think of people as unpredictable friends with minds of their own rather than as complex pieces of computer machinery programmed by external phenomena as the psychodynamists think or by random internal brain events as the medico-biologists would have had us believe. To think of humans as machines is anathema to the Moral Therapist, who repudiates all intellectualisations and factual analysis as being irrelevant to the therapeutic process where they are not positively harmful. His interest in the information produced by the individual is not so much in its content, but in the way it is freely exchanged, which is an integral part in the building of just that kind of successful relationship that is so vital to the proper working of the therapy.

We tell our friends about ourselves and they give us information about themselves in return. It is a two-way street of give and take. The actual information is of subsidiary importance but what is vital for the construction of a good friendship is the style, manner and generosity with which it is offered and received.

So the Moral Therapist learns about the individual not in the way that a scientist learns about the eating habits of laboratory mice or the pipe-smoking sage solves the clues to the sophisticated cross-word puzzle, but rather in the way that we learn about the next-door neighbour over the garden fence. He throws off the protective cloak of pseudo-scientific expertise. Instead he chooses to be a person first and last, realising that the greater his descent into impersonality the greater will be his failure in the field of helping others to help themselves. The main weapon in his armoury will be that most neglected and underrated but valuable commodity, common sense and the experience on which he draws will be the totality of his life's experience rather than the narrow, unverifiable and philosophically unsound mumbo-jumbo of the metapsychological system builders such as Freud.

Friendship is then the model for Moral Therapy. It is performed in the home, in the street, at the football match, in the pub. There is no place, in the absence of psychological illness, for the stereotyped confrontations in consulting rooms whose occult purpose is to ritualise as far as possible the relationship, so that the doctor or psychologist can retreat behind the paraphernalia of his professional environment and manipulate the 'patient' so that all risks to himself and his privacy are strictly minimised. Such subterfuges are clandestine methods of avoiding commitment. The risk to the doctor of such a commitment is that he will have great demands made on his time, and considerable calls made on his sympathy and patience. By avoiding commitment and involvement he avoids such risks. Unfortunately he avoids, too, the rewards of such a policy – namely, the trust and confidence of the individual, not in the doctor's superior wisdom as an expert but in his warmth and constancy as a human being. That faith is vital as a provider of the strength and support that will be required on the difficult path ahead when the individual breaks free from traditional landmarks and embarks on the rigorous journey towards increased self-respect. Without it there can be no progress.

Over the years we have become used to the 'patient' role and have colluded with the 'mind experts' in their ceaseless search to expand their fiefdoms, to increase the scope of diagnostic categories so that those who are well can be treated and regarded as if they are 'ill'. We do not expect, are perhaps faintly uneasy with, anything other than the hierarchical role in relation to the healer. Patients have to do little and there is a certain comfort in the passivity of their position. A 'good' patient obeys his doctor and puts himself in his hands. He asks few questions and does not argue. His faith in science and in any of the mysterious ritualistic procedures the doctor might employ, such as listening with a stethoscope to heart and lungs, or the word-association games of the analysts, heighten his suggestibility and make him more malleable. He is thus more susceptible to 'reassurance', and certainly for the time he is in the consulting room, and perhaps for some short time afterwards, he may feel an increased self-confidence as he is told by such an august figure that his fears are misplaced and his doubts unfounded. The doctor, too, is secure in this role. His privacy is protected and he can control the direction, length and content of the interview. In one sense he is totally in command, in another he may feel his impotence.

The hierarchical situation allows him to conjure up attitudes from the patient such as gratitude and transient bonhomie that allow him to feel that he has done some good. By keeping his distance he retains his authority and power to do things *to* the patient; by failing to get close he loses his ability to help the patient to do things *for himself*. To the practitioner of Moral Therapy, for the individual to be grateful or subservient is not an encouraging sign.

The more accurate and helpful view is that, in the surmounting of our difficulties, we ourselves are the architects of our own recovery, and the Moral Therapist has merely done what any concerned and trusted friend could be expected to do in the same situation. The respect that he may be afforded is not that of an inferior for a superior but of an equal for an equal. Some enlightened doctors subscribe to this view, but many more take effusive letters of thanks ('I could never have done it without you') as the highest compliment to their professional skills rather than as statements of dependency indicative of low self-respect.

Moral Therapy then rejects the expert/layman approach, both because it does not work and because it is based on a misconception. The misconception is that some people are experts at living by virtue of their scientific training and that this knowledge can be imparted in a way analogous to the tablets being handed down from the mountain. In fact there are as many successful ways of living as there are lives to be lived and all that can be done is to encourage others to live full and courageous lives within the framework that they have made for themselves.

Each style of life is an original work of art and any attempt to redirect it externally is an assault on the individual's creativity on which his self-respect ultimately depends. The hierarchical approach does not work because it tends to diminish the self-respect of the person. It is so prevalent because its correlate is an increase in the self-respect of the doctor who takes on the problems and responsibilities of the individual and deals with them for him, thus demonstrating to himself and the 'patient' his greater capability and strength. He is trained to take on this role and it comes easily to him. He is good at it and he enjoys it. It would be better if he were prepared to forego the pleasures of problem-solving, decision-making and responsibility-taking and help his patient to experience the successful and rewarding confrontation of difficulty. By mere reassurance he will in effect deny his patient's problem, and will end by reassuring nobody but himself, for the patient will not be convinced that his problem is insignificant if it was sufficiently real for him to ask for help in the first place. The doctor may see it as his task to instil confidence into his patient, but mere words, even from powerful authorities, cannot accomplish this. Only he and he alone can increase his confidence by his own efforts.

In Moral Therapy, then, friendship is the model for the relationship between helper and helped. It should, however, be realised that all friendships are a form of unwritten contract. As with a contract, friends enter into a usually unspoken agreement that they will in future react towards each other in certain generally specified ways. They will be pleased to see each other; they will support each other when either is threatened; they will be available for discussions; they will publicly admit their friendship; they will have each other's best interests at heart; they will attempt to share each other's joy and sorrow; above all, they will be predictable and loyal within the confines of the friendship. As with contracts there may be, apart from the general conditions, some more specialised ones in which for example one party to the agreement contracts to provide a particular service in exchange for the other's providing a different one.

It may be, for instance, that one uses the other as a semi-permanent shoulder to cry on in return for continual testimonials as to their wisdom, stability and sensitivity. Clearly there are as many types of friendship as there are friends but the unwritten contract, whilst always different in substance, will nevertheless be similar in form. Often contractual obligations will be broken in which case sanctions and penalties will be invoked. Your failure to seem pleased to see me may result in my being less available to discuss you on the telephone. My seeming to be depressed by your success may lead to you being unkind about me behind my back.

The contract of friendship is, then, a continually evolving phenomenon and the clauses are being continually rewritten and redefined. Occasionally the ultimate sanction is applied because of some particularly damaging breach and the contract is torn up and the friendship ended. More often the contract is renegotiated and on these occasions our friendship becomes stressed but ultimately recovers. I have elaborated this point to emphasise that friendship is never unconditional or it becomes slavery. It is just that the conditions are often so subtle that they are not understood even by those taking part in the friendship.

That they are often unrecognised, unspoken and unacknowledged does not mean that they are not there. In certain cases, however, old friends may be ill-equipped to help, owing in part to their attitudes, and in part to those of the person in trouble. Insecure and with low self-respect he may find the company of others, and particularly of old friends, a considerable strain. In his debilitated state he feels he cannot adequately fulfil his part of the contract of friendship and provide the liveliness and interest in their problems that friends so often demand. He does not want them to see him when he is 'down' and the contrast between his depressed and anxious state and their continued cheerfulness may make him feel worse. He may even blame them for his predicament, resenting the fact that his low mood and pessimistic attitude have made his friends avoid him. For it is one of our most fundamental desires to be loved deeply for ourselves alone despite anything we may do or say, and we tend to ignore the fact that such unconditional and unquestioning adoration is as rare as it is valueless. Thus we may come to resent our friends for their understandable reactions to our persistent misery and may seek to change them when we should rather be attempting to change ourselves.

Friends, too, may give us poor advice at such times. Encouraged by traditional attitudes they may try to reassure us by belittling and denying what we ourselves know to be a very unpleasant situation. 'Don't worry' and 'There is nothing wrong with you' are respectively an optimistic command that has little likelihood or possibility of being obeyed, and a mis-diagnosis whose inaccuracy is painfully obvious to the sufferer. He does not want his situation denied but rather admitted and alleviated, and he can have little confidence in those who show by their well-intentioned but misguided remarks that they are not really aware of the full extent of his suffering.

But there is another insidious factor at work tending to put distance between ourselves and our friends. Fundamental to our predicament is our lowered self-respect which may at times amount to an almost total self-loathing. Because we like ourselves so little it becomes increasingly difficult for us to believe that others do not share our view. If they appear to be fond of us they must be either stupid or weak and therefore unworthy of our respect and admiration. Another possibility is that they are merely pretending to like us. Thus, paradoxically, when our need for friendship is at its greatest we may feel that anybody who would befriend us is not worthy of our friendship. In these conditions of lowered self-respect old friends may become suspect whilst new ones are impossible to obtain. At times like this the requirement may be for the intervention of the concerned stranger rather than the old friend, and paradoxically the troubled individual may feel able to reveal himself more fully to such a person than to all but the very best and enlightened of friends.

The ideal person to take on this role is the very person to whom until relatively recently it belonged. The priest or pastor is well placed to step into the vacuum that may have been created by that unlikeability that flows from a severely compromised self-respect. As a newcomer to our lives he is free from the prejudices which friends may have. Solely interested in our well-being he will not be in the business of competing with us, as so many friends are. Interested in helping us he will not demand in exchange for his interest and concern any commodity that we, in our straightened emotional circumstances, may be poorly placed to provide. Firm in his own convictions and with a clearly defined sense of right and wrong he can serve as an excellent example, a living testimonial to the positive value of ethical structure, to the importance for self-respect of obedience to the dictates of a strong and well-developed conscience.

The very newness of such a relationship ensures that he will be free of the preconceived ideas and misapprehensions that the individual may feel characterise the attitudes of his friends. Above all, he will not recoil from allowing himself to feel for us and with us and from demonstrating that warmth of humanity which so frequently characterises those who have dedicated their lives to service with little thought or chance of material gain. Relating to us as a concerned but secure human being rather than as a cold, distant 'expert' he is far better placed to provide the support and advice that we may need as we fight our own battles. So, too, the articles of his faith, rather than standing in the way of a greater understanding of the individual's predicament, do in fact shed considerable light upon it. For Moral Therapy upholds that the root cause of unhappiness in this life is the failure closely to observe our own acknowledged moral commitments – that, at the end of the day, it is *badness*, defined as the contravention of our own conscience, that makes us miserable through the mechanism of guilt. Conversely it is *goodness*, defined as the close adherence to our own moral imperatives, that is the basis of a happy and mentally healthy life.

Insofar as mental health is prejudiced when we continue endlessly to do the things that we ourselves consider to be bad and wrong and conversely is strengthened when we strive mightily to do that which we earnestly believe to be good, the connection between morals and mental health is much closer than it has been fashionable to believe in recent times. Today it is a revolutionary concept to advance the theory that there is an element of 'badness' in the lack of success in life which has been characterised misleadingly as 'neurosis'. But it will help no one to deny that unsatisfactory behaviour, actions held to be unworthy by the individual himself, are, in the absence of diagnosed psychiatric illness, indicative of moral bankruptcy and therefore worthy of blame. Only an awareness and acceptance of this unpalatable truth can help us to find the right way forward.

To the extent that there is a continuum between felt worthlessness, lowered self-respect, and the psychological pain of the guilt feelings that accompany it and actual mental illness of the affective type, i.e. anxiety states and depressive illness, there is a closer connection between psychological illness and immoral behaviour than has for a long time been suspected.

As the natural guardian of a particular type of morality the religious practitioner may be far closer to a proper understanding of the root cause of psychological pain than the pundits of psychodynamism and its related creeds would have us believe. We have seen how in the form and style of his approach the priest and pastor has a distinct advantage over the distant professional. I would argue that in terms of the content of his philosophical method he is no less superior, providing good practical advice and avoiding the attempted 'explanation' of our predicament in terms of outmoded, out-dated and unproved theories.

Nor should it be thought that religious belief is necessary for such a person to be approached. It will not be demanded of the individual either that he believe or become a believer. But in fact he would do well to consider seriously the ethical codes laid down by the great religions. Tested through the years and usually coinciding closely with the moral codes of the vast majority of the society in which the particular religion is widely practised, religious canons may well provide the lifebelt that allows the troubled individual to learn to swim. They may provide him with the ready codified framework with which he can rebuild the structure of his life, recreate the ethical guidelines without which the way forward is always obscure.

So we should remember that there are those who will help us and demand little for their help. They are accessible and easy to meet, requiring no introduction, no letter of referral. Friends, as we all know, are difficult to make and people are surprisingly difficult to meet. It takes effort and skill, time and a degree of psychological health to make a friend in the ordinary way. Most of the time we take such attributes for granted, only realising their value when we seem no longer to possess them. However, the priest or pastor can be approached easily, requiring as introduction nothing more than the individual's failure to deal adequately with the problems of life. Thus the very characteristics that tend to preclude one from making new friends and keeping old ones are the means of obtaining the benefits of such a therapeutic friendship.

9
The Goodness of Guilt: The Royal Road to Self-Respect

It should be clear by now that Moral Therapy is more interested in action than in talk. But before embarking on a course of activity to increase self-respect, or to help another person to do so, we should understand the extent and quality of our own guilt feelings and those of others. We will discover the particular ways in which self-respect is compromised, seek out the nature of uniquely individual ambitions and longings. To do so, in every instance, we must first lay bare the moral code and uncover the areas in which it is being contravened. We must learn about the sort of person we feel we should be, come to an awareness of the moral imperatives of others. Only with this information can a proper plan of action be constructed. Whether we are dealing with ourselves or with others we should not forget that this is a process of pure discovery, never of imposition or fabrication. Never must we try to force any set of rules on to either a willing or unwilling recipient. What matters is the individual's own morals – for it is the dictates of his *own* conscience, not anybody else's, that he disobeys at his peril.

This is no difficult process because the information is readily available. We know only too well what makes us feel guilty, of what actions or lack of them we feel ashamed; of how pleased or displeased we are with our progress; how much we like or dislike ourselves. We know intuitively what decreases or increases our self-respect. In any one situation we have a shrewd idea of how we ought to behave, and genuine conflicts concerning the rightness or wrongness of possible courses of action are few. In those situations where our moral imperatives seem to be demanding different responses from us, one command will nearly always be stronger than another. There will, as it were, be a hierarchy of moral imperatives. So although we are often unwilling to admit them to others and quick to deny them in public, we are almost invariably aware of our shortcomings and of the ways in which we are contravening our personal morality, of the difference between good and bad.

It does not require sophisticated intellectual skills to persuade another to part with this information the better to position ourselves to help him. Far more important than the analytic powers of the 'expert' talk therapist will be the qualities of warmth and friendliness and the degree to which we have obtained the confidence of the person we are trying to help. Given sufficient trust it will not be too difficult to expose our secrets to another, and in our analysis of our own predicament we will not usually be mistaken.

This is of course in direct opposition to, for example, the Freudian approach in which the process of psychoanalysis constitutes a long, exhaustive, in-depth examination of the 'patient's' mind, requiring 'skills' which can only be acquired during a lengthy and expensive training and which prefers, even demands, that the relationship between analyst and analysed be as distant and impersonal as possible.

It is different, too, from the attitude of the medico-biologist who will tend to see his function as being to encourage his patient to air his problems in the pious hope that in the very act of doing so he will to some extent alleviate them. Having achieved this he may use the information acquired to determine whether or not some symptomatic relief from current problems may be provided by a chemotherapeutic reorganisation of his patient's brain biochemistry. Unable and unwilling to intervene in his patient's life in a more effective way he produces his tablets, blind reassurances and sympathetic ear hoping that such panaceas will tide him over until time and changed circumstances can effect a more permanent 'cure'.

In Moral Therapy, it is not considered a complicated process to discover what is going on in somebody's mind, what is worrying them, what they desire, of what their ambitions consist. If the relationship is right our friends will tell us their problems.

It is only when we attempt an altogether more ambitious project and try to discover why we are the way we are that the waters become muddied and the difficulties begin. For we cannot know for certain what chain of events has made us embrace a particular system of morals or why we feel the need to be a certain type of person. A thousand wise men could produce a thousand different explanations to account for our present situation and none could be convincingly confirmed or refuted as each would have analysed the same 'evidence' to reach their disparate conclusions. The Freudians, however, do not shrink from such a daunting task, failing to realise that it must be an impossible one as their heroic speculations can never be conclusively verified.

For the minds of others can never be known directly but only inferred from the overt evidence of activity and speech. We use analogy to predict the nature of postulated underlying psychological events and analogy is an extremely inexact tool, relying as it does on the unverifiable presupposition that the phenomena being compared are similar in all important respects. It is, then, conceit to imagine that another human being can be understood or explained in this way, and a hopeless quest to attempt to unravel the mysterious causal processes and past events that have conspired to produce the status quo. Such a formidable task would be as valueless as it would be impractical and time-consuming. Instead we should discourage all such speculative theorising and resist any attempt at intellectualisation and pseudo-sophisticated explanations of behaviour and feelings, concentrating rather on a straightforward commonsense analysis of the problems at hand, so that we can move on to the more useful task of helping the individual bravely to confront his problems, and of facing up to our own.

Unlike the psychoanalyst who feels that his job is largely completed once the subterranean processes of the psyche have been exposed and analysed, the concerned friend, having apprised himself of the problems, has *his* major work ahead. He helps elucidate problems so that the individual can increase his self-respect by solving them, whereas the psychoanalyst and to some extent the medico-biologists both subscribe to the view that the production of information by their patients is positively therapeutic *in itself*, and that the very identification of problems and their verbal admission constitutes the most significant factor in their solution. The practitioner of Moral Therapy, however, will regard the information-gathering process merely as a necessary prelude to that strenuous activity on his own behalf that alone will increase the individual's liking for himself.

It will be the present to which the enlightened friend will address himself, and on its implications for the future that he will concentrate. He will discover how the individual sees himself and his problems and will use what he learns to plan future activities. Offering no theories and explanations he will encourage the individual to talk freely of his dreams and schemes, of his desires and difficulties, of his guilts and fears, and as he does so the areas in which he fails to measure up to his own expectations, thereby prejudicing his self-respect, will emerge.

This pinpointing of the activities or lack of activities that make us feel guilty and diminish our self-respect is the fundamental task of Moral Therapy. The concentration on the here and now coupled with a lack of interest in the events of the past frees both parties from the need for sterile and unverifiable theorising about the relative significance of dimly remembered events. All energies can then be channelled into the more productive process of solving current problems once they have been identified, rather than in the manufacture of academic and usually inaccurate hypotheses as to their causation.

It may well be that the individual is little prepared for such a novel emphasis. The prevailing climate has ensured that most people expect a prolonged walk down memory lane to be the main feature in their relationship with an 'expert' therapist. Certainly they would not be disappointed by the Freudians in this respect. Similarly the employer of the medico-biological approach will often start by taking a careful history in order that he may come to 'understand' the 'sort of person' with whom he is dealing. Both will tend to view the present state of the patient as a form of conditioned response to past events for which the individual is only marginally responsible, and to the extent that it is largely predetermined it will be of subsidiary interest to them. Eager to play the game the individual may produce long lists of unfortunate events in his past that in his view have helped to cause his present predicament. He will present them proudly, secure in the knowledge that this is the very sort of thing that is expected of him. He may be unprepared for the studied uninterest with which the wise friend practising the principles put forward in this book will greet such unwelcome offerings. It is instead to the specious present and the future that such a person looks.

It may be that both the psychodynamists and the medicobiologists fail to realise the profound pessimism implied in their approaches. Believing themselves to be scientists engaged in unravelling the 'laws of human nature' they choose to ignore the infinite possibilities of the human spirit. A genuinely optimistic attitude on the part of a concerned and forceful friend may be all that is required to start the process that can turn the habitual failure into the habitual success and so we should refuse to retread endlessly the battlefields of past defeats, but instead concentrate on preparing the present ground for future victories.

Others may emphasise their greater realism, maintaining that a careful analysis of the past is the correct way to understand the possibilities of the future and that it would be unwise to hope for too much in situations where such an analysis indicates that the prognosis is poor. But without such hope we are condemned to certain failure, whereas the application of an enthusiastic optimism may be the one factor that alone is capable of turning the tide. In Moral Therapy, then, every day will be considered an opportunity for a new beginning whilst every yesterday will be consigned without ceremony to the scrap heap of history. We should dismiss the past both because it has no significant message for the future, and because, if it did, it would be wiser and more profitable to ignore it.

As we uncover the individual's ambitions and expose his ethics in order that we can help him to be more true to himself we should ignore the question of how he came to acquire this rather than another set of values; of whether or not such values correspond to those of the therapist; of whether or not such a value is 'right' for that particular person. Always the attempt will be made to help the individual to make the best use of the heritage that he *has*, so that he can be more true to it, rather than to try to recreate his whole life *de novo*. It will not be the response of the wise friend, when asked to point the way forward, that he would not have started from here. Instead he will seek to discover the hidden advantages of setting out from that ostensibly unpromising starting point.

It is the view of Moral Therapy that the individual's moral code and guilt system are developed early in life, shaped and directed by parental influences and those of the environment, and are constantly reinforced throughout the years. We are attached to them emotionally, and although in theory they can be changed with extreme difficulty, in practice this is neither feasible nor necessary. Thus the individual will never be asked to exchange one set of values for another, but rather will be shown how to use the value system that he has to greater advantage. He will never be told that he should not feel guilty but instead will be shown that he must cease the actions that give rise to that guilt; he will not be exhorted to redirect his ambitions and find new goals, but will be encouraged to strive more mightily and effectively towards old ones.

So Moral Therapy rejects the over-ambitious approach in which nothing less than the total re-education of the individual is attempted, in favour of a more conservative and realistic one. For why should a person who was unable to measure up to his old expectations be more likely to measure up to the new. The only way forward is for the individual to experience success on the road that he *himself* has chosen. He must learn to deal with the person that he is and the problems that he has before he can become the person that he feels he should be. The processes of laying bare the moral code, of understanding the ways in which self-respect is diminished and of analysing the nature and full extent of the individual's guilt feelings are to a large extent interdependent. Thus an understanding of the actions and thoughts that give rise to feelings of guilt will provide the surest signpost to the individual's ethical system and the areas in which his self-respect is threatened.

There should be no great difficulty in obtaining this information if the relationship between friend and troubled individual is the correct one, but there are several specific methods that can be used to simplify the task. These are not Machiavellian schemes for extracting information against the individual's will. Instead they comply closely with the unwritten conventions that we all use when getting to know somebody.

Good manners ensure that when we want to find out the opinions of others in sensitive areas we forsake the direct, frontal approach in favour of a more oblique one. Many people find it difficult to unburden themselves of their problems in front of others. So damaging and unpleasant for them are their feelings of guilt and self-loathing that they tend to deny them in an effort to shore up their compromised self-respect. They fear that if anyone else is allowed to see how much they dislike themselves that person might all too readily come to share their opinion. Words, however, are only one form of communication between people and are often intentionally misleading, as so many of us use conversation not to impart the truth as we see it but to implant in the minds of others the thoughts and attitudes that we would like them to have.

Actions are rather harder to fake. The protestation that an individual is happy and glad is contradicted by his miserable demeanour, sagging shoulders and general lack of interest and energy. We should not ignore these bodily manifestations of mood and not allow mere talk to form the basis of the analysis of an individual's predicament. Similarly, lack of self-respect will show itself more readily in general conversation than in a direct question and answer interchange. Ask somebody if they respect themselves and they must say that they do, so wary are they of revealing their weakness, and yet in ordinary conversation and in all their actions their low opinion of themselves may be all too obvious as ceaselessly they recoil from postulated future actions that they insist are beyond their capabilities and skills.

The individual's moral code, too, will be best revealed indirectly. A straightforward request that he expose it is more likely to reveal an ethical system that he feels might be acceptable to us and to conventional morality rather than the one that in reality he disobeys at his peril. He will be less inclined to dissemble when discussing general topics which on the surface appear to have little relevance to his personal problems. His view of what is right and wrong will emerge very clearly for instance in discussions about politics, economics, art, history and sexual matters. The books he reads and the television programmes that he watches and the attitudes that he has towards characters in films and the theatre will provide a far surer indication of his real feelings than can be revealed by the straightforward inquisitive approach.

Similarly the identification of the sort of people and their attributes that the individual admires and respects is a far surer method of discovering his ambitions and longings than asking him directly. Use can also be made of a person's daydreams and fantasies for, however unrealistic they may be, they will often provide a useful signpost to the direction in which self-respect is likely to be found. Such imaginings are often the clearest statements of at once people's wildest hopes and their most fundamental inadequacies and yet, knowing as they do that they are fantastical and therefore unlikely to be taken seriously, they can produce them freely and easily in the atmosphere of jocularity that they can expect them to occasion. In practising the principles of Moral Therapy with our friends and loved ones we will never foist our own values on to the person we are trying to help.

Approaching the relationship with no preconceived ideas the concerned friend will be genuinely interested in discovering that person's moral code, however bizarre and dissimilar from his own. His job is not to change the code, but to help to change the individual's behaviour until it is in *accord* with that individual's ethical value system, whatever that system may be.

It is important to be clear as to the implications of this. Firstly, in unusual situations it may be necessary for us to encourage behaviour that is directly contrary to conventional theories of morality and diametrically opposed to our own personal morality. For once we are convinced that another person firmly believes that he ought to embark on a certain course of action, we are bound to support that action if it is our primary concern to help him to avoid psychological pain. Moral Therapy maintains that mental health cannot long survive the continued contravention of one's personal morality, and its practitioners' prior consideration should be to act as the guardian of an individual's mental health rather than of the standards and rules of society.

Let us consider a difficult example that clarifies this point. An individual is deeply devoted to a political cause. Further he believes passionately that violence is both justified and necessary as a method of achieving his political objectives. He calls himself a freedom fighter, whilst the majority, who fail to share his ambitions, believe him to be a terrorist. All agree that he is an idealist although most believe his ideals to be misplaced and, according to *their* morality, his use of violence to be deeply wrong. In this hypothetical case it is agreed by all that his moral commands insist that he fight bravely and strenuously against his perceived enemy. Insofar as he fails to do this he must experience guilt and his self-respect must decline. Insofar as he courageously attempts to act as his conscience demands his self-respect must increase. In this situation the practitioner of Moral Therapy, whose own code may, indeed usually will, disallow violence for political ends, would have to admit that this particular individual would best preserve his personal psychological equilibrium by engaging in those violent activities in which he so passionately believes. For the hero of the French Resistance it would have been inimical to self-respect to shrink from killing Germans.

I have examined this rather harrowing example to emphasise the vital point that Moral Therapy does not seek to lay down general moral laws. It has no axe to grind, no propaganda to make. It is not in the business of exporting ready-made codes that it would urge others to accept. It is rather a process of discovery in which the codes of others are analysed, so that they can benefit from a closer obedience to their *own* unique disciplinary systems. In Western democracies the dictates of the law and the dictates of conscience tend to walk hand in hand, and in the majority of cases the law of the land will reflect the moral code of those who live in it. But if we are to avoid the Nuremberg factor, we would do well to admit the supremacy of personal moral imperatives and to follow faithfully, through thick and thin, the commands of our own unique ethical systems wherever they may lead us.

Moral Therapy is then deeply committed to the necessity for discipline, but not to a discipline that is externally imposed. For externally imposed discipline, by taking away the individual's freedom, renders him passive and uncreative and, insofar as he is not in control of his actions, he cannot take credit for them in terms of increased self-respect. That is not to say that institutionalised moral systems as exemplified by the great religions tend to sap an individual's self-respect. On the contrary the individual would be wise freely to choose a moral system based on such workable and pragmatic foundations as, for example, one of the Christian Churches. But one must differentiate between this *personal choice* of a disciplinary system and the external imposition of a disciplinary system. Thus the therapist will not give the individual rules to obey, but instead will discover that person's own rules and encourage him to obey them.

It is then immaterial to Moral Therapy whether or not the individual is a Catholic or a Jew, a Communist or a Humanist, a Protestant or a Buddhist, for as long as he has his own value system his mental health can be secured by the observation of its dictates.

In reality, we are seldom confronted by situations such as that of the terrorist/freedom fighter. The example is produced as a dramatic illustration of an important point, for it is vital that there should be no misunderstanding. Moral Therapy is not in the business of peddling a particular moral system, which is in some way regarded as superior to others.

In point of fact, the practitioner of Moral Therapy will encounter a remarkable similarity of moral values amongst the people that he meets. This will be due in part to standardisation of religious and educational processes and parental attitudes within the various cultural and economic groups, and more often than not his own personal code will be roughly in tune with that of the individual that he is trying to help. He can make use of this.

For example, a person brought up in a strictly religious and authoritarian family may attempt to excuse his extra-marital affair by pretending to embrace a moral system in which free love is not condemned and where there is a stigma attached to possessiveness and sexual jealousy. It may be correct that this is truly the case, but our suspicions should be aroused. It is just as likely that the individual knows in his heart that what he is doing is wrong and dislikes himself for his failing, experiencing considerable guilt because of his actions. However, the flesh is weak and he is unwilling to give up the considerable short-term physical satisfaction that the relationship provides, although by contravening his true code he is endangering his mental health. Thus, on an intellectual level, he espouses the permissive morality and uses his considerable rational powers to argue for the validity and usefulness of such a system. He may even persuade himself that his new morality is superior to the system provided for him as a legacy of his childhood and he may attempt to discard the old value system in favour of the new, imagining that one should be able to change one's moral system much as one might change one's car. But life is not that easy. However hard he might try, the moral notions of his childhood will not be changed and the guilt will remain until he ceases those actions that give rise to it.

118

So it may be that we dissemble in 'revealing' our moral codes to others. There will be situations also in which we ourselves are genuinely confused as to what course of action our conscience is demanding. Such conflicts of interest are much rarer than we might think and are often more apparent than real. We may pretend to others that we are confused about what action is the right one for us, but if we are honest with ourselves we will seldom be in serious doubt. This view would seem to be at variance with popular wisdom which tends to think of moral dilemmas as being everyday occurrences. This may be because when they do arise they are extremely powerful and frustrating and thus assume an importance that is full of dramatic potential, implying as they do that whatever action we take our self-respect must suffer in some area. Such a moral dilemma, involving certain sacrifice as our conscience seems to be pulling us in opposite directions, is a frequent subject in art and literature, in the theatre and the movies and thus gains a publicity out of all proportion to its frequency in our everyday lives.

Moral Therapy insists that conflict of interest problems *vis à vis* our moral imperatives are almost invariably smokescreens behind which we procrastinate and vacillate; intellectualisations and rationalisations whereby we avoid taking difficult but necessary decisions. A fundamental assumption in Moral Therapy, however, is that the guilt mechanism is not deceived. We might be successful at persuading others that we are doing the right thing and we might almost come to believe it ourselves but if we feel guilt about it then our self-esteem will suffer and we will have contravened the dictates of our own conscience.

Confusions may arise if we mistake our feelings of fear for a similar emotion, that of guilt. Often we are fearful of doing something or of leaving it undone. But because most of us feel that fear is usually an insufficient and unworthy spur to action we may pretend to ourselves that guilt rather than fear was the motive force behind our decision to behave in a certain way.

As an example, a man took on extra work in the office because he was frightened of his boss. He felt guilty that he was fearful, for in his code fear of his boss was an unworthy emotion and his self-respect declined. He explained to his wife and children that he felt he really ought to do the extra work as it would increase his chances of promotion, allow him to get on top of his job, shift a backlog of work, etc., etc. So plausible were his arguments that he to some extent came to believe them. All these explanations which he produced were true and the extra work did indeed provide tangible benefits for him. Deep down, however, he knew that the real reason for his compliance was fear and, despite the fact that all others were impressed by his diligence and industry and nobody thought the less of him, his guilt mechanism was not deceived and his self-respect decreased. Another person may actually have experienced a genuine moral command to do the extra work irrespective of his boss's feelings and in doing it *his* self-respect would have increased.

This example illustrates several points. Firstly there is no objective quality pertaining to actions that of necessity entails that a particular action or lack of it will inevitably result in feelings of guilt. Our guilt systems are our personal creations and are unique. Secondly it is often easy to persuade others that we are doing the right thing for the right reasons when in truth we are not, as other people can never know our innermost thoughts and feelings directly. Thirdly, in fooling others we may be able partially to fool ourselves, but fourthly in the end analysis we must always suffer when we contravene our moral code. The bottom line is whether or not we actually experience guilt and this is the surest indicator that self-respect and mental health are threatened. So guilt tells us of mental danger as pain tells us of physical danger. We don't wonder if we are in pain, and we don't wonder if we feel guilty. Both experiences are all too apparent.

Most of the problems that an individual faces will be of a spurious nature, produced by his natural unwillingness to face up to the hard and difficult task that lies before him. The wise practitioner of Moral Therapy will not be misled by clever arguments, whose purpose it is to prove that the individual is doing all that he can to obey his conscience, and yet still feels miserable and discontented. Contributions to charity, considerable public spiritedness and long lists of attributes and virtues may be produced to demonstrate his worthiness, but if his self-respect is low and he still feels guilty then he is not doing enough, or doing it for the wrong reasons, or is satisfying the moral codes of others rather than his own. The friend may need considerable tenacity to side-track the individual's determination to hamper efforts to help him help himself by his insistence that he is already doing as much as it is possible for him to do, and that therefore some external agent such as an 'illness' must be invoked to account for his predicament.

By following the guilt feelings, we will be led inevitably to the moral code and will come to understand how the individual is failing to achieve the goals that he has set himself. By watching his actions and listening to his opinions on a variety of topics, we will uncover the individual's attitude to himself and the areas in which his self-respect is low.

At this point, it should be emphasised that guilt is an emotion that admits of degree. When we contravene our moral codes in a minor way we experience low volume guilt. If the transgression is major, and is continued over a prolonged period, then the amount of guilt experience will be correspondingly large. It may well be that from time to time in a given situation, of the several actions open to us, each will involve some contravention of our moral code with consequent guilt feelings. As we have seen, such moral dilemmas are rarer in life than in fiction, but undoubtedly they do occur.

An example might be the situation in which a husband has broken his marriage vows and allowed himself to fall in love with another woman. He is still fond of his wife, who has learned of the situation, and demanded that he choose between them. For the sake of this discussion we will assume that he is faced with two basic alternatives, although in life there are always an infinite number of possible actions. What should he do? He will feel guilty to some extent whatever he does, and his self-respect must be diminished. However, there is always a hierarchy of guilt feelings in such a situation. He must ask himself which course of action will make him feel the *most* guilty, and therefore lead to the greatest diminution of his self-respect. In attempting to reach this most difficult decision he will examine his conscience and his moral code, considering carefully his feelings on the sanctity of marriage, the inviolability of promises, etc., etc. Deep within him the answer will be available, and he must follow the course that makes him feel least guilty, irrespective of other considerations. Usually it will be the hardest and most difficult of the possibilities, but the one that contains within it the most potential for increasing self-respect.

So isolating the guilt feelings is not a totally straightforward exercise as, to a limited degree, we may mislead ourselves and others with regard to the origins of these feelings. Similarly, it may not be easy to decide in hierarchical situations which moral imperatives are the most powerful and therefore which guilt experience will be the most profound if the command is disobeyed. This is the area in which we can all act as detectives, sifting the evidence, reading between the lines, watching behaviour and listening to talk as we seek to come into contact with the individual's genuine moral code. With very few exceptions it will be there to discover. Created by us and for us during the earliest years it is the framework within which we will operate for the rest of our lives. Changed only with the greatest difficulty it provides the scaffolding around which we construct our future.

10
The Cruelty of Kindness

In our efforts to help others, and as we try to extricate ourselves from unsatisfactory predicaments we should always try to concentrate on those areas in which self-esteem is high, taking every opportunity to accentuate the positive wherever we discover it. For every individual has the necessary equipment for leading a successful and contented life. Nobody actually is inferior, it is just that at times many of us *feel* inferior and act and behave in an inferior way. So often we are our own worst enemies in that all of our actions are aimed at short-term gratification at the expense of long-term self-respect, and most of our dissatisfaction stems from our own choice of the wrong path. Once this is realised the rectification of our mistakes is within our power. By choosing to change our actions, we can choose to become more successful people. All that is required is a supreme effort of will. It is not easy, but it is far from impossible, and all of us carry the key to success within us.

The well-meaning friend will seek out these hidden strengths and, by shining the spotlight on them will persuade the individual that they are alive and well, just waiting to be used. Our confidence and optimism should encourage that person in the belief that he is able to improve his lot and become more like the person he believes he should be. As he concentrates on the positive, so will he downgrade the negative aspects of the situation. All pessimistic talk about personal inadequacy and fundamental deficiencies of character will be strongly discouraged. Instead we should encourage others to indulge in immediate activity to counteract the depressed mood. It may seem harsh to appear uninterested and bored by pessimistic analyses and defeatist talk whilst being enthusiastic about optimism and positive things, but this is the way to condition the individual into feeling better. So often moods are habits that we have got used to. They need to be broken in the most efficient way possible. If we are not careful, misery and despair can become a way of life, an expensive attention-seeking mechanism, a learned way of looking at the world that can only do us harm.

Clearly a differentiation should be made between moments of intense sorrow and felt worthlessness and general and semi-permanent moods of pessimism and depression. At moments of crisis we should be as supportive and sympathetic as necessary. However, the truly concerned friend will adopt a much tougher stance to the more malingering type of negativism that is so frequently experienced.

Such is the state of current attitudes in psychiatry and psychology that a patient may feel it is his role to produce such depressed sentiments in order that the 'expert' can do away with them. The 'experts,' steeped in the tradition of liberalism, have cultivated sympathy to such an extent that they have forgotten their pragmatism. Endlessly they appear to provide the interested, sympathetic ear as their patients wallow in self-pity, since this they feel is the area of their expertise. Their attitude is the reverse of Moral Therapy's position, as they unwittingly condition their patients into attitudes of mind that are positively harmful to them. Because both feel that the expert's role is the solution of the patient's problems, problems automatically become the staple diet of the relationship. The patient is interesting and the professional interested only to the extent that the patient can produce examples of the things that are wrong with his life and personality. Both tend studiously to ignore the things that are going right, believing that here everything will look after itself.

Moral Therapy, however, believes that by concentrating on the building up of the positive aspects, the negative ones will disappear of their own accord. It is a question of different emphasis; of approaching the situation from a different angle. The traditionalists might feel that it is unkind not to allow the patient constantly to air his grievances and dissatisfactions, feeling as they do for some strange reason that this is in itself positively therapeutic. But by teaching the individual that such attitudes are unacceptable, and must and can be given up through an effort of will, and replaced with something of infinitely greater value, we are performing a far more worthwhile service.

Kindness and sympathy are attributes that, whilst they are always good for the person who possesses them, may not be so useful to the person on to whom they are projected. We should not shrink therefore, from being cruel to be kind, despite the initial resistance that such an attitude might bring forth in those accustomed to more generally accepted, though misguided, approaches. We may be accused of callousness, of lacking sympathy, of insufficient interest in the well-being of the individual we are trying to help. 'He is only interested in me when things are going well,' might be a common complaint. Of course, the truth is that we are deeply concerned that things should go well, but feel strongly that optimism is the best way towards that goal, and pessimism the least helpful.

So in Moral Therapy all the virtues and positive attributes will be steadfastly developed that they may be expanded at the expense of the more negative ones. The individual will be taught to concentrate on success rather than on the analysis of failure. Once he firmly believes that all is possible for him and begins to act in accordance with that belief, the way forward to self-development and increased self-respect will be clear. It will be the end of the beginning.

11
The Importance of Difficulty

To consider that one has the right to a 'good' or an 'easy' time is a dangerous fiction based on a misunderstanding of what our own best interests are. For there are no good times in the real sense of the word if we don't feel that we have recently and fully earned them. There are only scattered oases of predominantly physical or sensational transient satisfactions containing within them the seeds of their own destruction in terms of lowered self-respect. Maybe in our hearts we know the truth of all this, but in our actions we tend to behave as if it was not so. We may consider that after a bout of strenuous activity we have earned the right to rest and relax, to take things easy for a bit. But to relax after hard work is pleasurable only insofar as it is inseparable from the day's activity, the enjoyment that we appear to gain from it springing rather from this other source and in fact existing despite the relaxation rather than because of it. It has no lasting intrinsic value of its own. Thus a strenuous day at the coal face or in the office is followed by the unwinding in the hot bath, the relaxing glass of alcohol, the sedentary evening in front of the television. But it is the former and not the latter which contributes to the increase in self-respect which is the only lasting source of gratification. The relaxation panders to our desire for physical comfort rather than to our need for emotional satisfaction.

Relaxation is valuable, necessary and worthwhile for the efficient functioning of our bodies and minds, for our muscles and joints as well as for our psychological well-being, but unlike hard work it is not intrinsically good for us and should not be sought for its own sake. Unfortunately, many of us fail to see the truth of this and mistakenly believe that it is relaxation and leisure which are the real

126

goals in life and that hard work is a relatively unpleasant but unfortunately necessary part in the obtaining of them. In fact the real pleasure lies in the contemplation of a good job well done and in the actual performance of the task. The feeling of increased self-esteem may spill over into the rest period but cannot survive in the absence of the effort and struggle which preceded it. We may feel that we owe ourselves a 'good' time, but with continued inactivity and lack of application the time will soon cease to be good and we will be left with vague feelings of guilt which no amount of rational intellectualisations about how wrong we are to feel it can dispel. We may know that we have earned our rest, but unless we are constructive and active in our leisure time our self-respect will soon decline.

Such is often the problem of retirement and old age. All our lives we have worked and striven to earn the right to a peaceful and relaxed old age. Insurance policies have been taken out and the premiums paid, savings set by and children had so that we will be able to bask in the relative inactivity of our twilight years. By a life of toil we have earned the right to be lazy. And so, when the old person gives up his job and his role, his strife and his struggle he is frequently unable to replace it with something of value. As he does less his self-respect declines and his confidence in himself fails. Whilst confidence decreases so his bitterness increases as his expectations of tranquillity and peace evaporate. People sense the depressed and dissatisfied mood and explain it away, unthinkingly, as the 'problems of ageing'. If, however, the old person had retained his activity and interests, striving day after day to acquire new skills or perfect old ones, constantly fighting to overcome any physical deficiency resulting from the ageing process, then his self-respect and self-confidence will increase. He need never then accept the role that society so readily casts for those of its members who are different chiefly in that they have been alive for longer than most. By being interested he becomes interesting and he need never become 'old' in the traditional sense.

Moral Therapy, then, will seek to show people that in their own interest their goals must never be luxury and ease, but rather activity and difficulty. Thus it will involve to some extent a process of re-education in which the individual is encouraged initially to expect less from life so that ultimately he may gain more. As he begins to see life in a different and more realistic way he will begin to like and admire himself not because he is told to do so, but because, in the brave confrontation of his problems, he will realise that he is genuinely worthy of self-admiration. As he undertakes increasingly successful actions so his self-confidence will grow, and as he becomes more and more the person he feels he ought to be so his fear will diminish and, taking new pride in his achievements, his feelings of guilt and self-loathing will disappear. Always he should be encouraged to live an active and committed life following closely the dictates of his conscience. As he becomes more true to himself he will increasingly be able to shoulder responsibilities and to take decisions and to relate more effectively to others. He will be helped to analyse, to understand and to listen to his feelings of guilt, and will be shown that they can be ignored only at the greatest risk to his psychological equilibrium. As we learn to obey our own acknowledged moral commands our lives will acquire new purpose and direction. Fundamentally it will be a moral life, based on rules the validity of which we accept.

So important is it in life never to spare ourselves, constantly to drive ourselves on, to immerse ourselves in the struggle of problem-solving, that the search for difficulty can be a valuable pointer to those actions and behaviour which have positive implications for us in terms of increased self-respect. In the same way that guilt feelings warn us of inappropriate actions so the presence of difficulty signals a useful way forward. When confronted with various possible courses of action we should ask ourselves, 'Which is the most difficult?' In the majority of cases the most difficult choice will be the most desirable, for whatever else happens in the brave confrontation of difficulty our self-esteem must increase. The converse is also true. Insofar as we recoil from difficulty, seeking instead the easy way, we must like ourselves less, having missed out on a valuable chance to expand our self-confidence.

The test can be applied to the most important events in our lives, but also to the most mundane of everyday actions. Should we have an extra five minutes in bed? Yes or no? Which is the more difficult? *That* will be the correct choice for us. Of course, for most of us the difficult course will be to get up immediately, but that is not necessarily so. For the workaholic, obsessed with the need to get to the office, neglectful, perhaps, of his wife and her feelings, inconsiderate of her need to talk to him, for him to show her affection,

128

the most difficult course might be to linger in bed a little longer. Whatever is the most difficult action *for us* is likely to be the right one, and this example helps clarify the intensely individual nature of our experience of difficulty. For me to lose weight, to demonstrate affection, to be untidy and to understand computers may all be difficult. For you they may be easy. For me to diet successfully, smother my wife with love, make a mess around the house and write a computer programme would increase my self-respect immeasurably. For you such actions might make you hate yourself. The search for personal difficulty is then a uniquely individual search in the same way that the experience of guilt is different for all of us. But although we have different ideas about what is difficult and about what is right and wrong, we do not have a problem in recognising difficulty or moral imperatives. In both situations a hierarchy applies. Of the various difficult courses open to us, which is the *most* difficult? Of the various actions and behaviour that will tend to diminish guilt feelings, which will bring about the *greatest* diminution?

I am not suggesting that we should go out immediately and attempt the most difficult task that we can think of, but rather that, of the jobs and courses of action that we deem *appropriate* for us, to select the most difficult is usually the right thing for us to do. Thus it is not suggested that the innumerate but successful literary editor should give up his job and enrol as a computer programmer or that the sufferer from vertigo should take up tightrope walking. Instead I maintain that in our everyday lives we should ensure that we are extending ourselves, pushing ourselves, developing ourselves by subjecting ourselves to the test of difficulty, without which self-esteem must always elude us.

Should I protest when somebody is rude to me, to my wife, to my child? It depends. Which is the most difficult path for me? It will usually be the one that tends to diminish rather than increase our guilt, as increased difficulty and diminished guilt tend to walk hand in hand. I may take what is for me the easy way. I laugh off the insult, feeling secretly guilty while doing so as I contemplate my felt inadequacy. When I discuss it at home later I rationalise my failure. 'It was the civilised response.' 'The man was drunk.' 'He is always like that.' 'He didn't mean it.' But my guilt mechanism laughs at my attempted rationalisations, at my doomed excuses, as it squirts psychological pain into my psyche. I know only too well that I avoided the difficult course – did what for me was the wrong thing. So now I feel pathetic despite the fact that I had more than adequate warning, that I knew all along what I should have done. I have only myself to blame.

Once again one must emphasise that what was 'right' for me may well be 'wrong' for you, as there is no such thing as universally 'right' behaviour if the criterion of rightness is the choice of action which in the long run will produce the greatest overall diminution of guilt. You may be quick to anger, accustomed to hit out, either verbally or physically at the very slightest provocation. You may be ashamed of this your aggressive tendency. Punching the offender is then for you both the easiest way and the one most likely to produce guilt feelings, turning the other cheek the most difficult and the most likely to increase self-esteem. Supposing on the other hand you revelled in your aggressive assertiveness, were actually proud of your 'manly' reactions, and that to punish the offender verbally or otherwise would be not only easy but would not produce guilt either. In such a situation the turning of the other cheek would certainly be more difficult but it would not be *appropriate* – not really a course of action even to be considered. It is only in selecting from actions deemed to be appropriate for us that the test of difficulty is useful. Of course, when confronted with such an unusual attitude towards behaviour that verges on the unacceptable we should ask ourselves whether or not we are dealing with a sociopath to whom guilt feelings are alien and for whom, consequently, the Moral Therapeutic approach is null and void.

So of the courses of action open to us, those which we consider as realistic options, the difficult path will be the one to tread. This implies that we should seek a life of asceticism and self-denial if we are not naturally self-denying and ascetic, a life of hedonistic pleasure-seeking if we are – always providing that we are dissatisfied, to some extent guilty, in our original situation. In turn this implies a life full of movement and action as we attempt to become more nearly the person we feel we should be. This brings us to another tenet of Moral Therapy: all action, change, movement and exercise of responsibility, all decision-making tend to increase self-esteem in that such actions are often difficult, representing the hardest choice, the greatest risk, the leap from inertia to action, from stasis to mobility, from being to becoming.

Change for change's sake is not a motto on which many would look favourably, with its implications of revolution, impermanence, the abandonment of security and comfort, its pungent whiff of danger, its intimations of imprudence. However, I would argue that change, provided of course it is congruous with our moral imperatives, is good for us. Changes in oneself or one's circumstances usually involve decisions. Decisions are difficult to make and imply responsibility for and control over one's own destiny. Often they involve actions and the expenditure of energy. They stress us and they test us. As such the decision-making process is a method of increasing self-respect, whereas vacillation, indecision, fear of responsibility and inertia have the opposite effect.

In the decision-making process we imprint ourselves on life, choosing our own direction, impinge ourselves on events rather than merely drifting on the tide, floating with the current. It matters not that later we may change our minds. What is important is that we should demonstrate to ourselves that we have minds to change, minds that are ours to control, that life is something to which we happen rather than something that happens to us. The decision to change our circumstances or attitudes brings home to us the fact of our independence and helps to destroy the myth of determinism.

We must exercise the decision-making process in the same way that we exercise our bodies, and should practise it constantly until it comes easily to us. As with our choice of the difficult path we can start slowly and build up to more complicated decisions. I am not suggesting that we should simply pluck some unconsidered decision from thin air, and, acting on impulse, project ourselves into the unknown, but rather that with regard to the various *appropriate* decisions and changes which we have recently wondered about implementing we should come down on the side of action as opposed to passivity. It may be, for example, that we have for many years been dissatisfied with our jobs, in which we are bored, unfulfilled, unstretched, our talents poorly occupied. Above all, perhaps, we just don't 'admire' the job we are doing. And yet it represents security, there is a mortgage to be repaid, we are not as young as we were, millions are out of work, etc. etc. We may feel guilty that we don't possess the courage to change, to take the risk, to be adventurous when the arguments of reason counsel caution. Our self-respect is low in this area and we like ourselves less. In the hierarchy of guilt we feel more guilty about staying in the unwanted job than in the exposure of our families to financial risks and uncertainty if we give it up. What is the most difficult decision? To hand in one's notice. To decide to act. To make the change.

Of course, it could be argued that every day we continue in the unsatisfactory job we are to some extent making a daily decision not to leave, but that is not a decision in the true sense of the word. The real decision is the one on which we ruminate during every lunch hour, every morning when we get out of bed. We recoil from it, from the responsibility that it brings, from the action and expenditure of energy it will involve, from the danger and excitement that it represents. Moral Therapy is on the side of bravery and courage, of risks and adventure as long as they remain in harmony with the individual ethical code. If our advice is asked, and we are convinced that the signpost of guilt is pointing in the direction of change, then we should encourage our friend to leave his job, to clear his decks for action, to take life by the scruff of the neck and to shake it. He will not regret it.

If on the other hand the guilt mechanism points the other way, convincing him that his action in giving up his job would be wrong, bad – that he would be neglecting the needs of his wife and children, indulging himself in his own fantasies at the expense of others for whose welfare he is responsible, a dilettante, unreliable, untrustworthy – and if such guilt feelings swamp any such emotions he might feel at retaining his boring job then we must encourage him to retain it.

Now his task is no longer to decide to change his job, but to decide to change his attitude towards it, for if we cannot allow ourselves to change unsatisfactory circumstances then we must change ourselves.

In effect, then, Moral Therapy asks you to do what others so frequently tell you not to do – to learn how to take decisions lightly. If the guilt mechanism is consulted the decision will not be wrong and the value will lie not in the change of circumstances which results from the decision but from the decision-making process itself. To remain static, avoiding change, emphasising the difficulty involved in taking control and initiating movement, is never in our best interests but it does have the spurious advantage of safety, security and familiarity, which is why so many of us prefer to suffer the pain of low self-respect which inactivity brings. Predictability and lack of uncertainty have strong attractions even when misery is the devil you know. But we must dare to change and encourage others to do the same.

12
Activity Therapy

In the same way that the body needs food, the mind requires stimulus if it is to do its job properly. Like muscles it must have exercise in the form of input, of sense-data, if it is to become strong and efficient. So as we work our bodies in order to become fit we should do the same for our brains. The converse is also true. If our minds are under-utilised and lacking in stimulation they become flabby, atrophied, sluggish, and our mood correspondingly depressed and anxious. In Moral Therapy constant mental activity is advocated. This may take the form of bombarding the brain with information from the senses, or of concentrated and goal-directed thought.

It is important that stimulation of the senses should involve the activation of the mental processes rather than the mere passive acceptance of sense-data input. Thus massage, whilst pleasant, is of limited value as psychic food. Exercise or the solving of complex problems is, however, of the utmost usefulness. Purposeful physical labour is always positively beneficial and the more strenuous the more valuable. We all know this. The devil finds work for idle minds no less than for idle hands. We all know that keeping busy is the best method of escaping uncomfortable psychological feelings, and that brooding inactivity is the very best way of prolonging them and of making them worse.

And yet why is it that the 'experts' seem so often to suggest the very opposite, pushing pills, relaxation and passive introspection – suggesting that talk is the magic panacea? Are not these the worst possible methods of escaping our psychological torment? Do they not fly in the face of common sense, of our most profound experience? 'Keep mother busy' is the time-honoured advice when father has died. 'Don't dwell on it,' 'Let's get ourselves out of the house,' 'Throw yourself into your work.' These are the sorts of

methods that sensible people use to deal with psychological pain –
far superior to the introverted philosophising, the doomed search
for cause and effect, the gnawing away at the bone of the problem
in ceaseless and circuitous talk which is so often advocated by the
cosmetic psychiatrists, who have nothing to sell but their witch-
doctor charisma, their naked appeal to the twentieth century's
equivalent of superstition – the uncritical belief in 'scientific expertise'.

The mind can be diverted from gloomy preoccupations by giving
it tasks to perform, jobs of a difficulty sufficient to demand all its
powers of concentration. Insofar as those tasks are difficult and in
tune with moral imperatives, they will increase self-respect as well
as banishing the psychological unpleasantness of the moment. The
senses can be stimulated together or separately. We should acquire
a visual eye, train ourselves to 'see' both in the formal sense by
exposing ourselves to the visual arts and in the more natural one by
learning to concentrate with our eyes on the beauty of the ordinary
things around us. Music, too, has the power to lift the spirits and we
should experiment with it, catholicising our tastes and seeking out
more difficult works. All the time we should be stretching ourselves,
flexing our mental muscles not necessarily in the narrow intellectual
sense, but in the wider field – in the business of experiencing life.

Often neglected is the sense of smell. Of all the senses this is the
one that we have learned to dampen and to ignore. We should recreate it, amplify it, using the information from the olfactory sense
to bombard the brain with messages for processing so that it expands its capacity, learns to handle more input, improves our ability
to relate to and to gain from our environment. We should experiment, too, with touch and taste, always learning new skills, immers-
ing ourselves in the active experience of life guided always by the
voice of conscience and the pursuit of difficulty. The theatre, art,
music, literature are there for all of us but because for many they
involve difficulty and the expenditure of energy we avoid them,
failing to realise the value of such exertions. Unemployment is one
of the great evils of our age, and immensely prejudicial to self-
respect, but it can be a time of opportunity, too – a time to learn new
skills and to perfect old ones, to expand our interests. If the attitude
is right, and no force prevents it from being so, we can emerge from
the test stronger than before, more resilient, more self-sufficient,

liking ourselves more as we contemplate the way we have overcome difficulty. The alternative is to succumb, to accept the illness role that so many would force on us, to take the path of 'neurosis', citing the excuse of our circumstances, to give up responsibility for our lives.

Whether in work or out of it we must keep ourselves busy and active – not in the semi-mindless activities of the less enlightened hospital occupational-therapy department, of 'patience' and other time-filling activities, but in purposeful actions which are congruent with our ambitions and conscience, which require self-discipline and hardship. This is the path we must follow, and we must encourage others to do the same.

For many centuries man has known that regular exercise makes one feel better. It is good for the body and good for the mind. It is only very recently, however, that psychiatrists have suggested that increased physical fitness and exercise programmes might alleviate the symptoms of moderate anxiety and depression although they point out that it is unwise to begin a programme of exercise without first consulting your doctor, if you are over forty. This is not as odd as it might seem. Firstly, few have suggested that exercise has a place in the treatment of actual psychological illness. Psychotic endogenous depression, for example, would not be expected to improve with exercise whilst other effective methods of treatment exist for this condition. Rather the areas in which depressive symptoms seem to respond to exercise are those which include the field of so-called 'neurotic' depressions, those modifications of normal mood which I would maintain result from the choice of an inadequate lifestyle, from a failure to live up to one's own expectations and to observe one's own standards. It could be argued therefore that exercise as a therapy has been ignored by the psychiatric profession because the people for whom it might be of use are not really ill at all, although they might hover on the borders of illness.

There is another and perhaps more important reason for the lack of interest in exercise as a therapeutic tool. Although adherents of the biochemical – the volts and pills men – are easily distinguishable from their more philosophically and psychotherapeutically-oriented colleagues, both groups tend to be thinkers rather than doers whose actions, such as they are, consist largely of talking, prescribing, of achieving the 'brilliant' insight – phenomena usually much admired by acolytes steeped in the same traditions of knowledge. Most of their work is done sitting down, pens and words are their stock in trade, and their most formidably exercised muscle is the tongue. If it could be conclusively proved that exercise had a part to play in psychiatric treatment, resulting for example in the provision of a gymnasium in the psychiatric wing of every hospital, then it could be expected that their sedentary way of life might be to some extent rudely disrupted. Sweating and working out with his patients is not the average psychiatrist's forte, and he might well be emotionally inclined to view with a jaundiced eye the experiments which seek to prove the efficacy of intense physical activity in relieving the symptoms of human psychological suffering. Such people might find themselves drawn to a consideration of the undoubted inadequacy of the trials and tests that have been conducted so far to investigate the effects of exercise on 'neurosis', and in this they would not be entirely remiss.

It is well known, for example, that some subjects will work hard simply because they want the experiment of which they are a part to be a success. They pick up on the experimenter's enthusiasm and apparent interest and repay him by actually getting better. The end result may be the same but the causation is different. Others, whilst feeling no better, may fudge the results of the questionnaires which attempt to measure their mood because they do not want to let the experimenter down. Conversely, those of a contrary disposition, may disguise any felt improvement for a variety of reasons – because they are unwilling to give up the illness excuse for example, or because they are loath to admit that anything as relatively straightforward as hard physical exercise can ameliorate moods which they would prefer to believe are the results of infinitely complex and fascinating causal processes.

In Moral Therapy, however, such considerations pose no problems. Psychological illness has been excluded. We are only interested in leading more fulfilled lives and helping others to do the same. Common sense and personal experience point to the efficacy of exercise in this respect. That is enough.

Exercise works to increase self-respect in several different ways. Firstly, there are the physiological benefits. Regular exercise helps to protect the body from coronary artery disease and strokes by lowering blood pressure, reducing weight and ameliorating blood fat levels. It aids the digestive system, promotes healthy sleep patterns, improves respiration and conditions the muscles. When we are physically fit we *feel* better. Few could deny it.

Secondly, exercise results in an improvement in our personal appearance and in the shape of our bodies. This results in increased self-respect as we realise that through our own efforts we have changed ourselves for the better.

Thirdly, regular exercise is difficult in that it requires considerable will power. In keeping at it we are showing ourselves that we possess strength of character. As we overcome the difficulty involved in the expenditure of energy and the decision to act we will reduce guilt and like ourselves more. On this renewed confidence in ourselves we can build, branching out into other areas of achievement.

Fourthly, exercise breaks the spiral of a depressed and anxious mood. We are not likely to indulge in unhelpful and pessimistic ruminations if we are extending our bodies in strenuous exertions. At the end of a 4–5 minute mile there are more pressing considerations than our previously unhappy psychological predicament!

Finally, as the strength of the body flows through to the mind, uplifting us both spiritually and morally, there is less time and inclination for the less health-making leisure activities such as smoking, drinking, over-eating and drug abuse described in the next chapter. So, those of us who would practise the Moral Therapeutic approach to life should take regular exercise and encourage our friends to do likewise.

13
Body Maintenance

Moral Therapy believes that bodily health cannot be ignored in the battle for increased self-respect. In contrast to other theories, the vast majority of which tend to concentrate on thoughts and ideas to the exclusion of physical health, Moral Therapy argues that we should pay as much attention to the body as to the mind. There are two basic reasons for this. Firstly, many though not all of us believe that it is our moral duty to look after our bodies. We may deny this while scorning those who, we feel, are over preoccupied with their appearance and their health. However, most of us, if we are truthful to ourselves, would feel guilty if, through neglect, we have allowed our bodies to deteriorate in terms of increased weight, lack of physical fitness, chronic smokers' cough, etc., etc.

Knowing how difficult and time-consuming it is to lose weight and to exercise, whilst at the same time being addicted to the transient pleasures of fattening foods and the sedentary life, we may choose to consider that we don't have the 'will power' or the 'strength of character' to do anything about it. But by being out of condition we are admitting to ourselves and to the outside world that we have little respect for our bodies.

It may be that for a few such an attitude is healthy to the extent that they exclude their bodies when calculating their self-respect. The moral code of such a person might demand that he ignore his bodily health and appearance to free him, for example, for a more serious concentration on his art. He might truly believe that to care for his body is a weakness and demonstrates an unworthy obsession with appearances and that his body should be regarded as an old and dirty car, whose chief purpose is to get him from A to B. But this is an unusual and rather rare attitude. Most of us have been brought up to believe that our bodies are a precious gift that should be maintained and utilised to the very best of our ability.

139

Despite this, many of us spend more time improving the condition of our cars, houses and businesses than in doing something about our physical health. Neglect of our bodies is then an important source of guilt feelings and of diminished self-respect, and it is but a short step from losing bodily control to losing mental control. If we cannot resist temptation to the detriment of our bodies, why should we be in any better position with regard to our minds? It may seem far-fetched to suggest that there is a connection between the piece of chocolate cake and the extra-marital affair, but insofar as both involve a failure of self-discipline and diminished self-respect, there is a significant similarity.

The second reason why Moral Therapy is more than usually interested in the physical state is because it is well known that physical states have a large and important influence on mental ones. A sound body is an excellent method of insuring that the basic conditions are fulfilled for the attainment of a sound mind. The precise nature of this mind/body interaction has puzzled philosophers and scientists throughout history. The fact remains that a poor physical condition is often related to a depressed and anxious mood, whilst there would appear to be at least some correlation between extreme physical health and mental well-being. Moral Therapy would not want to over-emphasise this second fact, and does not maintain that perfect physical condition is sufficient for mental health as, in the absence of a strictly observed personal morality, it is of little worth. However, the achievment of a good physical condition is an important therapeutic tool in that it tends to diminish uncomfortable moods on a purely biochemical level, whilst contributing to an increase in self-respect on a psychological one. Certainly the mind can be more readily approached through physical activity than by introspective theorising, and if we are feeling gloomy we are infinitely more likely to ameliorate our mood by embarking on some strenuous activity rather than by attempting the intellectual discovery of the causes of our emotion. The former will give us the satisfaction that always accompanies positive action; the latter is doomed to failure, both because we can seldom be sure of the cause of our moods and because even when we are the discovery of the cause seldom results in its alleviation.

The body, then, provides an excellent starting point on the journey towards increased self-respect. In general it is relatively easy, with encouragement, to embark on a programme of exercise, dieting and body maintenance. As the days go by the results are readily apparent for all to see, and we reap the twofold benefits of the feeling of increased physical well-being coupled with heightened self-esteem. So we should be on the lookout for any decline which can be reversed and that will then serve as a springboard from which we can launch ourselves forward on new and more successful careers.

Self-respect is not gained immediately, at a stroke. It is a steady, hard, uphill struggle which one embarks on stepwise, taking things one at a time, building confidence as one goes along. To start with the most difficult task, hoping for an instant increase in self-respect, is both dangerous and foolish carrying with it the strong possibility of failure with a consequent lowering of self-esteem. The resulting dissipation of enthusiasm may endanger our confidence and hinder our potential for growth. We should start to build self-respect at first in easy stages and then in progressively more difficult ones. The previous success will provide the impetus and strength of purpose so necessary for the achievement of much harder objectives. There are no sudden and instant cures in Moral Therapy.

Thus the fat person will find a new spring in his step as he loses weight and also will experience an uplifting sense of physical and consequent mental contentedness. This will be combined with a pride in his achievement, in his self-discipline, in his ability to control his desires, change his behaviour and resist temptation. His action in losing weight and the increase in self-respect that it brings will give him a taste for attempting yet more ambitious projects and so this relatively straightforward treatment may serve as the first brick in the foundation of the building of his self-esteem.

Similarly, in the absence of physical or psychological illness, rectification of a poor nutritional state may alone be sufficient to improve one's mental state. So we should be sure to eat properly and regularly.

If we are having problems sleeping this in turn may be a symptom of anxiety and depression. Or it may be that we are overworked to the extent that our competence to do so efficiently is diminished. Sleeplessness often responds well to simple, straightforward measures. Intense physical activity is a wonderful way to tire the body and calm the mind, with a resulting improvement in sleeping.

141

There are even simpler measures such as the avoidance of caffeine and spicy foods late at night, taking a hot drink before going to bed, reading for half an hour to clear the mind of the day's worries, ensuring that we are neither too hot nor cold during the night by more efficient organisation of the blankets, room temperature etc. All these methods are infinitely preferable to the easy and dangerous solution of sedative drugs which ensure immediate sleep whilst compromising self-respect, risking dependency, and upsetting normal sleep patterns to the extent that on withdrawal successful sleep is even more difficult to obtain than before.

It may be that our general appearance is unprepossessing and unsatisfactory. Is our hair too oily, or too dry and brittle? Do we suffer from dandruff? Is our scalp in poor condition? Is our skin greasy and pale, perhaps with spots and blemishes? Are our teeth well cared for? Are they clean and without cavities? Do we have bad breath? Are our ears full of wax? What is the state of our personal hygiene? Do we smell unpleasantly of sweat? Are our finger nails well manicured or long and untended. Are they clean, dirty, or stained with nicotine? And what of our feet? Are they in good condition or uncared for with long, uncut toenails? Are we generally obese ... and out of condition? What is the state of our musculature? What is our exercise tolerance? Do we look as if we could run a mile without doing ourselves serious damage? Do we hold ourselves up straight and look other people in the eye, or do we slouch and evade their glance, hinting at a correspondingly inadequate mental state? Do we have any habits that we might well wish that we were without? Do we pick our hair, feet, the skin around our nails, or do we bite the inside of our mouths, our lips, our nails? Do we grind our teeth? Do we appear embarrassed and apologetic about our bodies and, if not, then what is our attitude towards them?

In general, medical men and certainly psychologists pay scant attention to these points, although many of them cannot be ignored entirely. They are regarded as being beyond the scope of the physician's proper interest, part of the individual's private persona. The doctor might feel that it would be impolite to comment on them, that they were a potential source of embarrassment to be avoided or glossed over. And yet they are valuable signs that all is not well with the individual. He may worry more about his unsatis-factory aesthetic appearance than about the hernia that the diligent doctor has discovered, the varicose veins and the heart murmur. That he is letting himself run to seed says much about his self-attitude and general mental state. So the concerned friend will seize on those phenomena that the traditional physician will note but discard as being beyond his rightful domain and sphere of influence. For these are the things that we can do something about. Nor should we wait for our friends to point out such deficiencies, but instead should not attempt to suppress our awareness of our own inadequacies with regard to body maintenance.

It is not generally realised how psychologically debilitating un-wanted habits can be and here we are merely discussing unattractive personal traits rather than the use of drugs etc. A tendency to pick at oneself is off-putting to others and their distaste communicates itself in subtle ways to us. We ourselves would like to be without the habit, but somehow the effort of will required seems out of propor-tion to the disadvantage of the activity itself. We need encourage-ment, somebody who cares, to give us the initial motivation to assert our will and to make that first choice to refrain and to help us renew our decision when we find ourselves lapsing from grace.

Above all we need to elevate what on one level is a rather trivial little failure in life into a test case of our resolve. By putting our self-respect on the line in a situation that is well within our powers to master, and yet at the same time involves considerable toughness of will, we learn success and can build on our achievement. Our friends can serve as witnesses to our investment in this struggle, being not uninterested observers but rather cheerleaders, the roar of the crowd encouraging us in our endeavour, men in our corner ever ready with advice and support.

Who would deny that in looking better we feel better? It is no coincidence that popular clichés provide better advice on how to deal with psychological distress than the boring and convoluted theories of the 'experts'. After all, this 'science of the mind' is a latecomer to the scene and people have been dealing with un-pleasant psychological feelings for thousands of years. We all know the value of the psychological uplift provided by efforts to improve our appearance and that low feelings do not long survive intense and

143

rewarding physical activity, such as digging the garden or going for a run or a swim.

We must not shrink from discussing those inadequacies of appearance and body maintenance whose rectification can be expected to provide a psychological boost to the individual. A trip to the hairdresser, to the dentist, to the health food shop, to the chemist, to the chiropodist, to the gymnasium, running track or swimming pool, to the sun, to the beach, to the tanning salon may be amongst the very first activities in which we indulge in the long battle for increased self-respect.

This is by no means to advocate that the basic goal of man should be to maximise his aesthetic appeal, nor does Moral Therapy suggest that the cult of the body is even of prime importance in the maintenance of mental health. It is not a charter for narcissists or an encouragement of vanity. Rather it holds that the body is often the best and easiest place to start in the long struggle against psychological discomfort. It is accessible to us in a way that the workings of the mind are not, and such is the intimate connection between mind and body, between physical and psychological wellbeing, that the benefits of physical improvement are inevitably reflected in more positive mental attitudes. For such reasons Moral Therapy will discourage obesity and bad habits such as smoking and the abuse of alcohol.

Obesity is one of the great problems of our age, and is invariably caused by the combination of eating too much and of doing too little. In our current climate of aesthetic values, it is thought unsightly. In our present state of medical knowledge it is known to be positively harmful to health. It is, given the similarity in the moral codes of those of similar upbringings, almost invariably damaging to self-respect and a source of guilt feelings. And yet it is a problem the solution to which is within the capabilities of all of us and so can be used as an excellent first step in Moral Therapy. If the individual can be encouraged to solve his weight problem it will be a not insignificant victory with positive implications for his self-esteem.

Alcohol

Alcohol is a potentially dangerous drug. There are a large number of ways in which it can damage physical and psychological health. In most cases the heavy drinker will suffer diminution of his self-respect as a result of his drinking behaviour. In knowing that his abuse of alcohol is harming his body as well as his relationships and career prospects, and in realising that he appears to have little control over it, he will experience guilt as he contravenes his moral code. This is always assuming, of course, that his moral code dictates that he should be in control of himself, should not be weak, and should not give in to self-destructive impulses. In effect most of us *do* subscribe to such a code and, insofar as it is severe, alcohol abuse will tend to cause guilt and unhappiness for the individual quite apart from the consequences of actions undertaken whilst under the influence of alcohol.

At this point, we should be clear about the definition we are using. In Moral Therapy a person will be said to be abusing alcohol if his alcohol intake is sufficient to cause damage to his physical or mental health, to his ability to carry on successful relationships with friends and loved ones, or to his occupation and career prospects. Most of us have no wish to impair our performance in any of these areas and will think the less of ourselves if we do.

As usual at this stage, the proviso must be made that hypothetical cases can be postulated in which what would for most of us be considered abuse of alcohol may for others be a useful and even necessary adjunct to their careers and lifestyles. Many great artists find in drink the liberation from more ordinary conventions that tend to hamper their originality and creativity. There may be careers in which to remain abstemious would actually hinder efficient working relationships, and where relatively heavy drinking is both accepted and expected. Many people, too, would maintain that to be drunk occasionally is good for you, and might feel that the sober and abstemious person is too calculating and controlled for his own good, unable to trust himself to have a good time and let himself go, too wary perhaps of showing weakness, too obsessed by what others might think about him.

However, these are the exceptions that prove the rule to be true and in general most of us will like ourselves less for drinking too much, and to that extent should be encouraged to cut down as an efficient method of increasing self-respect. The reduction in alcohol intake will be a powerful force for good in other areas of the individual's life, as the increase in self-respect will permeate all his activities and attitudes.

We should be clear that from the viewpoint of the Moral Therapist there is a considerable difference between alcohol and the 'hard' drugs that will be discussed later. Alcohol has been used by man since as far back as 6,000 BC and for hundreds of years the drinking of it has been considered a socially acceptable activity, and widely regarded as normal. Few social gatherings are not lubricated by alcohol of some kind. Some doctors have suggested that a drink in the evening is positively medicinal, helping one to relax after the stressful activities of the day.

The point of all this is that moderate drinking is regarded by many as an activity that is in no way harmful to them, and insofar as it contravenes no moral code it produces for them no guilt feelings or decreased self-respect. At the other end of the spectrum is the down-and-out alcoholic on skid row, who drinks all day and whose life revolves around his drinking. Physically and mentally he is a wreck, perhaps drinking methanol because it is all that he can afford. He can't control his drinking and he can't abstain from it. Such a man will be beyond the help of Moral Therapy. He is ill and he will need specialist medical help to deal with his malnutrition, vitamin deficiencies and any other physical illnesses secondary to this, eg. pneumonia, chest infections etc. At some stage, he will probably be put in touch with Alcoholics Anonymous, whose contribution to the alleviation of the problem of alcoholism is without parallel. It is interesting to note that this organisation adopts a very firm moral tone, and aggressively promulgates the Christian ethic. In the twelve steps that they recommend an alcoholic take on entering their community, Step 4 suggests that the individual makes a 'searching and fearless moral inventory' of himself.

At these two ends of the alcoholic spectrum, Moral Therapy will have no contribution to make other than the vitally important one of realising that there is no use for its methods in these instances. No greater harm can be done to a person than misguidedly assuming that one has the panacea for all ills or possesses expertise in a narrow and specialised field, where the skills and experience of others are infinitely greater than one's own.

Moral Therapy will be interested in the middle ground. Here the drinker will be caused problems by his drinking, but will still be to some significant extent in control of it. It will be an activity in which he over-indulges because his will power appears insufficiently strong to avoid it; he will dislike himself for gratifying his short-term desires at the expense of his long-term needs; he may feel guilty and worthless. Low in spirits and anxious he takes a drug that depresses his central nervous system, thereby providing some short-term relief from his anxieties, a quick fix of self-confidence. As the effect wears off he realises that he has chosen an unworthy path that leads in the opposite direction to a lasting increase in self-respect. As the hangover sets in, physical and psychological discomfort are added to the low mood that he had sought to escape. Thus the vicious circle is set up. He drinks to avoid guilt, unhappiness and felt worthlessness only to have these feelings exacerbated by the supposed cure.

Moral Therapy seeks to reduce the need for the 'comfort' of alcohol by replacing it with something of greater value. The individual will be shown how to obliterate his low feelings by strenuous activity in all sorts of different areas, including exercise and bodily improvement. Swimming a mile will be every bit as efficient a way of escaping the metaphysical blues as the drinking of alcohol. But because it is good for you, makes you feel better physically, look better aesthetically, increases self-respect and diminishes guilt, it can have only positive implications for peace of mind.

Of course, the presence of our low spirits has the effect of making such activity an extremely difficult and, on the surface, unattractive proposition. The gin bottle is a less exacting and ostensibly more comforting one. It is at just this point, however, that the intervention of the concerned and forceful friend practising the principles of Moral Therapy can tip the scale in the direction that will result in increased self-respect. Not only will he suggest activity, he will participate in it as far as he possibly can. The individual will, therefore, learn how to react to negative moods by positive actions, as he finds out by trying them that they work. Without the enthusiastic directive of his friend he may never have made the discovery.

The doctor will be well versed in the various signs that point to alcoholism or give early warning that the individual is heading towards such a state. All of us after over-indulging experience the well-known withdrawal effects of the hangover. We feel sick, psychologically ill at ease, tired, shaky and with an aching head and a vicious thirst. These are caused by tiredness, the dehydration effect of the alcohol, increased levels of the alcohol metabolite acetaldehyde in the blood, and the presence of substances known as congeners in the alcoholic drink, which give it its distinctive colouring and taste. Mixing congeners seems to produce particularly bad hangovers. Fructose and high dose vitamin C may have some beneficial effect, but by far the best method of alleviating hangover symptoms is to remain in bed and allow time to do its work. There is no evidence that exercise or stimulant drugs, eg. the caffeine in coffee, have any significant effect in speeding alcohol metabolism.

Between the person who suffers the occasional hangover, and the person who is addicted to alcohol to the extent that only by continued drinking can he ward off classical alcoholic withdrawal syndrome, there is a wide gap. In its severest form the alcohol addict may suffer from delirium tremens. Before this stage is reached the withdrawal period may be characterised by profuse sweating, intense anxiety, and gastro-intestinal upsets with vomiting and diarrhoea. The alcoholic may tremble uncontrollably and demand alcohol constantly.

In the early stages the individual might increasingly resort to alcohol to escape problems, saying things like 'I need a drink', rather than 'I would enjoy a drink'. He may become uninterested in the taste of the drink, being primarily concerned with its psychotropic effect. In this stage he may begin to drink secretly, going to moderate lengths to mislead others close to him about the amount that he is drinking. A person who has formerly drunk only on social occasions might start to drink alone. He begins to frequent drinking establishments in a regular way, making new friends in those places who share his preoccupation with drinking. In expansive mood he will invite these new friends back to his home and entertain them generously to the irritation of his wife and family. He feels increasingly guilty and depressed and drinks to avoid these feelings. He gets drunk more frequently, suffering constant hangovers and tolerance develops so that more and more alcohol is required to produce the same effect. This is probably because enzymes are induced in the liver so that it becomes more efficient at metabolising blood alcohol. The drinker moves from drinks such as beer and wine to those with a higher alcohol content such as spirits. Rather than sipping drinks he tends to gulp at them and he begins to avoid regular meals. His expenditure on alcohol increases and he spends less on food. Alcohol begins to preoccupy his thoughts and his day revolves around his visits to the bar or pub. A particularly sinister sign is if he loses his memory for events of the night before, despite being apparently conscious of all that was going on. Passing out and having to be put to bed is also a sign that things are moving fast down the slippery slope. Arguments and strife at home will be more prevalent as the wife gives voice to her worries, and resents the time spent on the drinking activity and the unsavoury friends that go with it. Colleagues at work are worried that things are not as they should be as ability to concentrate and work efficiency tails off, ambition is lacking, energy is decreased and self-confidence disappears.

The boss may notice alcohol on the individual's breath in the early morning (alcohol takes 24 hours to leave the body). Gradually he becomes less predictable, emotionally incontinent, expansive but unrealistic, and increasingly unreliable. His libido may increase, but his sexual ability declines. Others may notice that there is a falling off in his personal appearance. Increasingly he seems unable to stop once the drinking has started, and most nights and some lunchtimes he is quite noticeably under the influence of alcohol.

In the early stages the heavy drinker will be amenable to the methods of Moral Therapy. In the later stages, he will be beyond Moral Therapy's help as the problem becomes more severe and the decline gathers momentum with work and social relationships suffering to a greater degree. Now self-respect declines dramatically and the person suffers uncontrollable guilt and anguish as a result of his alcohol-induced excesses. He fights to regain his lost control over his habit, and for a few days goes ostentatiously 'on the wagon'. He misses more and more meals as he is too busy drinking, and feels too queasy to manage a substantial diet. Finally, in an effort to ward off his vicious hangovers and the guilt that accompanies them, he starts to drink in the early morning. At this point the alcoholic has reached the stage at which he needs desperately to be withdrawn from alcohol if he is to survive, and must be under medical supervision as the consequences of sudden withdrawal are severe. He will need tranquillisation, high-dose vitamin replacement (especially B group vitamins), and possibly fluid replacement. Above all, he will require professional nursing care.

Smoking

The smoking of tobacco cigarettes is an activity that has been conclusively proved to be extremely damaging to physical health. A heavy smoker can expect statistically to lose over eight years of his life compared with a non-smoker. The increased mortality from the chronic lung diseases such as bronchitis and emphysema has a more or less straight-line graphic relationship to the number of cigarettes smoked per day; and the cessation of smoking lowers the death rate in these conditions. Smoking cigarettes is also a clearly identified cause of lung cancer (carcinoma of the bronchus). Stopping smoking reduces the risk of death from lung cancer by about 50% in five years, but over a fifteen-year-period death from this unpleasant disease is still twice as high for smokers as for non-smokers. Data would also indicate some connection between smoking and the much rarer cancers of the mouth, lips, larynx, oesophagus and bladder. Smoking is also an associated factor in ischaemic heart disease in which the excess death risk is over twice that of non-smokers.

Heavy smoking during pregnancy is associated with slow-growth of the foetus and low birth-weight babies, with increased risk of intra-uterine and perinatal death.

Nobody needs to be told that cigarette smoking is intensely addictive and that the average smoker is enslaved by his habit. He suffers from bad breath and his clothes are semi-permanently covered by ash. He coughs unpleasantly in the mornings and manufactures unsavoury smells in enclosed places to the considerable discomfort of others. The fumes that cigarettes produce permeate the clothes of non-smokers and infiltrate their lungs with a damaging effect on their health. It is aesthetically unpleasing and socially aggressive. To the extent that smokers are damaging themselves and irritating others, most would wish that they could be freed from their compulsion. Insofar as their will power is insufficiently strong to enable them to break their habit, their self-respect declines, and they experience guilt at the contemplation of their weakness. We should encourage such people strongly to take action and give up smoking, in the same way that we exhorted others to return to their proper weight and avoid obesity. Nobody has ever suggested that it is easy to give up smoking, or to stick to a weight-reducing diet, but both are within the capabilities of all of us. In making a start at learning to control himself and attain difficult objectives the individual will reap the benefit in other less easily accessible areas. He will find that in the losing of weight and avoidance of cigarettes his general mood will improve as he begins to like himself more.

It may be asked what methods should be used to help the individual to give up cigarettes. There are very many methods including hypnosis, slow tapering off, oral substitutes, aversion therapy (smoking associated with electric shocks), monetary fines, programmes designed to make the addict repulsed by his habit (like making him sit in a small smoky cubicle and chain-smoke endless cigarettes). All these have significant disadvantages in that they all seem to be designed to minimise the sense of 'I did it all myself' that Moral Therapy is so anxious to develop. In Moral Therapy the main advantage in giving up smoking is the increase in self-respect that must surely follow from it. So the individual will be encouraged to see it primarily as a test of his will power. Is he strong enough to master himself? Is he capable of freeing himself from this slavery? If he can prove himself in this area, he can prove himself in others. It can be the first significant victory in the war against felt worthlessness. We should seek to mobilise the individual's self-respect in the campaign, and impress upon him that it is a test of his resolve generally, and not just an attempt to rid him of an unpleasant and unhealthy habit.

In order to maximise the increase in self-esteem, the smoker should be encouraged to make a solemn commitment never to smoke again. There will be no half-way measures. Each time he fails, he will renew his commitment. He must never give up. For if he reneges on one commitment, it makes it easier to go back on others. So each battle, however unimportant it may appear to be on the surface, will be fought tenaciously and courageously. If we don't respect our behaviour in small things, we will be unable to hold our heads high in matters of greater importance.

So by discouraging obesity, smoking, and excessive alcohol intake, the practitioner of Moral Therapy will help to alleviate those seemingly intractable problems that the psychodynamists and medico-biologists seem powerless to solve. By his oblique approach to those apparently inaccessible areas in which thoughts and ideas live and mysterious brain biochemical events occur, he will achieve far more than by the frontal approach favoured by the traditionalists. The individual must be encouraged, first, to act positively as from these actions positive thoughts will come. He will learn to like himself by watching himself do the things that he feels are admirable. Never must he be allowed to fall into the pit dug for him by the psychodynamists in which he attempts to straighten his thoughts and attitudes as a *prelude* to successful action. All that will happen in such cases is that the pit will become deeper and deeper as the intellectualising processes expand, as in Parkinson's Law, to fill the time available for their contemplation. Correct conclusions in this shadowy world are rare commodities. If they exist at all they are seldom recognised and never achieve a higher status than acts of faith, believed in with varying degrees of conviction by the psychodynamist and his unfortunate patient. And all the time, as these directionless meanderings continue through the meadows and fields of ghostly lands with names like 'the unconscious mind' or 'the id', the patient continues to suffer, isolated and introspective, unable to influence his destiny, as his psychodynamist pilot steers him along paths that have no existence except in the narrow speculative theories to which that particular therapist adheres. In Moral Therapy talk will be considered the enemy of action. First we must act and then we can assess action. The discussion of what action is suitable should be minimal, as we ultimately know what actions we should pursue. Always we must avoid the pitfalls of talk about talk about talk, an obsession that has bedevilled the successful development of people throughout this century, causing untold misery as 'patients' are encouraged to find excuses for themselves, rather than encouraged to go out and act in the way that alone can contribute to an increase in their self-respect.

14

Sex, Marriage and Moral Therapy

Nowhere are the views of Moral Therapy more easily clarified than in a consideration of its positions regarding the institution of marriage and the biological activity of sex. All of us are aware that in recent years we have been living through a sexual revolution during which traditional values have been cast aside. The pace at which these standards have been discarded and replaced with more radical views has been remarkable.

Once again one need look no further than Freud and his disciples in the search for the people who are mainly responsible for current attitudes in this field. That their ideas have become so popular can be explained only in part by their intrinsic attraction, and by the fact that these philosophical 'breakthroughs' found a kind and hospitable environment and climate in which to flourish. And so at the turn of the century the process started as a revolt against prevalent attitudes before expanding into the current state of permissiveness in which all values are discounted in favour of the unbridled pursuit of personal and transient pleasure, which has as its lowest common denominator the superficial gratification of the senses experienced through sex.

The reader by now will be no stranger to the view of Moral Therapy that so often what we desire is not what we need and that often we appear to be the worst judges of our own deeper self-interest. He will realise, too, that the surface appearance is more often than not belied by the inner knowledge of inadequacy and experience of guilt and lowered self-respect that ensure that the individual will more than pay the price for the contravention of his ethical system in the currency of psychological pain, and this despite the fashionable views and teachings of society that are too often publicly held but privately disavowed.

First let us consider the institution of marriage. Moral Therapy holds that marriage need have little or nothing to do with sex, a view that is more widespread in this world than 'sophisticated' Western attitudes might indicate.

Marriage represents a total commitment; the deepest evidence of love, affection and respect; a fundamental promise; the welding together of two spirits; a mutual onslaught on loneliness; a shoring-up of defences; a path towards selflessness without self-neglect or diminished self-esteem; a secure environment for the procreation of children; an efficient economic unit; a firm foundation from which both partners can build self-respect and in loving each other learn to like themselves more. Our marriage partners are above all our special friends who we care for as for ourselves; who will shield us from harm, from degradation, from unnatural stresses.

At the start of this union we enter into a solemn and binding promise in a ceremony witnessed by friends and loved ones. The promise is comprehensive, all-embracing, involving a commitment to stand by our partners when the going gets rough – to love, cherish, honour and obey in sickness and in health, in poverty and in wealth for ever.

What has happened to this most useful and efficient institution in the sixty-odd years since Freud's theories propounded the misleading and unhelpful view that the id, the primeval driving force of the personality, permeates us with a libidinous energy that directs us inexorably towards activities that, despite outward appearances, are expressions of attempts to achieve what basically is a sexual gratification? Certainly marriage has not prospered since the promulgation of these speculative and unverifiable theories. As divorce rates in the western hemisphere approach fifty per cent whole new industries have grown up to deal with and profit from this unhappy state of affairs. Marriage counsellors, divorce lawyers and family therapists practise their 'skills' but achieve little except to give an aura of respectability to marriage breakdown and therefore facilitate what is the most disastrous step that two individuals can take. The damage to self-respect caused by the failure to live up to the most important commitment that we make is inestimable, whilst the guilt that we suffer from the contravention of our moral code is often unbearable. And yet the mind pundits, mouthing watered-down versions of the Freudian myth, assure us that our primary responsibility is to ourselves and our self-gratification. This they interpret as a right to freedom, a right to happiness, a right to sexual pleasure, a right to the avoidance of hardship, of unpleasantness, of difficulty. If marriage has become too difficult and is hampering our self-development in this permissive age then we are encouraged to cast it aside, and move on to the fresh pastures and greener grass on the far side of the hill, again to repeat our errors, compound our mistakes and learn to like ourselves even less as we struggle from failure to failure in our misguided pursuit of a success that seems permanently to elude us.

Moral Therapy will try to give the individual a clearer view of the realities of life. He must realise that, although marriage is an institution of inestimable value, it is not easy but tough. He must accept a life of hardship, not of ease. He should know that there will be difficulties and problems but he should know, too, that he must always be determined to deal with his self-admitted responsibilities, not to deny them; to strive bravely to keep his promises and maintain his commitments, not to renege on them. As the stresses and strains of marriage arise, he must struggle manfully to cope with them, secure in the knowledge that this is the nature of marriage and that in successfully surmounting difficulties both partners will like themselves more and increase their love for each other as steel is tested in the fire, as the broken bone heals stronger than before. He should realise that to break up the marriage would not solve problems for him but create them. For if he cannot deal effectively with a situation that he has freely and so enthusiastically chosen, he is unlikely to do better elsewhere.

Divorces happen because the motive, the will to make the marriage a success, is lacking. People are misled into believing that circumstances have conspired against them; that the pressures are too great; that the partner has changed; that greater pleasures and opportunities lie elsewhere. But people *do* change as do circumstances and if we give the proper emphasis to our commitment then *we* must change too. In overcoming marital difficulties both partners will achieve an increase in self-respect and diminution of guilt that will always outweigh that admission of failure that constitutes divorce.

It should be a rare thing indeed for us to counsel divorce because it is a very rare thing for anybody to benefit from it. Whatever attitude we might hold superficially most moral codes are contravened by that breaking of important promises that the divorce process involves. Moral Therapy seeks to conserve that which is good by encouraging decision-making and change. This seeming paradox is at the heart of its doctrine. For if things are going badly we should not remove ourselves from them but instead should seek to change them, to remould our present situation so that original promises can be kept, not broken, fundamental commitments adhered to rather than abandoned.

Divorce and breakdown of marriage are about mistakes, but not about mistaken choices of partners. Instead it is about mistaken decisions, mistaken attitudes, mistaken behaviour. Our ability to reshape and re-fashion our relationships, whilst maintaining them, is infinite. All that is required is commitment and determination.

The promises that we make in our marriage vows are to our partners, but they are also to ourselves. We neglect and negate them at our *own* peril, as well as that of the relationship. Faithfully we keep them for our own benefit and for that of our marriage. There may today be little or no social stigma attached to divorce, no external sanctions mobilised against us, but we will know what we have done and our guilt mechanism will not be deceived or quieted by those fashionable liberal attitudes that tend to regard a change of marriage partner as being analogous to a change of living place or a change of occupation. If we are to increase our liking of ourselves we must keep our promises and maintain our marriages whilst re-organising our behaviour and attitudes the better to achieve that purpose.

It seems that sexual difficulties are one of the most frequently blamed 'causes' of marriage breakdown. It may be that all sexual activity between partners has ceased and that they no longer find each other physically attractive, although in other ways they remain fond of each other. Each partner may find themselves strongly attracted to other people and may be involved with them in an extra-marital sexual relationship. The strains, trials and tribulations that such illicit activity can have on the marriage are usually significant, whether or not the wronged partner is aware of what is going on. A guilty husband in the vast majority of cases will suffer from guilt knowing that he is breaking the promises that he so solemnly made. He exchanges that psychological pain for the transient pleasure of the sexual relationship, but he feels resentful that he is not contented. Why should he feel so guilty, he may argue, when he is merely indulging in a little harmless extra-curricular activity? After all he is in good company, for it would appear that many others are doing the same thing. He may feel that it is his partner's fault that he no longer finds her attractive. She may feel that it is *his* behaviour that has caused her ardour to cool. When we know we are behaving in an unsatisfactory way and we have nobody to blame but ourselves, we attempt to find a scapegoat and the marriage partner is conveniently at hand. Always we listen to, and are influenced by, those pundits who are so willing to tell us that we owe it to ourselves 'to have a full and active sex life', that sex is something that nobody should be without, a *sine qua non* of human activity, the ripest plum on the tree of life. Nobody today thinks of it merely as a means to an end. Instead it is now widely considered, thanks partly to Freud and his co-conspirators, of prime and vital importance in itself, permeating and instigating behaviour, whether recognised or not. Some would go so far as to judge the success of a marriage or relationship in terms of whether or not sexual activity was mutually satisfactory. Good sex is something that we are entitled to, we are told. Others have it and so should we. If something appears to stand in the way of our natural right to sexual fulfilment, we should consider seriously doing away with it. Others may take a less liberated view, but still fall into the trap of overvaluing and giving far too much weight to what should be considered a relatively unimportant part of human behaviour.

Moral Therapy has no truck with such 'liberated' views. It may well be that we have come to feel intellectually that it is vital to have good sex and that we owe it to ourselves to experience it. Furthermore we are encouraged to believe, by the media and the protestations of others, that nearly everybody else apart from ourselves is busily enjoying a satisfactory and fulfilling sex life. In reality very many people find that sex is a relatively unimportant and overrated part of their lives and are happy to do without it. They can take it or leave it as it is a matter of small concern to them. When, however, sexual activity cheapens and demeans us, causes pain to those we love and results in our breaking our most formal and binding commitments, few of us will like ourselves more by indulging in it. Despite our intellectual standpoint our deeper emotional instincts will tell us that we are unworthy. In contravening the dictates of conscience, we will like ourselves less and suffer the pain of guilt. In Moral Therapy, then, extra-marital sex will be disallowed because in the vast majority of cases it will contribute neither to our self-esteem nor to our mental health.

Moral Therapy is also interested in giving the lie to popular misconceptions in this area that have grown up in an intellectual climate that has for too long been dominated by theories whose wide acceptance has been founded on the fact that they have pandered to, and encouraged, the expression of man's baser desires at the expense of his more fundamental needs. Once the theory that man is governed by unconscious and primitive urges for pleasure and gratification that can only with difficulty be repressed, controlled or redirected has gained wide credence, then full and unfettered freedom of sexual expression tends immediately to become valued as a very natural and consequently proper activity. It follows from this elevation of the desire for physical gratification to a point where it is used to explain all our motives and ambitions that those who do not divine such urges in themselves are mistaken, or are in some way seriously deficient and are in need of help.

Most of us, however, despite the advice of the intellectuals and mind pundits, embrace a more commonsense view. We have been brought up to believe in keeping our promises, in marital fidelity, in the valuelessness of casual and irresponsible sex. We know that we indulge in such 'pleasure' illicitly and that there will be a price to be paid. Other such 'pleasures' exist, of which drugs and alcohol are good examples. We indulge in them moderately or immoderately knowing that they are not good in themselves and will provide no lasting benefits. They are used for what they are, for the immediate satisfaction that they provide, as 'rewards' for hard work, as relaxants to banish strain, as part of our habitual behaviour that we are unwilling or disinclined to resist. At the very best we might argue that they 'do us no harm'. Few would go so far as to argue that they are fundamentally and positively beneficial – that their use or abuse signals a natural and healthy self-expression that we repress at our peril. And yet prevalent attitudes towards sexual promiscuity reflect the view that not only is it harmless but that in some way it is harmful to suppress it. 'It can't do any harm to have a discreet affair', 'If nobody knows, then nobody can be upset', 'It doesn't mean anything, I still love my wife', 'It's unnatural to do without sex', 'I owe it to myself to have a good sex life' are all sentiments that are frequently expressed. Whilst some would be prepared to go so far as to maintain that such behaviour is valuable, important, good in itself, others prefer to emphasise its harmlessness, its inconsequentiality, its naturalness and point to its prevalence in order to justify it. But in truth all these protestations reflect an unsuccessful attempt to conceal what the individual knows in his heart – that he is behaving badly and suffering the consequence in the psychological pain of guilt.

Moral Therapy takes the hard and uncompromising view that all 'pleasures' that tend to decrease self-esteem should be avoided, for in reality they will not be pleasures in the only valuable sense of the word but will instead be the cause of guilt feelings. Transient pleasures are easy, not difficult, and it is their avoidance that constitutes the harder and therefore the more valuable alternative.

To those who would ask whether Moral Therapy advocates a life free of sex for the married person who no longer desires or is desired by their partner, the answer is 'yes'. Sex is not of necessity important. It can be dispensed with, and very frequently and in many successful relationships it is. When the truth of this assertion is widely recognised and the stigma of 'an unsatisfactory sex life' is removed many will come forward to admit that for them sex is not as important, pleasurable or essential as so much of popular wisdom would have it be. Today an unsatisfactory sex life is regarded as a disease, and those who suffer it are encouraged to consult the expert, a doctor, a sex therapist, a marriage guidance counsellor. It is not considered natural to miss out on this central and seminal activity, this fount of all pleasure, this ultimate expression of life energy. Sex in short is considered to be too good to miss – food, warmth and water are considered to be hardly more vital for our continued well-being.

In truth, to dislike sex need be of no greater significance than to dislike oysters. It is a question of taste. Some feel the need for it, others do not. Some are good at it, others bad or indifferent. Yet publicly to admit that you dislike or are indifferent to sex or worse that you are bad at it would be to give rise to a series of responses that would be as inappropriate as they would be predictable. People would feel sorry for you, would disbelieve you or would scorn you. Recommendations might be made as to what course of action should be taken. Speculations would be made and hypotheses advanced concerning the causal processes involved in your descent into this 'unhappy and unnatural' predicament. In all cases it would be assumed that this unhealthy *status quo* could not be left undisturbed, in view of the deep unhappiness that such attitudes must of necessity cause. Even if it was believed that you had come to some uneasy arrangement with your own inadequacy, there would be sympathy for the unfortunate marriage partner who would be assumed to be suffering intolerable deprivation as a result of being denied the fundamental human right to a full and satisfying sex life, a right that is for some reason considered as basic and inalienable as the right to freedom before the law and the right to vote.

Moral Therapy maintains that, of the many different types of pleasure, sexual satisfaction is not of necessity the *primus inter pares*. From this it follows that in the absence of illness or physical disability, which should always be excluded by a doctor, the so-called sexual dysfunctions such as premature ejaculation, impotence, frigidity, vaginismus and anorgasmia do not represent real inadequacies. In the majority of cases they represent a dislike or fear of sexual activity which may be totally natural and normal. In all these cases the problem will disappear if the individual merely refrains from all unpleasurable sexual activity.

It is difficult to overestimate the opposition that exists to such a simple solution despite the undoubted fact that many of those who lead the most conspicuously successful lives, Roman Catholic priests for example, have done so whilst voluntarily denying themselves all sexual contacts. It seems extraordinary in the presence of so many examples of the lack of importance of a busy sex life to psychological health that the idea should be so prevalent that to be sexually incompetent represents an inadequacy for which expert intervention is automatically required. But it is part of the great tendency of our age to attempt to make patients of us all.

As an example of Moral Therapy's attitude towards sexual problems let us consider the plight of the premature ejaculator.

Premature ejaculation is one of the most common sexual malfunctions, causing much unhappiness and discomfort. Very often the person who suffers from this condition is unaware that techniques exist that have a very high success rate in solving this problem. Because he feels he wants to be able to satisfy his wife, and also that it is his duty to do so, his self-esteem is often seriously compromised by his inability to control his orgasm, and he may feel extremely guilty about this failure. Because he is naturally shy of discussing such problems he is not well placed to receive good advice. His doctor will be able to put him in touch with those whose job it is to explain and organise the behaviourist 'squeeze' technique, pioneered by Masters and Johnson, by which this seemingly intractable problem can be overcome. For premature ejaculation is a failure of bodily function and in such situations the doctor will always seek specialist help, unless the problem falls within his own particular area of scientific expertise.

Premature ejaculation interestingly highlights a grey area where the individual's actions are making him feel guilty, but he apparently is not in a position to do anything about it. It would be simplistic to suggest that he can just cease to ejaculate prematurely in the same way that one might suggest that he ceases to be unfaithful to his wife. However, Moral Therapy maintains that there are always courses of action open to us to alleviate our guilt feelings. In this case the natural tendency might well be for the individual to do nothing, talk to no one and merely suffer in silence, whilst hoping that things would improve by themselves. The more courageous approach is bravely to confront the problem, seek advice on how it should be conquered, and then for the individual to mount a frontal assault on it with all his energy and enthusiasm. In overcoming his problem he has the double benefit of a more satisfactory sex life and a large increase in his self-respect, resulting from the contemplation of his hard and successful campaign.

Again it is worthwhile to point out that in Moral Therapy nothing is a problem if it is not regarded as being so by the individual. It may well be that the individual is a person who regularly ejaculates within seconds of penetration, but who truly believes that there is nothing wrong with this. He may make the very valid point that for him sex is a method of procreation, and nothing else. He may argue that his behaviour in this respect is very similar to that of other higher primates in the animal world, who find that speed is of the essence in their performance of the sexual act. In the animal kingdom, when the risk of intervention is considerable, it clearly does not pay to hang around! If the Moral Therapist is convinced that such arguments are not mere casuistry designed to paper over genuine guilt feelings, he will not suggest intervention in this area. His only concern is the mental health of the individual, which in this case would remain unthreatened.

The more traditional approach would involve an attempt to widen the issue. Forgetting that his only real responsibility is to his patient, the medico-biologist, well-versed in the liberal attitudes of the age, might 'know' that sex is a wonderful experience to be enjoyed for its own sake and that any failure to extract maximum pleasure from it must carry with it important implications for his patient's psychological well-being. He would also be interested in the predicament of his patient's wife. Why should she be denied the pleasures of a full and satisfying sex life?

The psychodynamist would be far too interested in the occult causes of this condition to worry too much about whether or not anybody closely involved with the situation regarded it as a serious problem. For him such speculations as to whether or not it represented a subconscious act of aggression towards his wife perhaps occasioned by his latent homosexuality, would be the only valuable way to proceed. Both approaches are widely different, but in that they both fail to discover the individual's true attitude towards 'the problem of his premature ejaculation', and tend to insinuate that this phenomenon would be a problem whenever it occurred, the net result is that they find themselves in the position of having to persuade the individual that he really does have a problem. Effectively they would be attempting to force guilt and low respect on to their patient against his will. Is he secretly an aggressive latent homosexual? Is he a selfish chauvinist who has no feelings for the rights of others (e.g. his wife)? Is he so short-sighted that he can forego the excitement of prolonged lovemaking?

But if the wife objects to her husband's inability successfully to control his orgasm, then, if he does not truly regard it as a problem, it becomes hers alone and not his. For in the same way that some people experience no moral imperative that they should take care of their bodies, so some others hear no ethical commands that they should receive and dispense pleasure in the sexual act. It may not be the view of traditional wisdom and may be contrary to society's dictates, but if the individual is honest to himself in holding these attitudes, then we do him no service in trying to disabuse him of them. They may be unusual, but they are in no way mentally unhealthy.

The female sexual dysfunctions consist chiefly of inability to become sexually excited (frigidity), inability to have an orgasm during sexual intercourse (anorgasmia), and the tendency to experience intense vaginal spasm on attempted penetration (vaginismus). Once organic causes for such conditions have been excluded, an attempt should be made to discover whether or not the individual is really worried about their condition or is merely reflecting the attitudes of others, e.g. boy-friend, husband, well-meaning friends, etc. For it should be remembered that there is no law of nature which says that all of us should be able to enjoy sex, and if we are unable to do so we are not necessarily deprived, rendered in some way crippled and incomplete as so much of traditionalist psychodynamist doctrine would suggest. The 'frigid' person may be free to channel her energies into, for her, more productive areas whilst the person who has never had an orgasm need not necessarily worry that she has missed an experience which, although universally regarded as pleasurable, can seldom be said to increase one's self-respect. Continually Moral Therapy would emphasise that in the world of the mind nothing *has* to be. It may be usual to worry and feel guilty about frigidity, anorgasmia and vaginismus, and in these cases specialist help can be sought, although information about methods of dealing with these situations is available in books which require no specialist knowledge to understand. However, in very many cases the individual pays lip-service to the fact that she regards these conditions as serious problems because the world tends to view them as such, because there are sections in psychiatric texts concerning them and because 'experts' have invented long names to describe them.

Moral Therapy upholds that in cases in which the woman feels that sex is unpleasant, unsatisfactory, lacking in aesthetic appeal, and demonstrates this attitude by her 'frigidity', preferring to concentrate her energies on other activities, then rather than attempting to change her attitude she should be encouraged to avoid the sexual activity that she finds so distressing. If sex makes her feel guilty she should give it up. If avoiding sex makes her feel guilty she should indulge in it. If she feels guilty in both situations she should follow that course of action which she truly feels will give rise to the least guilt, to the least diminution of her self-respect. Whatever happens in this way and in the particular circumstances she will maximise self-esteem. It is as simple as that.

15
Drugs and Moral Therapy: No Escape from Reality

We have considered the case of drugs misprescribed by the medical profession and the dangers of drugs such as alcohol and nicotine, which we prescribe to ourselves. Now we come to a discussion of those drugs which are obtained illegally. As a general principle Moral Therapy maintains that in so far as their use tends to contravene private individual moralities, such substances are potent sources of guilt and lowered self-respect.

Many attitudes and behaviour propensities are implied by the use of drugs and all are potentially damaging to self-esteem. The drug user will demonstrate a desire to escape problems rather than facing and solving them; a willingness to surrender control of himself, rather than striving to maintain it. He will indulge in attempts to gain bogus 'insights' and experiences on the cheap rather than by working for them; tend to withdraw from active participation in life rather than attempting to contribute to it; be prepared to harm his body and mind, rather than seeking to maintain and develop them; show preference for the easy rather than the difficult way; seek to avoid responsibility for his actions; be prepared to hurt and frighten those who care for his physical and mental well-being; be willing to exchange the future for the present; and above all he will demonstrate to others a weakness of character and a failure of will. Let no one doubt that the use of drugs is not conducive to contentedness. Some may desire and want them, but never do they need them, and we should ensure that our friends recognise this. At no stage, unless physical or mental illness is thought to exist, or to be about to exist, should psychotropic drugs of any sort be countenanced.

If an individual shows that over a period of time he is unable to desist from a drug habit and is addicted in the medical sense of the word to the extent that physical dependence with tolerance has occurred, e.g. to one of the dangerous narcotic analgesics such as heroin, then that patient should be referred immediately to specialists who are trained to deal with these problems.

Traditional therapists and doctors often see it as their task to busy themselves with attempts to understand the drug user and his problem. In time-honoured fashion they will try to explain the reasons that led him to this unhappy state of affairs. Was he predisposed towards alcohol abuse by his 'inadequate personality' or perhaps he had become, in Freudian terms, fixated at the oral stage of his sexual development, seeking pleasure by putting things into his mouth (e.g. drink, cigarettes)? Or perhaps again it is the fault of that long-standing scapegoat society itself whose capacity for causing the individual intolerable stress is continually emphasised by those of a liberal disposition. Endlessly such 'experts' will seek for excuses so that the individual can be forgiven his unfortunate behaviour and be absolved from all blame. After all, they might argue, alcoholism does run in families so perhaps there is a genetic component, an enzyme deficiency, a chemical imbalance which determines this unfortunate person's condition and therefore removes that responsibility for his own actions which alone would provide sufficient grounds for his feeling of guilt. Needless to say the individual is not persuaded by such well-meaning arguments and continues to be racked by guilt at what he knows ultimately to be his own failure.

But the short answer is that the taking of drugs provides instant pleasure, occasionally coupled with instant oblivion. In facing difficulty and psychological discomfort the individual, by using his drug, escapes his stress at the cost of increased guilt and lowered self-respect. He exchanges current gratification for long-term psychological pain. It is a very ordinary human reaction analogous to, although vastly more dangerous than, the enticing but fattening pudding or the sleep in the sun when there is work to be done. No further explanation is necessary, and we should see it as our job not to understand the use of drugs but to prevent it. Drug abuse signals a weakness of character and a lack of foresight that the individual must eliminate if his self-respect is to increase. It is a straightforward problem to be confronted in a straightforward way – 'If thine eye offend thee pluck it out.' This is not to imply that the breaking of a drug habit is easy. It is far from that. But although difficult the task is not complex in that the objective is clearly visible and the methods, although involving hardship, are there to be used.

As with all such problems in Moral Therapy the taking of drugs will be used in a positive way to build the individual's belief in himself as, by breaking their hold on him and reversing long-established behaviour patterns, he will experience a significant success and learn to like himself more.

The position of Moral Therapy with regard to cocaine and heroin is quite clear. Whilst it recognises that we may all need occasionally to escape 'the intolerable clutches of reality' the easy way of achieving this should always be avoided. Physical exercise on the one hand and immersion in literature and the arts on the other are infinitely more acceptable ways of removing ourselves from the humdrum reality of everyday life. They are more difficult and therefore more rewarding, having positive implications for self-respect. Half an hour of intense physical effort can provide a sensation of transcendence of reality and euphoria every bit as rewarding as that provided by any drug. Similarly when we wish to get away from our worries and anxieties we must learn to immerse ourselves in books, plays, hobbies. It will not be easy but it will be worthwhile and far preferable to the synthetic moods created by the swallowing of chemicals.

While bending our minds in this irresponsible way, we may see in the eyes of others the low opinion of ourselves that we strive so ineffectually to escape. So the user of cocaine, for example, begins to mix preferentially with those who share his habit, seeking to escape the adverse judgements of others, making the mistake of failing to realise that the harshest and most omniscient judge of all will be himself. Others are persuaded with considerable tenacity to do as he does. He uses his influence over those that feel they have reason to defer to him, girl-friends, subordinates, those new to and impressed by his 'sophisticated' milieu who feel they must observe all its rituals to gain acceptance. All are encouraged to try it 'just once' – and the pleasure will do the rest. It is difficult to overestimate this peer group pressure with its implied threat of sanctions in the form of personal and social disapproval if the individual does not conform to the drug-taking behaviour: a girl is in love and wants to please her loved one; a house guest does not want to spoil the party; a stranger wishes to be a stranger no more; a friend is frightened of losing the benefit of friendship; a subordinate wishes to ingratiate himself with a superior. In each case the spurious arguments are trotted out as the 'conversion' process gets underway. 'What possible disadvantage can there be in trying cocaine? It is not a hard drug like heroin. There are no side effects, just a wonderful experience. It is not addictive. You don't have to inject anything. Why are you making such a big thing out of it? Have you no spirit of adventure? What an old stick-in-the-mud you are! You are spoiling our party. Let's just forget about him. Let him be a bore. I can take it or leave it, but he's frightened that he may be too weak and will get hooked. Please do it for me just this once. Trust me. It's fantastic stuff – better than anything you are likely to get anywhere else. This is the time and the place to try it. Everybody takes it. It's better than alcohol. It's less dangerous than cigarettes. It will be legal soon. How can you know about it until you have tried it? Use my silver spoon. Use my hundred dollar bill. Let me show you. Just sniff. Just once and then we promise not to badger you any more. He's frightened of letting himself go. He's weak. He's wet. He's pathetic. If you take it I will love you more, like you more, help you more. If you don't take it I will love you less, like you less, help you less.' So the charade continues. The pressure to conform in a drug society is every bit as formidable as the forces favouring conformity in society at large and all of us who have been to a party and tried not to drink alcohol have experienced it to a minor degree.

What of course is happening in such situations is in fact a mirror image of the sentiments most often declared. For it is the person who resists the pressures who is strong and if he is successful then all who witness his stand will admire him for it. They do not like him less, they respect him more. It is themselves that they like less as they sense the disapproval that his behaviour implies. They know he is strong as they call him weak. They know they are weak as they pose as the strong, the brave experimenters, the adventurous pioneers.

For those reasons we are never justified in trying drugs, even though we believe them to be relatively harmless. Our refusal must be a matter of principle, a way of enhancing self-respect, of increasing our stature. If it starts as that, then the arguments of those who would persuade us to use a drug just once are without avail. For we elevate our refusal to the level of a conscious test of our will power in which our self-respect will be compromised if we succumb. There can be no value in experimenting with drugs since they can never in the absence of illness be of permanent benefit to us. They may please us but they must harm us, and we should always avoid them.

Moral Therapy would urge that we unfurl the standards of our own personal morality when we are confronted by temptations, and encourage others to do the same. We must learn to be proud of our moral system, of our ethical code, and should not be afraid to give voice to it, to display it at all times and in all situations. For some years we may have felt the climate to be unfavourable to such declarations of sentiment – that others will mistrust us, pour scorn on our 'old-fashioned standards', think of us as narrow, bigoted or 'square', out of tune with the permissive age in which anything goes, and in which experiences are to be had for their own sakes – a world in which knowledge and freedom are the gods, and in which self-discipline and personal restraint are regarded as unnecessary hindrances to our 'personal development'.

It is enough to say no, because we feel it is right to say no. We need justify ourselves no further. The time has come once again to place our individual morality in the forefront of our lives – to live according to our ethical code and to be proud that we are doing so. Only in this way can we regain our self-respect and our mental health. For the truth is that, in this unhappy century, morality has not ceased to exist but has been forced by the dictates of fashion to lie dormant. As a result we have indulged in behaviour and activities that are basically alien to us, and have reaped the whirlwind in terms of guilt and lowered self-respect. On every side, the mind pundits have urged us on. 'You have a right to be happy. A right to a full and pleasurable sex life. You have the right to be free from guilt, to be equal, to be comfortable, to be loved.' Insofar as you do not experience these things, there is a malfunction either in the mysterious depths of your psyche or in the little understood biochemical pathways in your brain, in society itself, or in those who misuse and maltreat you.

And so, the myth is disseminated and the 'experts' carve out their fiefdoms, posing as the only ones who can rectify the imbalances that have occurred in our minds, in our brains, in our lives. They shrink from all talk of right and wrong, good and bad, morals and ethics. Are they not scientists interested in the workings of the human machine, which they interpret according to the rules of their narrow disciplines? So the individual is left, bemused and uncertain, encouraged not to use the rudder of conscience, to ignore the pilot of personal morality as he drifts directionless across the bewildering sea of life.

Moral codes, insofar as they are associated with that dreaded emotion of guilt, are to be thrown overboard. After all, it is argued, we did not freely choose the moral code that we have. Rather it was a thing forced upon us at an early age, when we could not be considered arbiters of our own destiny, by parents, by schoolteachers, by that scapegoat for all ills 'society itself'. Now, it is suggested, we should discard our moral codes where they are too exacting, where they give rise to guilt, where they displease us, where they conflict with the new permissiveness. They should be replaced with something more sophisticated, more in tune with the times, something that enables us to become more plastic, less hidebound, less rigid, more 'free'. All the time this facile talk assumes that personal codes can be shed at will; that we can change ourselves as easily as we can turn the pages of a book, when in fact our ethical systems are as deeply ingrained in us as the eyes are set in our heads, as our heart beats within our chest.

Our moral systems may not be perfect, but they are all that we have. In all their most significant features, they cannot be changed and we ignore them at our peril. We may act against them, but we can never feel good about doing so, and we must suffer the inevitable psychological pain of guilt. So instead of recoiling from our moral imperatives we must embrace them, for however outmoded and out of tune their rules may be we can never successfully contravene them. We must resist the siren voices of those who would lead us astray by painting a picture of the world that bears little resemblance to reality. Life is tough, hard and very frequently unpleasant. Much of the time we are all unhappy, discontented and

170

sad. When we are thus it is not necessarily a sign of malfunction. It is as natural to be unhappy as it is to be happy, and 'expert' intervention is required no more in the one case than in the other.

So many of our crises and expectations are built on misconceptions regarding the nature of life. When we hear somebody describe life as nasty, brutish and short we smile and wonder what is wrong with him, despite our inner awareness that there is much truth in the remark. Paradoxically, by reaching an awareness that our expectations are too high, we may be able to come to terms more comfortably with our predicament. Only then can we acquire the knowledge that all satisfaction in this life must be earned – that it will require effort and hardship on our part to achieve it, and that 'expert' intervention is at best irrelevant and at worst a hindrance to our attainment of that contentedness.

Attitudes must change. Increasingly we must live and be seen to live in harmony with the dictates of our own conscience. Nor should others be left in any doubt what those rules are. We should not be afraid to wear our own personal morality on our sleeves, and should encourage others to do likewise. As we begin openly to live by our own rules, and as we expect less from life, realising that all our worthwhile achievements must be paid for by our own efforts if we are to increase our self-respect, guilt, anxiety and despair will begin to fade and our mental health will improve. Then we will be able to afford the luxury of finding other employment for those psychologists who have made it their business to pander to people's misguided desires to escape their problems and responsibilities. As with other industries that have become obsolete and irrelevant, the practitioners of the various talk therapies will become redundant as the concepts that they have fought so hard to promulgate, and in which they have such a vested interest, are discarded as unnecessary and misleading. Doctors, too, will be able to concentrate once again on their primary function of dealing with physical and genuine psychological disorders, rather than ladling out biochemical panaceas to little effect and at considerable risk.

Such is my dream. It is my hope that this book is one small step towards making that dream a reality.

171

Appendix –
A Layman's Guide
to Psychiatric
Diagnosis

How is the diagnosis of real psychological illness made? The illnesses are taken in turn. A brief introduction is followed by a chart in which the symptoms and signs of the particular illness are listed in the left-hand column and explained in the central column. In the right-hand column are listed the various steps taken by the psychiatrist to identify the particular symptoms and signs in the Mental State Exam (abbreviated M.S.E.), in the Psychiatric History (abbreviated P.H.), in the Physical Exam (abbreviated P.E.) and in the Pathological Investigations (abbreviated P.I.).

The psychiatrist assesses the patient in the Mental State Exam under the following headings:

Appearance and Behaviour

Form of Talk

Mood

Thought (including abnormal experiences referred to environment, body or self)

Obsessive/Compulsive Phenomena

Phobias

Cognitive State, including Orientation, Attention and Concentration, Memory, Intelligence and General Information

Insight

The psychiatrist assesses the patient in the Psychiatric History under the following headings:

Reason for Referral

Patient's Complaints

History of Present Condition

Family History, including Past Medical and Psychiatric History

Personal History, including Past Medical and Psychiatric History

Use of Drugs or Medicines

Present Life Situation

Assessment of Pre-morbid Personality

Corroboration from an Informant

We will examine each category within my classification framework in turn, starting with schizophrenia.

Schizophrenia

Schizophrenia is a remarkably common disease and nearly 1 per cent of the world's population will suffer from it at some point between adolescence and late middle age. Although the word means literally 'split personality' public understanding of the term, as a personality split down the middle into two equal, conflicting, discrete and well-organised parts on the Jekyll and Hyde model is erroneous. Rather, in schizophrenia the personality is shattered, fragmented, disintegrated, in the way that a pane of glass is smashed by a hammer. All behaviour, thinking, emotion and volition become disorganised, dissociated and, as a result, there are bizarre changes in actions, thoughts and feelings. The patient is totally unable to demonstrate the relatively well-functioning, albeit opposite and conflicting, personality structures seen in the rare 'condition' of 'Split Personality Disorder', which psychiatrists prefer to classify as being hysterical in nature. Thus remarks of the kind 'I'm a bit schizophrenic about this', implying 'in two minds' or 'undecided' are actually an abuse of the word schizophrenia.

Schizophrenia is best thought of as a group of illnesses sharing common symptoms and signs, and as such is a syndrome. There are theories as to causation, but as yet the underlying pathological process has not been elucidated, and so these theories remain speculative. What is certain, from work on twins separated at birth from schizophrenic parents in conjunction with single egg and other studies of twins, is that the tendency to develop the symptoms of schizophrenia is passed on in the genes from parents to children. On this genetic weakness, this potential vulnerability, various environmental factors can work to produce the characteristic syndrome. Amongst these would appear to be physical stress such as illness and child-birth, mental stress accompanying turmoil and disaster in personal life, and a hostile, aggressive, overbearing family structure in which strong feelings and emotions are constantly expressed. It seems that such phenomena go to work on the inherited defect to produce an illness whose final common pathway at least is a biochemical one. It is not the case, as maintained by some, that schizophrenia is an 'understandable' reaction to a difficult or contradictory environment, representing a more or less intelligent escape from unbearable stress. Those who would maintain that to suffer the symptoms of schizophrenia is not to be severely ill are wrong. They are misguided and they mislead. It is a dangerous and serious mental illness and must always be treated as such by a qualified psychiatrist and by nobody else. To attempt, as many do in America, to treat the full-blown condition, in which first-rank symptoms are present, with insight therapy, or worse with psychoanalysis is, in my view, little short of malpractice. Such an approach is harmful and positively distressing for the patient and is always contra-indicated.

What the sufferer from schizophrenia needs is not metapsychological clap-trap, but anti-psychotic medication. The discovery of the phenothiazine drugs has revolutionised the treatment of the condition. They are very effective in controlling the frightening delusions, hallucinations and strange experiences which characterise the disease. These and related drugs have helped to empty the hospitals of schizophrenic patients – no mean achievement when one considers that until fairly recently nearly one-quarter of all the hospital beds in England were occupied by schizophrenic patients.

Clearly it is important to be able to recognise the symptoms of such a disease. If treatment can be started early, the decline in what is often a chronically progressive condition may be arrested, and so in this section we shall see how the diagnosis of schizophrenia is made. We cannot be as good at diagnosing the illness as most psychiatrists, especially in those 'borderline' cases where the diagnosis is in doubt. Their experience counts for a lot and they will always consider the differential diagnoses such as amphetamine, alcohol or L.S.D. abuse, various organic diseases of the brain, or affective psychosis – all of which may produce symptoms similar to those found in schizophrenia. However, by carefully following the chart below I would estimate that more than 80 per cent of the time the intelligent layman would make the diagnosis correctly and in more than 90 per cent of cases of genuine schizophrenia his index of suspicion would be sufficiently aroused for him to consult a professional. In such a review there is little room for theory – the objective is diagnosis so that treatment can be instituted, but first a brief word should be included on prognosis.

Today psychiatrists have more or less abandoned their attempts to classify 'the schizophrenias', which in the end have always defied neat categorisation. It is useful, however, to divide them into two broad groups which could be called 'Good prognosis' schizophrenia and 'Poor prognosis' schizophrenia. Good prognostic factors include acute onset of illness later in life, a clear precipitating cause (e.g. childbirth), the presence of perplexity with some mild disorientation and clouding of consciousness, the presence of a marked emotional component either excitatory or depressive, the fact that the patient is married or has good social ties, a family history of emotional illness, a high intelligence, a 'good' previous personality, and the absence of a family history of schizophrenic illness. Poor prognostic factors include insidious onset of illness early in life, absence of a clear-cut precipitating factor, a withdrawn, shy, introverted and rather 'odd' previous personality, absence of any perplexity, absence of elevation or depression of mood with emotional flatness or 'blunting', the single state or social isolation, a family history of schizophrenic illness and a low I.Q. The psychiatrist will inquire about such factors in the M.S.E. and P.H. as well as trying to eliminate other possible causes of the symptoms.

The diagnosis of schizophrenia can be made with the greatest certainty in the presence of one or more of Schneider's 1st Rank symptoms of the disease. If you can elicit one of these symptoms, then nine times out of ten you will be correct in your diagnosis. However, approximately

20 per cent of schizophrenics with a poor prognosis do not show 1st Rank symptoms and, of those that do, about 10 per cent do not suffer from the disease. Still, a nine out of ten success rate is better than that achieved in many medical or surgical diagnostic categories. We will deal with the 1st Rank Symptoms separately.

Before he begins to elicit and analyse the symptoms and signs the psychiatrist will consider the general background.

P.H. 'Family History':

Note any family history of schizophrenia or affective disease, both important diagnostic and prognostic indicators. Note the sort of people the family are, the intrafamily relationships, stresses and strains. Are they aggressive, overbearing, the type of people who revel in expressing their opinions and feelings?

P.H. 'Personal History':

Note any abuse of alcohol, stimulant drugs or hallucinogens. Has he ever been prescribed anti-psychotic drugs?

Has there been any recent illness?

Is there any past history of schizophrenia or affective disease? Any emotional or psychiatric problems associated with pregnancy?

What is the present life situation? Married? Single? A loner? Gregarious? Has it changed recently? Any particular strains and stresses of a psychological nature?

What was the previous personality like? The flavour of the delusions often mirrors it. Thus the suspicious, irritable, over-sensitive person might show a paranoid psychosis. The schizoid personality, cold, withdrawn, introverted, a dreamer, seems more liable to develop the disease and is associated with a poor prognosis.

Is there a manipulative, attention-seeking, histrionic flavour to the personality, the sense that the symptoms are being used for some advantage or gain? If so this may be a pseudo-psychosis, a feigned illness – although the patient may be only partially aware of what he is up to, or not at all aware. Try and elicit an *approximate answer*. Such a person when asked to add 2 and 2, might answer with a cunning smile 'Five'.

Talk to an informant and try to find out when things began to change.

P.E.:

Exclude any organic disease, especially in the Central Nervous System.

1st Rank Symptoms	Description	Diagnosis from M.S.E etc.
Thought Insertion	The patient feels that strange things are happening to his thoughts, that in some way they are not controlled by him, are possibly controlled instead by some external agency. He may express the idea that alien thoughts, not essentially 'his', are inserted into his head.	*M.S.E 'Thought':* A thorough Mental State exam will always seek to exclude such phenomena even if the index of suspicion of schizophrenia is low. Say something like – 'You won't mind if I ask you some questions which may appear rather strange to you. It's a procedure we go through with everyone – just routine.'
Thought Withdrawal	Alternatively they may appear to be suddenly plucked out from his brain, withdrawn from his mind, leaving him, momentarily, with no thoughts at all.	Then ask – 'Have you ever had the feeling that people or things have been interfering with your thoughts – putting things into your mind, perhaps, or taking them out?' and 'Do you have the sensation sometimes that people might be able to know what you are thinking or that you know what others are thinking?'
Thought Broadcasting	Yet again he may believe firmly that his thoughts are available to, can be directly experienced by, others. As he thinks them, and in the absence of speech, they are in effect broadcast so that those around him and even those distant from him can know exactly what he is thinking. Occasionally the patient feels that in the same mysterious way he 'knows' what others think and this in the absence of any claimed telepathic or clairvoyant powers.	
Somatic Passivity	The patient believes that either the whole or part of his body is in some bizarre way no longer controlled by him, but is instead controlled externally. He may feel that strange bodily changes are taking place because of this.	*M.S.E 'Thought':* 'Do you ever feel that you are not in complete control of your body, or of some part of your body?' 'Do you think there is anything strange going on in your body?' 'Do you think your body is externally in-fluenced in any way?'

Passivity Feelings with Respect to Actions, Will and the Emotions	There is the feeling that actions, emotions and the patient's will power are externally controlled or influenced. With respect to his thoughts, feelings, desires and consequent behaviour all or each may appear to be foisted on him so that the whole or a part of his being feels totally passive, and to that extent does not 'belong' to him.	*M.S.E. 'Thought':* 'Do you ever feel that you are made to do things, think things, want things or feel things – by some force that is outside your control?'
Audible Thoughts	The patient actually 'hears' his own thoughts being spoken out loud, or whispered, inside his head. This may take the form of 'Thought Echo' in which immediately he has had a thought it is at once repeated to him 'verbally', echoed in his head. Alternatively he may 'hear' his thoughts immediately before they are conceived, as if they were being dictated to him.	*M.S.E. 'Thought':* 'Do you ever hear your thoughts spoken out loud inside your head?' It is important to ascertain that the thoughts are actually 'heard' as the spoken voice is heard, not *as if* a voice was heard, as in 'I heard a voice saying to me, "Now come on, for God's sake pull yourself together."'

1st Rank Symptoms cont	Description	Diagnosis from M.S.E etc.
Voices Discussing or Arguing about the Patient	The patient 'hears' two or more voices talking about him. Often these voices are threatening, critical, abusive, ordering him about, swearing obscenities or muttering wordlessly. These hallucinations, externally uncaused perceptions, are often extremely disturbing to the patient and he may try to answer the voices back.	*M.S.E. 'Appearance and Behaviour':* Does the patient appear to be hallucinating, e.g. carrying on conversations with thin air, talking to imaginary people? *M.S.E. 'Thought':* 'Do you ever hear voices discussing you, talking about you or to you when there doesn't appear to be anyone there?' Find out when these voices are heard. Hallucinations on falling asleep or waking up are quite common and are not significant. Find out if the voices are male or female; ask if they are recognisable. 'Do you hear them in the same way that you hear my voice?'
3rd Person Commentary	The patient 'hears' voices commenting on his actions in the third person, saying things like, 'Look at him. He's going to make a cup of tea. Isn't he stupid? Now he's turning the kettle on.'	*M.S.E. 'Thought':* 'Do you ever hear voices which discuss what you do – comment on your actions?'
A Delusional Perception (Autocthonous Delusion).	A delusion is a false belief held in the face of all evidence to the contrary. It is unshakeable, being held with extraordinary conviction, and is totally inappropriate to the individual's cultural and intellectual background. A genuine primary delusion is pathognomic (absolutely definitive) of schizophrenia. It consists of a totally incomprehensible deluded belief following instantly and apparently	*M.S.E. 'Thought':* 'Have you ever had a strange experience which was particularly meaningful for you – that made a great difference to your life, which represented a turning point for you?'

caused by, an in fact unrelated perception. The weird association between perception and belief occurs suddenly, often in the setting of a strange mood known as the delusional atmosphere in which the world is experienced as being charged with a sense of mystery and importance, the feeling that something vital is going to happen. An example: 'I was walking down the street when the man in front of me reached up to scratch his beard. Suddenly I knew I had been sent to save the world.'

It is possible to diagnose schizophrenia in the absence of 1st Rank symptoms, but it is more difficult.

Symptoms/Signs	Description	Diagnosis from M.S.E etc.
Schizophrenic Thought Disorder (In a clear consciousness)	Disorders of thinking in schizophrenia vary from the subtle to the florid. There is a loosening of associations, an abnormal association of ideas that manifests itself in the phenomenon of *tangential thinking* – it being difficult to follow the patient's drift, to get to the bottom of what he is saying. Abstract thought becomes a problem and he becomes increasingly *concrete* in his thinking, taking things too literally, unable to handle quite simple concepts. There is an oddness, a vagueness, an incoherent illogicality, an elusiveness about his speech and he may dwell on matters metaphysical, mystical, religious whose natural obscurity is well suited to papering over the difficulty he experiences in retaining meaning in his comments. Amongst pseudo-philosophical ramblings strange words, existing in no dictionary, may appear. These *neologisms* are invented words, often created by cobbling together parts of existing ones. In florid thought-disorder, speech may lose its meaning completely, the patient mumbling a hash of real and invented words in a so-called '*word salad*'. Sometimes associations fail altogether and the patient experiences a moment when thoughts appear to stop, the phenomenon of '*thought block*'.

Consequent upon the general breakdown of the thinking process is a gradual loss of goal-directedness, of ambition, of sense of direction. | *M.S.E. 'Thought':*
'Do you have difficulty in thinking and concentrating, in getting your thoughts together?'
'Do you ever feel there might be something wrong with your mind?'
'Do you find you can think as clearly as you used to?'

Note the coherence and cogency of the thought processes. Do there appear to be gaps and frequent changes of topic? Are associative powers impaired, with tangential thinking? Any strange words? Is the talk woolly, odd, evasive, vague, difficult to follow, inappropriate? Does thought appear occasionally to be blocked?

M.S.E. 'Cognitive State: Intelligence':
Test for concretism and powers of abstract thinking by asking the patient to explain the meaning of proverbs. In concrete thinking the meaning of 'people in glass houses shouldn't throw stones' might be 'If people throw stones about in glass houses they will break the glass'. Make a rough assessment of intelligence.

P.H. 'Personal History':
Progressive difficulty in thinking may result in a deteriorating school and academic record, |

In general terms schizophrenic thought disorder may manifest itself as nothing more than a subjective feeling on the part of the examiner that something odd or indefinable is going on.

and later on in an inability to keep jobs which become steadily more menial and undemanding. This is the phenomenon of *downward drift*, common in schizophrenia. Note the start of the decline and its speed. Hobbies and interests may reveal mystical-type preoccupations.

Symptoms/Signs cont	Description	Diagnosis from M.S.E etc.
Emotional Disturbances	In 'good prognosis' schizophrenia there is often a marked affective component in which the patient is depressed, elated, irritable or shows lability of mood. In 'poor prognosis' disease the predominant feature is often a progressive *loss* of emotion, a shallowness of affect, a 'couldn't care less' attitude, which may seem callous and cruel. Occasionally there is *incongruity of emotions*, an inappropriate response in which the patient appears cheered by sad events, and may cry at happy ones. The observer may sense a lack of rapport, an inability to sympathise or empathise with the patient, a failure to 'get through' often described as the feeling that some invisible barrier exists between examiner and examinee. This *blunting of affect* may proceed until the patient is totally oblivious to the needs and desires of others, becoming increasingly withdrawn and isolated, preoccupied with himself. On the way towards this state he may feel that the external world has become in some way unreal (*Derealisation*) or that his own body seems strange, odd (*Depersonalisation*). Often it is difficult to differentiate between a schizophrenic psychosis and a manic or depressive one. It is important to discover whether or not emotional disturbance *preceded* the loss of contact with reality. If it did, then this would tend to shift the diagnosis towards that of affective psychosis as would the fact that the delusions themselves had a marked depressive or grandiose flavour.	*M.S.E. 'Appearance and Behaviour':* Does the patient look sad, excited, irritable? Do his behaviour and gestures show indifference to others? Is he pleasant and cooperative, or distant, withdrawn, unhelpful, unfriendly? Is he relaxed or tense and restless? *M.S.E. 'Mood':* Is the mood constant, appropriate, congruous with the content of the talk and with the situation? Is there evidence of flatness or blunting, or of shallowness and superficiality, a silly fatuousness of affect? *M.S.E. 'Thought':* 'Do you ever have the feeling that your body is in some way strange or odd, or that the everyday things around you seem weird and unreal?'

| Catatonic Motor Behaviour (Excitement or Stupor) | In acute catatonia the patient may adopt strange physical attitudes, which are often accompanied by feelings of extreme fear. Periods of prolonged immobility (stupor) may alternate with sudden periods of excited overactivity, often of a violent kind. These strange posturings tend to have peculiar significance and symbolic meaning for the patient, who is often acting under the influence of hallucinatory voices. In chronic states and in catatonic excitement there may be curious repetitive stereotyped movements, tic-like mannerisms and facial grimacing.

The phenomenon of *waxy flexibility* may be shown in which the patient maintains a bizarre posture for long periods, taking up a new one when the examiner moves his limbs to a different position. His body shows a characteristic 'waxy resistance' to the re-positioning.

There may be *automatic obedience* in which the patient follows all instructions slavishly, or *negativism*, an apparently perverse determination to be generally contrary. *Echolalia* (the remorseless repetition of recently uttered syllables or words) and *Echopraxia* (the copying of actions) are sometimes seen as variations on the theme of automatic obedience. *Perseveration* refers to the pointless repetition of a movement which has been previously requested. | *M.S.E. 'Appearance and Behaviour':*

Do attitudes have purpose and meaning? Are gestures, expressions, and other motor activity normal and appropriate? Is posture normal?

If inactive does he resist when his limbs are moved? Does he seem aware of what is going on around him? How does he respond when asked to do things, to react to situations? Does he appear to be reacting to hallucinations? Test for automatic obedience, negativism, echopraxia etc.

Are the eyes of the stuporose patient open? Do they follow movement? What is his response to different stimuli? Is his position comfortable or awkward and constrained?

P.E.

All stuporose patients should have a thorough physical examination with special interest paid to the Central Nervous System. |

Symptoms/Signs cont	Description	Diagnosis from M.S.E etc.
Disturbances of Will and Motivation	Often central to the schizophrenic predicament is a gradual loss of the power of the will, a sort of global indecision, lack of thrust, drive and ambition which manifests itself in an increasingly apathetic lethargy and eventually withdrawal, introversion and immobility. Purpose is lost and decision-making becomes increasingly difficult as the patient becomes less active and energy declines. Spontaneity, enthusiasm and competence diminish, and this, coupled with emotional disturbance and difficulty in thinking, reduce effectiveness drastically, leading to a downward drift through the echelons of the socio-economic hierarchy.	*M.S.E. 'Appearance and Behaviour'*: Is the patient withdrawn, lethargic, apathetic, uninterested, indifferent? *P.H. 'Personal History'*: Does the school and job history show gradual deterioration and the life-style show increasing withdrawal and isolation?
Other hallucinations (Apart from 1st Rank Symptoms)	Auditory hallucinations are by far the most common in schizophrenia. Visual hallucinations are relatively rare, but can be especially frightening. They are usually experienced more as disturbances of visual perception rather than as well-organised complex 'visions'. Tactile hallucinations occur quite frequently, the patient often complaining of tingling or shooting sensations. He may describe the feeling of insects crawling on the skin or of animals inside his body – like Marshal Blücher who told the Duke of Wellington that he could feel an elephant in his tummy. Once a false belief has been constructed to 'explain' an hallucination it is a delusion. Hallucinations involving the senses of smell and taste occur occasionally. Derealisation and Deper-	*M.S.E. 'Thought'*: 'Have you ever had strange visual experiences?' 'Have you ever had peculiar feelings in your body?' 'Have you ever experienced odd tastes or smells?' 'Have you ever heard voices, or odd noises, when there was nobody around?'

sonalisation are disorders of perception and therefore hallucinations, but they often accompany a depressed mood, or indicate the beginnings of schizophrenic blunting of emotion.

		M.S.E. 'Thought':

Other Bizarre Delusions
(Apart from delusional perceptions)

Unlike autochonous primary delusions secondary delusions are false beliefs which have their origin in attempts to 'make sense' of bewildering experiences such as passivity feelings, hallucinations and delusional perceptions. For example a passivity feeling with regard to thought with the sensation that thoughts no longer belong to the examinee might lead to the delusion that his brain has died. Delusions are often persecutory with the belief that the patient is being influenced, followed, harassed by such shadowy organisations as the K.G.B., the Mafia, the C.I.D., the Fascists, the Communists etc. Or they may be primarily hypochondriacal with bizarre delusions of bodily disease such as the feeling that one's bowels are blocked with cement. Erotic delusions may result from tactile hallucinations, the patient believing that his genitals are being manipulated. Sometimes the delusions are grandiose, the patient feeling he is a special person with exceptional powers, God, perhaps, or Royalty. Occasionally they are depressed with delusions of wickedness or sin. If the content of a delusion is strongly grandiose or depressive and nihilistic (with feelings that parts of the body have died) then suspicion should be raised that the psychosis is emotional rather than schizophrenic. This is one of the most

M.S.E. 'Thought':

'Do you think that people treat you as they should?'

'Does anybody or any group of people pay special attention to you?'

'Do you feel that anybody is actively trying to harm you?'

'Do you think that you are in any way a very special person – especially good or particularly bad for instance?'

'Do you feel that you have done wrong, or have been punished in any way?'

'How is your physical health?'

'Do you ever have the feeling that the radio or the TV refers to you or what's happening to you?'

'Do you believe that strange forces from outside are controlling you or influencing you in any way?'

(cont.)

Symptoms/Signs cont	Description	Diagnosis from M.S.E. etc.
	difficult and important distinctions to make in psychiatry because the treatment and prognosis of the two conditions is different.	
	Common in schizophrenia are delusions known as *ideas of reference.* The patient comes to believe that events mentioned on the TV or radio, or songs on the record player in some way refer to him personally, have some special meaning for him. A football match for instance is being played for him, the words of a song have been written specifically with him in mind.	
	The content of delusions is often religious, mystical, political or scientific and will reflect the patient's emotional, intellectual and personality traits – be in a way his own artistic creation. They also reflect the spirit of the times – radio waves, X-rays and atomic energy tending to have taken over from God and the Devil as instruments of control. Sometimes clear-cut delusions are absent, but there may be over-valued ideas, vague hints of telepathic powers, of the possession of finely tuned intuitions, which border on the delusional.	
Behavioural Changes	Eccentric behavioural changes can be a consequence of all the above symptoms. The family will notice this first. There may be increasing 'oddness' with disorganisation of behaviour, withdrawal and a characteristic falling-off of activity and competence. Personality change may be sudden or gradual, the formerly	*P.H. 'Personal History':* Look for downward drift. *M.S.E. 'Appearance and Behaviour':* Is there evidence of a falling-off of self-care, lack of cleanliness, poor grooming etc.

Ask the informant about any changes in personality or behaviour.

prudish girl becomes promiscuous, the abstemious man abuses alcohol, the neat person becomes untidy. It is the unusual nature of the behaviour *vis à vis* previous behaviour which is significant.

| Insight | In schizophrenia most patients show no insight at all concerning the unusual nature of their predicament, seeing no reason to explain what is often extraordinary behaviour. Schizophrenia is, therefore, a condition we recognise in others rather than in ourselves. | *M.S.E. 'Insight':*
'Do you think that you are ill in any way – that you need help?' |

Disorders of Mood and Emotion (Affective Illness)

All of us are at some time or another depressed, most of us occasionally elated. Our depressions may be very deep indeed. Bereaved, assailed by financial difficulties, thrown out of a job, retired from work, unable to cope with the children, lonely and alone, in poor physical health, or abandoned by loved ones, we may experience the depths of despair and misery. And yet we bounce back, life goes on, we recover our equilibrium. Was our misery an illness? Certainly it was understandable, not in any way odd or peculiar, a quite reasonable response to appalling circumstances. It was to some extent self-limiting, too, as we came gradually to terms with our changed predicament, learned to adapt to new circumstances or worked to change them. From both our ups and our downs we tend to return to our normal mood. Or do we?

Sometimes our natural depressions seem to get out of control, at others a black mood seems to descend upon us like a cloud appearing suddenly in a clear blue sky. In the one case our reaction to the cause of our sadness seems out of all proportion, a gross exaggeration. In the other, both we and our friends may not be able to point to any cause at all for our mood of despair, which seems to spring from within rather than represent any reaction to external environmental conditions. In either case the mood darkens inexorably, slipping and sliding, in a way apparently beyond our control, into a deep abyss. All our efforts and those of our friends to remove us from it seem doomed to

fail. To the informed eye our thoughts, behaviour, emotions and appearance may indicate that a whole new situation has arisen, the symptoms pointing unequivocally to the fact that we are in the grip of an emotional illness.

The professional might be able to see at once that the range of normal mood variations has been exceeded, that our mood is no longer an understandable, even appropriate, response to stress; that we are reacting too deeply, for too long; that we are in danger as surely as if we had pneumonia, and that we need medical help. Further, we are in pain, the acute psychological misery with which even the most intense physical discomfort cannot be compared. We suffer it and are disabled by it. We are mentally ill, and our illness is potentially life threatening. Failure to recognise such a condition could easily be fatal, whilst its diagnosis can result in effective treatment. But how do we recognise it? We are not told how to do it, and yet approximately 2.5 per cent of men and 4 per cent of women can expect to suffer from a manic-depressive reaction in the course of a 75-year life.

Obviously, then, it is important to know how to differentiate between emotional illness and normal depression or exaltation of mood. In this section we will look at the ways in which psychiatrists go about making the distinction. If we are ill we must know it so that we can seek treatment, and we should know how to recognise the condition in others so that we can advise them to do the same. If we are not ill, and others are not ill, then we should know that too. For so many of us, though, we are frankly failing to make the best of our lives, fail to enjoy them, fail to give enjoyment to others. Feeling guilty about our failure we take no steps to succeed and our guilt is compounded. Illness offers us an excuse at the cost of self-respect and of future success. It is vital that this unsatisfactory avenue of escape be denied us. In the absence of illness we must feel free through our own efforts to improve our lot, to try harder and to do better; to give success a chance.

There is no broad agreement in psychiatry about just how the emotional illnesses are best classified, but several different approaches have been used. The most widely accepted distinction is the *Uni-polar/Bi-polar one*, which has much support from genetic studies.

Bi-polar affective disorders usually consist of periods of prolonged excited, manic mood alternating with periods of depression, the mood returning to a possibly rather precarious normality in between the mood swings. Less often, manic moods alone are seen in the Bi-polar disorders. In the Uni-polar disorders, phases of depression appear in the absence of any episodes of manic excitement.

Evidence suggests that, as in the case of schizophrenia, the dispositional tendency to suffer these illnesses is passed on in the genes, and that environmental factors then work on the inherited vulnerability to produce the illness. Some individuals, with a heavy genetic loading, are almost certain to be affected, come what may, whilst others with a minimal inherited pre-disposition may require considerable environmental stress to precipitate the signs and symptoms of disease.

Situations in which depression descends with unremitting ferocity and severity in the absence of any apparent cause, in which there are marked physiological symptoms and in which there is such gross disturbance of mood that contact with reality is severely diminished or lost altogether, might be thought to represent those instances in which serious defects in brain biochemical functioning have been inherited. On the other hand, those depressions which appear to result from a reaction, albeit possibly an over-reaction, to an 'understandable' precipitating factor, in which biological disturbance is not marked and in which contact with reality is not lost, could be considered to be examples of situations in which a relatively mild hereditary weakness has been amplified by environmental stress to an extent that manifestation of illness has resulted.

Symptoms and signs of the usually more severe, often psychotic, apparently 'un-caused' *endogenous depression*, in which the depressed mood seems to spring from within, include early morning waking, diurnal mood variation with the mood worse in the morning, a qualitative difference in which the depressed mood is quite different from mere 'sadness', psychomotor retardation, a relatively short time-span, a tendency to affect older people, significant weight loss, a history of previous attacks and a family history of depression. In contrast is the less severe, 'neurotic' as opposed to psychotic, *reactive* depression, which represents an understandable reaction to a precipitating cause. In such depressions the mood is more akin to normal sadness and the depth of the depression is usually not so great that the sufferer cannot, at least momentarily, be distracted from it possibly by removal from the situation which seemed to cause it. The sleep difficulty in reactive depression tends to be in getting off to sleep and, if there is mood variation during the day, the mood tends to worsen in the evening as tiredness increases. Biological features such as anorexia and weight loss tend to be less marked and are often absent. It may be significant that there is an association between the tendency to suffer depressions of the reactive type and various character traits and personality types. Thus obsessionality, 'inadequacy', histrionic tendencies, and hypochondriasis seem to correlate with the propensity to suffer reactive depressions.

It has been suggested that endogenous and reactive depressions are qualitatively different. One strong argument for the truth of this is the fact that the usually more severe endogenous depression responds better than the less profound, reactive depressions to both anti-depressant medication and E.C.T.; another is the genetic evidence referred to above. If that is the case we need, perhaps, look no further in our search for the borderlines of illness – endogenous depressions representing the illness category, reactive ones being merely the response of a self-pitying and histrionic 'weak' personality to stress.

There are problems, however, in taking this attitude. Firstly the distinction between endogenous and reactive mood change is often not as clear as opposing lists of characteristic symptoms might superficially indicate. Not

'uncaused', and sometimes reactive depressions show severe biological disturbances. In short there is often considerable overlap in the symptoms displayed by each of the two supposedly different groups, whilst many psychiatrists have seen what was initially a clearly reactive depression merge imperceptibly into one with florid endogenous type features such as delusions of worthlessness, severe psychomotor retardation and marked diurnal mood variation. This has led some to suggest that the endogenous-reactive distinction is to be thought of as a continuum, the one picture shading into the other, no fundamental qualitative difference separating the two poles.

Secondly, whether or not reactive depression represents a genuine illness, it is indubitably true that it often represents a significant threat to life. Because activity and volition are to a large extent preserved in such conditions in contrast to the endogenous situation in which the patient is often severely slowed down in both his behaviour and thinking, the sufferer may be able to summon up the energy, initiative and will power for an often violent attempt on his own life.

That having been said, and reactive depressions having been included within the illness category, it is true to say that in the majority of cases they represent the milder instances of depressive illness, differing only in degree from normal depressed moods and being to some extent due to behaviour and attitudes of the patient for which he is ultimately responsible. This is no reason for withholding medical treatment but after remission of symptoms the wrong attitudes which have to some extent caused them will have to be confronted by the individual if he is to escape the treadmill of psychiatric recidivism.

illness or is he merely a bit depressed. It is one of the questions that he asks and answers frequently and it is important that he gets it right, bearing in mind the considerable danger of suicide in clinical depression.

So now we will see how the psychiatrist sets about answering the question 'Does this patient suffer from a depressive

DEPRESSIVE ILLNESS

Before he begins to elicit and analyse the symptoms and signs the psychiatrist will consider the general background

General Background	Description	Diagnosis from M.S.E etc.
	In both Uni-polar and Bi-polar affective illness there is often a family history of emotional illness. Often a particular drug used successfully to treat a family member will work well with the patient. The presence of such a family history might help to confirm the diagnosis. Obviously, too, it is vitally important to know if the patient has suffered a depressive illness before, and how it responded to the particular treatment. Physical illness frequently causes depression. Viral infections, particularly influenza, are often the culprits. Chronic painful illness of any sort can be a *(cont.)*	*P.H. 'Family History':* Ask for full details of family psychiatric history, including diagnosis, treatment, response to treatment, length of illness etc. *P.H. 'Personal History':* As above for personal psychiatric history. Ask about all details of past medical history and present physical health, including details of childbirth. *P.E.* A thorough physical exam is performed to exclude physical illness.

General Background cont	Description	Diagnosis from M.S.E. etc.
	cause. The following conditions seem especially likely to cause depression:	*P.I.* Basic pathological investigations in suspected depressive illness would include:
	Parkinson's Disease	Full blood count (Anaemias, infections, chronic disease)
	Myasthenia Gravis	Urea and Electrolytes. Liver Function Tests
	Multiple Sclerosis (Often mildly euphoric instead)	Skull X-Ray (Tumours)
	Systemic Lupus Erythematosis	Chest X-Ray (Bronchial Carcinoma, T.B.,
	Post Syphilitic General Paresis of the Insane	Heart disease)
	Epilepsy	Thyroid Function Tests (Hypothyroidism)
	Hypothyroidism (Myxoedema)	VDRL/TPHA (Syphilis)
	Hyperparathyroidism	
	Cushing's Syndrome	
	Addison's Disease	
	Head injuries	
	Brain tumours	
	Strokes	
	Athero-sclerotic and other dementias	
	Anaemias. Iron, B12 and folate deficiencies	
	Chronic Disease e.g. Heart disease, Cancer	
	Chronic infections e.g. T.B.	
	Depressions are relatively more common after child-birth and in the menopause.	*P.H. 'Use of Drugs or Medicines':* Ask about medicines prescribed and about use of alcohol and other drugs.
	Several drugs can cause depression, including the following:	*P.H. 'Present Life Situation':* Ask about stressful life events.
	Reserpine	'What's been happening in your life re-cently?'
	Alpha Methyldopa (e.g. Aldomet)	
	L-Dopa	Try to discover what the patient is worried
	Steroids	

Barbiturates
Amphetamines (e.g. Durophet)
Benzodiazepines (e.g. Valium, Librium)
Alcohol

Many people attempt to curb the anxiety which so often co-exists with depression and to lift their sad mood by abusing alcohol. 15 per cent of suicides are alcoholics whilst 50 per cent of males making suicidal type gestures do so to some extent under the influence of alcohol. Abuse of other drugs is common in depression.

There is a correlation between the amount of stressful life events and the development of depressive illness. Loss of a loved one, or a bereavement are particularly significant but any drastic change in circumstances, even potentially happy ones such as marriage or a new job are stressful and it seems to be the stress which triggers off biochemical change which may manifest itself as depression or mania, characteristically a week or two later.

about, what he sees as the cause of his depression. Then get the chronology right. It may be that the depressed mood preceded the loss of a job or a loved one and possibly was a causative element in that loss rather than a result of it.

Symptoms/Signs	Description	Diagnosis from M.S.E etc.
Change of Mood	It is vital to establish that there has been a significant mood *change*. In Uni-polar and Bi-polar conditions the swings of mood run self-limiting courses in time even when untreated. Severe chronic depression is relatively rare although devastating and hard to treat when it occurs. Some people appear semi-permanently sad and unhappy, pessimistic and dreary, strong indications that they are living their lives unwisely rather than evidence of illness of the affective type.	*M.S.E. 'Mood':* 'How were you feeling before your mood changed?' 'What sort of person would you say you were usually?' 'Do you feel you are not your old self at all?'
Depressed Mood	The commonest symptom is an all-pervading sadness, a despondency that is persistent throughout the day and from one day to the other, and from which there is no *significant relief*. The mood comes to dominate all thought, action, perception and motivation, to colour and influence all experience. In severe endogenous illness it may transcend mere sadness and consist of a feeling of flat emptiness, of 'deadness', of almost physical illness which is impossible to bear. In the less severe reactive depression the difference in feeling from the normal depressed mood is quantitative rather than qualitative, and it may be possible briefly to distract the sufferer from it, although he will return immediately to his preoccupied, brooding ruminations as he picks away in his mind at the cause of his condition like a hungry dog at a bone. As the illness progresses in severity the gloom is unremitting, remorseless until the patient is blunted, drained of emotion, incapable of expressing	*M.S.E. 'Appearance and Behaviour':* Does he look gloomy, sad, tired, worn down with the cares of the world, his posture slumped, signalling defeat. Does he look listless, lifeless, perhaps shedding quiet tears? Has he neglected his personal appearance? *M.S.E. 'Mood':* 'How are your spirits?' 'How do you feel in yourself?' 'How would you describe your mood at the moment?' Is the mood constant? Can he be made to smile or cheered up in any way? Ask 'If 0 represents the depths of despair and 10 the heights of happiness what number would you put on your feelings?'

feeling, of having a good cry, which in the early stages of the condition he had cried frequently.

If asked to rate his mood numerically on a 0–10 scale with 0 the abyss and 10 the heights of ecstasy he may describe his mood as 'Zero, or less.'

In contrast the normal depressed mood tends occasionally to relent, is not so persistent, is recognisable as having been experienced before. It allows brief periods of distraction tending to descend again when we are bored, under-employed, under-active, concentrating too much on ourselves and our thoughts. We may even recognise that we are to some extent indulging ourselves, wallowing in our misery, acting the role of the depressed person and that we could at a pinch snap out of it.

Sleep Disturbance, and Early Morning Waking	Sleep disturbance is a characteristic symptom of depressive illness. Classically, early morning waking is a pointer to the endogenous type of illness. The patient wakes unusually early in the morning, perhaps at 4 a.m. and cannot get back to sleep again. He lies there, staring at the ceiling, brooding and ruminating on his sorry state. Or the problem might be constant waking during the night (middle insomnia). Difficulty getting off to sleep (initial insomnia) tends to be a problem in the reactive depressions. Rarely excessive sleeping may be a symptom of depressive illness. However, in the large majority of cases normal or marginally excessive sleeping is an important indicator that the individual is not suffering from clinical depression, is not ill at all. If somebody tells you he is depressed and yet is sleeping well then there is seldom cause to worry.

M.S.E. 'Mood':
'How are you sleeping at the moment?'
    Get all details.

Symptoms/Signs cont	Description	Diagnosis from M.S.E etc.
Diurnal Mood Variation	In severe depressive illness the mood is often worse at a specific time of day. In the endogenous depressions this tends to be in the morning on wakening. Reactive depressions may show no such variations, and if they do the mood is usually worse at night. It is rare for normal depressed moods to show diurnal variation, although such depressions are often exacerbated by tiredness.	M.S.E. 'Mood': 'Is your mood worse at any time of the day?'
Anorexia and Weight Loss	Over 90 per cent of those suffering from genuine depressive illness will lose their appetite. 80 per cent will have lost 3lbs or more since the onset of the depressed mood, and in the absence of dieting. Often weight loss is severe. Very rarely there may be weight gain, but far more frequently increased food intake, appetite, and weight gain are a powerful indicator that the individual is not ill, although he may well be unhappy.	M.S.E. 'Mood': 'How is your appetite?' 'Have you lost any weight recently?' Find out how much and over what period.
Constipation	Approximately one quarter of those suffering from depressive illness are constipated. Obviously this symptom is of limited diagnostic value on its own, but taken with others it may be significant especially if severe.	M.S.E. 'Mood': Ask about change of bowel habit.
Amenorrhoea	Periods may stop in depressive illness.	M.S.E. 'Mood': Ask about periods.

Loss of Sexual Interest	Approximately half of those suffering from depressive illness complain of decreased sexual interest. This is more common in the endogenous than the reactive type. In the normal depressed mood this is not usually the case – in fact sexual longings and fantasies may be increased.	*M.S.E. 'Mood':* Ask about sexual interest and sexual activity. 'Have you noticed any change in your sexual desires?'
Loss of Energy and Increased Tiredness	A particularly common symptom in depressive illness is to feel drained of energy, constantly tired. Such feelings are common, too, in normal depressed moods. The difference in the two cases is one of degree. It is necessary to find out the extent to which normal activities are interfered with.	*M.S.E. 'Mood':* 'Do you find you are able to get things done in the way that you used to?' Find out the extent of the disability. Just mildly tired? Or having to lie in bed all day?
Thoughts of Hopelessness about the Future	The depressed mood in illness colours all thoughts with a grey pessimism. The future looks gloomy and there seems to be no light at the end of the tunnel. When asked about the future the ill patient may say 'I have no future. It's hopeless.' In contrast, in normal depressed moods, we retain an idea of what the future might hold for us 'if things changed', and we remain aware of the fact that life will go on. Intellectually, if not emotionally, we know that we will not always feel like this. In true depressive illness, however, the patient may feel, literally, that there is no possible escape from his predicament.	*M.S.E. 'Mood':* 'How does the future look to you?'

Symptoms/Signs cont	Description	Diagnosis from M.S.E etc.
Thoughts of Suicide, Death and Other Morbid Pre-occupations	Such feelings of hopelessness, springing from a profoundly depressed mood and often accompanied by those of apprehensiveness and foreboding, may lead to thoughts of suicide, or self-harm together with morbid thoughts of death and destruction. The patient may feel he would be 'better off dead' and sometimes, so gloomy is his view of life and the world that his wife and family would be better off dead too. Suicide is a grave risk in depressive illness and 15 per cent of those suffering from severe depression in which contact with reality has been lost will succeed in killing themselves. However, although thoughts of suicide are extremely common in depressive illness and the discovery of such ideas should make one extremely suspicious that psychopathology does exist, their existence alone is not of necessity indicative of mental illness. It has been reported for instance that during the course of a single year in the 1970s 9 per cent of a general population sample in the United States reported feeling suicidal at one time or another. Obviously it is important to be able to make some assessment of the likelihood of suicide and psychiatrists do it all the time. Actual, as opposed to attempted, suicide is more common in men, whilst suicidal gestures, involving deliberate self-harm and with varying degrees of genuine suicidal motivation, tend to be performed by women. Self-poisoning, often with aspirin or anti-depressant medication, is	*M.S.E. 'Mood':* 'Have you had any morbid thoughts recently?' 'Have you ever felt that life wasn't worth living?' 'Have you ever felt like putting an end to it all?' If suicidal thoughts are mentioned, then ask about method and any steps that have been taken towards acting on intentions. Evasive answers at this stage are particularly significant. Assess the strength of suicidal intention. 'Do you really want to die, or do you just feel that things can't go on as they are?' 'Have you ever tried to kill yourself in the past?' Assess the seriousness of the attempt, including violence of method, likelihood of success in terms of being found before tablets have had time to work, making of wills, giving away of possessions, degree of premeditation. Was he pleased or sorry that he didn't succeed? Assess the depth of the depression. Prominent biological symptoms and the presence of depressive delusions are sinister. *M.S.E. 'Appearance and Behaviour':* Look for anger, agitation, tenseness and restlessness. These are worrying. In contrast the

the commonest method. Spring and early summer is the most usual time, and peak incidence is in the 70s for men and the 60s for women. The following factors seem to be related in some way to suicide:

Single status
Living alone
Large, socially disorganised urban areas
Rootlessness
Childlessness
Some significant loss e.g. money, job, loved one
Abuse of alcohol and other drugs
Chronic, painful physical illness
Unemployment
Family history of emotional illness and/or suicide
Previous suicide attempt

The presence of several of the above factors should put one on guard.

Symptoms of depressive illness which indicate increased risk are prominent agitation, anxiety and tension, severe sleep disturbance, strong feelings of guilt, anger and inadequacy, and the presence of psychosis with delusions of worthlessness or of physical illness. The co-existence of schizophrenic symptoms with those of depression often results in particularly violent suicides.

Nearly all suicides communicate their thoughts and intentions to others at some time. In the absence of clearly manipulative mechanisms, and against a background of depressed mood such remarks should always be taken seriously. If the individual has selected *(cont.)*

and actions are sluggish and retarded probably won't be able to summon up the energy and initiative required for a successful suicide attempt.

P.H. 'Family History':
Any family history of suicide or emotional illness?

P.H. 'Personal History':
Any previous history of suicide attempts or emotional or other psychiatric illness?

P.H. 'Use of Drugs or Medicines':
Any abuse of alcohol or other drugs?

P.H. 'Present Life Situation':
Assess present social situation in light of factors related to suicide.

Symptoms/Signs cont	Description	Diagnosis from M.S.E etc.
	in advance and considered a specific method, and furthermore has taken steps to put that particular method into practice e.g. has obtained the pills, reconnoitred the roof of the tall building, bought the sharp knife, then the risk of suicide is correspondingly greater.	
	If there has been a previous 'suicide attempt' its circumstances must be carefully analysed. A valium overdose in a busy household has different implications to a gunshot wound to the head which does the individual considerable damage. In considering whether or not a patient can safely be sent home after a gesture involving some minor degree of self-harm, such factors as the presence or absence of support at home, availability of suicidal tools such as dangerous medicines, and the stated intentions of the patient will all be taken into account. A spontaneous promise from the patient that he will not try to harm himself is of considerable value.	
Feelings of Physical Illness	It is extremely common for depressed people to feel ill and those people who are ashamed of their depressed mood, or who refuse perhaps even to themselves to acknowledge it, may go to their doctors with complaints of physical illness. Depressive illness is often intensely anxiety-provoking and it is seldom that anxiety and depression do not co-exist to some extent. Physical symptoms complained of tend there-	*M.S.E. 'Mood':* 'Have you been worried about your health recently?' *P.E.* A thorough physical examination should be given to exclude illness. It will tend to reassure the doctor more than the patient.

frequently affected by over-stimulation of the autonomic nervous system e.g. nausea, vomiting, disturbance of bowel habit giving rise to worries about bowel cancer; palpitations causing fears about heart disease; headaches precipitating worries about brain tumours; tightness in the throat raising the spectre of 'growths', etc. Such patients often deny that they are primarily depressed, preferring to believe that theirs is a physical illness to which they are reacting with natural worry and apprehension exacerbated, perhaps, by the failure of the medical profession to recognise the extent and seriousness of their physical disability.

Repeated investigations and examinations may do little to reassure such people, and indeed this resistance to informed reassurance coupled with an often unshakeable determination to remain pessimistic about prognosis, far from usual even in those with genuine and severe physical illness, is a strong hint that underlying depressive processes are at work. Such determination to believe oneself ill in the face of all logical evidence to the contrary falls short of the delusional, but helps to differentiate between those of us who merely worry a bit too much about our health and those who do so because their all-pervading pessimism has reached 'illness' proportions. Thus severe and unreasonable hypochondriasis in conjunction with other, especially biological, symptoms of depression is a useful diagnostic indicator to affective illness.

Pathological and other investigations are performed both as a routine 'screen' and for the above purpose.

Symptoms/Signs cont	Description	Diagnosis from M.S.E. etc.
Delusions of Physical Illness and Associated Hallucinations	The preoccupations described above may merge by degree into unshakeable convictions, the certain 'knowledge' that illness exists and illness often of a bizarre and unusual nature. Such beliefs may be accompanied by, or are sometimes attempts to explain, the weird tactile hallucinations described above. The patient may come to believe that his brain is frozen, his insides are rotting, or that they are twisted into knots. He may come to believe that he has actually died. What's more he may believe that such terrible afflictions are well deserved, an apt punishment for his unsatisfactory thoughts and behaviour. These psychotic symptoms are an infallible pointer to illness and their depressive content and the background of worsening depressed mood from which they spring help to differentiate them from schizophrenic symptomatology. Strong feelings of strangeness in one's body (Depersonalisation) often herald the onset of such ideas.	*M.S.E. 'Mood':* 'Do you ever feel that you may be severely ill?'
Feelings of Guilt, Self-Reproach, of Being a Bad Person	Such feelings are of course extremely common in everyday life. Often we have good reasons for feeling guilty and self-reproachful, a bad person, because all too often that is just what we are. However, such feelings when they occur in the presence of hard evidence of depressive illness may well be pathological. In this case the guilt and self-blame serve no useful purpose except as an indicator of illness. Typically they are	*M.S.E. 'Mood':* 'Do you ever think of yourself as being a particularly bad person?' 'Do you feel excessively guilty?' 'Have you ever felt that you are wicked or evil?' 'Do you feel sometimes that you are completely worthless?'

shortcomings, increasingly introverted, mulling over his inadequacies to the exclusion of all productive thought. There is an odd irrationality, too, in the quantity of guilt produced, an incongruous inappropriateness of response to what might be quite innocuous behaviour. Changing behaviour to that which might tend to diminish guilt feelings is irrelevant, both because of the lack of energy, inability to concentrate and take decisions which characterise depressive illness and because 'better' behaviour, once instituted, has no effect on the feelings of guilt. In these situations guilt and felt worthlessness have taken on an identity of their own as overvalued ideas rather than as useful spurs to more worthwhile behaviour.

Feelings of Social Incapacity Leading to Withdrawal	Feeling intensely and irrationally unlovable, and in fact hardly the life and soul of the party, the sufferer feels increasingly socially inadequate and as a result withdraws from people.	*M.S.E. 'Mood':* 'How do you get on with people?'

Symptoms/Signs cont	Description	Diagnosis from M.S.E etc.
Delusions of Guilt, of Being a Wicked and Evil Person, and Associated Hallucinations	Imperceptibly the feelings discussed above may metamorphose into full-blown delusions, into psychosis. Or the psychosis may descend suddenly with little warning. The patient comes to 'know' that he is thoroughly evil and may feel that he contaminates others with his wickedness. He feels he should be punished and is worthy of the most terrible fate. Sometimes he hears voices which accuse him and threaten him. In the grip of these delusions he	*M.S.E. 'Mood'*: 'Do you think of yourself as being evil or wicked?' 'Do you feel excessively guilty?' 'Have you ever felt you are being punished for something?'
Delusions of Persecution and Punishment	may come to believe he is actually being punished, possibly by actual physical illness. Or he may believe he has committed unspeakable crimes and attempt to turn himself in to the bewildered police. Alternatively he may believe that others, knowing of his badness, are persecuting him and he may develop ideas of reference in which people, the TV and the radio refer to him and his miserable nature.	*M.S.E. 'Thought'*: 'Do you ever have the feeling that people are ganging up on you?'
Delusions of Poverty	Such is his despair he may believe that he has lost all his money, can hardly afford to eat. Such psychotic delusions are the cause of intense psychological pain and not surprisingly suicide becomes a significant risk.	
Apathy Inactivity	In some instances of depressive illness, inactivity and apathy, the loss of all feeling, are particularly marked leading in severe cases to impaired thinking and loss of mobility, a state known as *psychomotor retardation*. This may leave the patient totally immobile or	*M.S.E. 'Appearance and Behaviour'*: Does he react at all, seem aware of his surroundings? Does he co-operate or seem to have difficulty in obeying instructions, appearing bemused, perplexed, bewildered, unable

Loss of Energy and Increased Tiredness

...in and taste for life, indecision, and difficulty in concentrating. The difference between these normal phenomena and the experience of them in depressive illness is largely one of degree. In depressive illness loss of energy may mean that all movement is an effort – lifting things up or walking across the room may seem almost impossible and the patient may actually take to his bed or sit all day in a chair, perhaps in a darkened room, crying gently. The tiredness is mental as well as physical and there may be the subjective sensation that the thought processes have slowed down, become so sluggish that thinking about anything is difficult.

Slowed Thought Processes

Loss of Concentration

Concentration in these circumstances becomes increasingly impaired, both because thinking is a problem and interest in the external world is reduced. The patient can no longer concentrate on the TV and radio, finding it difficult to follow the drift of conversations and the plots of soap operas. Reading, too, is an effort, no longer a pleasure, and a page is read over and over again because its meaning is not retained. Books and even magazines are eventually discarded.

Loss of Decision-Making Ability

Decision-making may seem impossible, calling for non-existent energy and motivation. The depressed patient may not even be able to pick up the telephone to call for help from friends from whom he has tended to withdraw anyway. As he sinks deeper into the slough of despond he has no energy, and little interest in feeding himself.

Such debilities are usually slowly progressive in depressive illness and are unremitting, not varying

(cont.)

diminished activity and movement, the patient slumped morosely in the chair, gloomy and despondent, resigned to his fate?

M.S.E. 'Form of Talk':
Is the talk slow, flat, expressionless, lacking in spontaneity, sparse and colourless, giving the impression that all conversation is an effort? Is the patient mute?

M.S.E. 'Mood':
'Do you find you have plenty of energy at the moment?'
'How do you spend your day?'
'Do you find that your thoughts come to you in the normal way?'
'Do you have the feeling that your thoughts are slowed down in any way?'
'Can you concentrate on the TV, on the radio, on a book?'
'Can you read a book or an article through from start to finish?'
'Do you have a problem taking things in?'

Symptoms/Signs cont	Description	Diagnosis from M.S.E etc.
	significantly from day to day. Environmental factors, friends, stimulation, and so on, seem to make no difference to the severely depressed patient, who seems to have lost all capacity for enjoyment of once pleasurable activities. It is the change from previous attitudes and behaviour, and the unremitting and irresponsive nature of that change allied to the qualitative severity of its symptoms which allow one to differentiate between illness and normal depression of mood.	*M.S.E. 'Cognitive State: Concentration':* Is attention easily aroused, sustained? Is patient easily distractible? Perform the 'Serial 7s' test. The patient is asked to subtract 7 from 100 and to keep on doing so until nothing is left. This is a test of concentration, not of intelligence or arithmetical ability. You and I are expected to do this in two minutes or under and to make no more than two mistakes!
Loss of Interest in Life and Inability to Enjoy Previously Pleasurable Activities	If we can be lifted out of our mood, become our normal relatively cheerful selves, for an hour or two, it is extremely unlikely that we are ill. So, too, if we are usually of a permanently pessimistic inactive, indecisive disposition and there has been no significant change in our outlook, then our predicament is unlikely to be due to depressive illness.	*P.H. 'Assessment of Pre-morbid Personality':* Is this reduction in energy, apathy, etc. a new phenomenon representing a marked change? Try to get corroboration from an informant.
Agitation	In marked contrast to the apathetic, slowed-down, retarded depression described above is the depressive state whose most prominent symptom appears to be a severe agitation. So stark is occasionally the contrast between the so-called agitated and the retarded depression that for some time a classification of depressive illness was based on this distinction. In the agitated depressions anxiety, tenseness, restlessness, anger and irritability are the salient features, and activity, albeit often purposeless, is in-	*M.S.E. 'Appearance and Behaviour':* Does the patient look anxious, tense? Is he restless, hostile, pacing the room nervously, wringing his hands, fidgety, unable to sit still, on the edge of the chair, scratching and rubbing at himself, sighing constantly, licking dry lips?
Anxiety, Anger, Irritability, Tenseness, and Restlessness		*M.S.E. 'Form of Talk':* Is the voice tense and shaking, the words catch-

...creased rather than diminished. Characteristically there is little decrease in energy or lack of drive, although the very considerable psychological angst suffered by the patient diminishes powers of concentration and makes work difficult.

The anger, irritability and frustration coupled with an often severe sleep disturbance, and the frequently retained energy levels make those suffering from agitated depressions particularly likely to succeed in a suicide attempt. The elderly seem prone to such depressions.

M.S.E. 'Mood':
'Do you feel tense, anxious, all "strung out"?'
'Do you feel cross with anyone in particular?'

Symptoms/Signs cont	Description	Diagnosis from M.S.E etc.
	In general the 'hardest' symptoms of depressive illness are the biological ones appearing against a background of depressed mood in a person who was not previously depressed. Severe sleep disturbance, marked anorexia and weight loss and significant diurnal mood variation are probably the most useful tell-tale symptoms and signs, particularly when there is a family or personal history of affective illness. They are useful, too, because they are not widely recognised as being evidence of depressive illness and help to differentiate between genuine cases and those who for some reason would exaggerate the severity of their condition.

Retardation, apathy and severe concentration impairment are also important indicators, as are marked agitation, suicidal ideation and feelings of hopelessness about the future. Any psychotic features of which the flavour is depressive should point firmly to the diagnosis of depression in the absence of 1st Rank symptoms of schizophrenia. Inappropriate and excessive feelings of guilt, worthlessness and of being a bad person are also of considerable diagnostic significance. In the absence of a cluster of the above symptoms depressive illness should be diagnosed with extreme caution. Depressive illness should always be treated by a psychiatrist. Anti-depressant tablets are the first-line treatment and are reasonably effective, especially in the endogenous type depressions. E.C.T is extremely effective in 70 per | |

cent of cases, especially in severe depressions in which retardation, delusions and weight loss are prominent features.

MANIA AND HYPOMANIA
(Phases of Bi-polar Manic-Depressive Illness)

Mania and Hypomania, differing from each other only in degree, are states of sustained, increased and abnormal excitement. In Bi-polar manic-depressive illness they may occur alone or interspersed with periods of depression. They are not difficult to recognise in others and the diagnosis is relatively simple once physical illness, alcohol and drug abuse and Schneiderian 1st Rank symptoms of schizophrenia have been ruled out.

The patient in the grip of a hypomanic mood swing often has little or no insight into the nature of his abnormality. Sometimes, although not always, it is a pleasant experience with the elevated mood increasing self-confidence and giving rise to feelings of intense well-being and euphoria. The hypomanic state, however, produces all sorts of problems for the individual and his family. Considerable damage is often done to his health, to his social and work situation, and to his finances – all bitterly regretted when the mood returns to normal. He must be treated, if necessary against his will, and we should all be in a position to notice the warning signs, at a stage perhaps when insight is not too greatly impaired and when psychiatric intervention can prevent precipitous decline.

Often there is a history of past episodes of emotional illness or of affective illness in the family, and these should be asked about in the Family and Personal History. Abuse of alcohol and drugs of the amphetamine type can result in hypomanic behaviour and should not be overlooked in the Psychiatric History. Stressful life events which may have precipitated the attack should be pinpointed and inquiries made about the previous personality, which is often of the 'up and down' or cyclothymic type.

Symptoms/Signs	Description	Diagnosis from M.S.E etc.

Usually Gradual, but Sometimes Sudden, Onset of Sustained Excitability, with Mood Elevation	Occasionally out of the blue, or sometimes in response to a stressful event or situation, the patient begins to exhibit uncharacteristic behaviour as the result of a significant and prolonged upswing of mood, which is both inappropriate and incongruous. It appears that periods of frustration are particularly liable to occasion hypomanic mood swings in the susceptible. Both happy and sad events can precipitate the elevated mood.
	
	The mood is cheerful and elated, euphoric, but it can change quickly to one of anger and irritation when the patient is thwarted or criticised. There is often an infectious jollity which communicates itself to those around – at first amusing, later tiring. The mood may be labile, changing suddenly to sorrow and sadness before swinging up again. Because he feels so good he comes to believe he is a wonderful chap and is correspondingly self-assertive. This may progress to the belief that he has unusual powers and talents and is a special person.
		M.S.E. 'Appearance and Behaviour': Is he restless, unable to sit still, over-active, uncontrolled? Is he untidy, his clothes in chaos, his appearance neglected?
		  Ask how he spends his day.
		  Get corroboration from an informant.
		
		M.S.E. 'Mood':
		'How are your spirits?'
		  Ask him to rate his mood on the 0–10 scale.

Symptoms/Signs cont	Description	Diagnosis from M.S.E etc.
Increased Energy, Activity, and Distractibility	Under the influence of his heightened mood the hypomanic engages himself busily in frantic, ceaseless, and often unnecessary and uncharacteristic activity – from dawn till dusk and, more worrying, from dusk till dawn. He is easily distracted, tending to leave jobs undone as he loses interest and takes up new ones. His energy appears boundless, and although he may look worn out he does not feel tired. Restless and more sociable than usual he has a prodigious appetite for work of all kinds.	*M.S.E. 'Appearance and Behaviour':* As above.
Sleeplessness	Long after everyone else has gone to bed the hypomanic is still busy, doing the housework, perhaps, or waking friends and business associates with 'vitally important' telephone calls in which harebrained schemes are mooted. His need for sleep seems to be considerably decreased as the routine of the household is severely disrupted.	*M.S.E. 'Appearance and Behaviour':* Does he look tired? Ask about sleep.
Pressure of Thought	The patient may have the feeling that his thoughts are coming to him faster than usual, are particularly clear and lucid, that his mind is working at high speed. At the same time he finds that each new idea seems to breed another, opening up new areas to be explored.	*M.S.E. 'Thought':* 'Do you have the feeling that your thoughts are coming faster than usual?'
Flight of Ideas	There is a loosening of associations and an increased tendency to distractibility in thought until the ideas which he expresses seem hardly to be related at all, tending to fly about all over the place. This may be progressive until each new word seems to suggest a	*M.S.E. 'Thought':* Does he keep to the point or is he discursive and incoherent?

new association and speech becomes peppered with rhymes and puns, which the patient finds hilariously funny.

Pressure of Talk	He becomes increasingly talkative, resisting or ignoring interruptions. The stream of talk becomes a raging river, the words pouring out in an exhausting rush with the subject changing from second to second. His voice may be hoarse from overuse.	*M.S.E. 'Form of Talk'*: 'Do you feel you have to keep talking?' Is he over-talkative, changing the topic frequently, distractible, commenting on insignificant events in the immediate environment?
Delusions	Delusions spring in an understandable way from the mood disturbance. Characteristically they are grandiose, the patient believing, perhaps, that he is Christ or some powerful and impressive figure – Royalty for example. He may feel that he can control and influence events, the weather, or the flights at London Airport. Paranoid delusions are not uncommon, the patient feeling that others are trying to harm him because they are jealous of his powers or his exalted rank. Delusions tend to be fleeting rather than fixed, the patient incapable of holding on to a particular idea for any length of time.	*M.S.E. 'Mood'*: 'Do you feel that you have any special and unusual powers?'

Symptoms/Signs cont	Description	Diagnosis from M.S.E etc.
Abnormalities of Behaviour	Feelings of omnipotence lead to marked irregularities of behaviour. There may be over-spending, uncharacteristic extravagance and generosity, and unwise business investments. There is increased interest in sex and often a loosening of inhibitions leading to unacceptably overt sexual behaviour and 'dirty' conversation. Disinhibition is reflected in odd and unusual clothes, an excess of make-up, in exotic headgear. Abuse of alcohol and other drugs is common. Appetite is voracious, but weight is not gained. The patient becomes increasingly sociable, making many new friends often met during drinking bouts in pubs. He may bring them home in the middle of the night to the irritation of his long-suffering family. He begins to neglect his appearance, having little time for such mundane matters as cleanliness or the changing of clothes. Singing, dancing and violent behaviour are quite usual as hypomania progresses to frank mania. Mania and Hypomania are susceptible to treatment. In the acute stage, excitement is well controlled by drugs such as Haloperidol. After two or more such episodes long-term therapy with Lithium may be required. It is an extremely effective although rather toxic drug, whose serum levels should be monitored closely.	*M.S.E. 'Appearance and Behaviour':* Note any unusual clothes. Is he disinhibited, swearing, using bad language etc?

Clinical Anxiety

This is discussed in the chapter entitled 'The Mind Sweets: Bitter Pills for Anxiety'.

Obsessive/Compulsive Illness

In this relatively rare condition the patient complains of persistent and recurrent thoughts, impulses to act, ideas or images, which he recognises as silly and without value and which he finds unpleasant. Compulsions consist of behaviour (or the avoidance of behaviour) admitted to be pointless and absurd which is performed with very great reluctance in order to relieve a state of unbearable tension. Only by indulging in the compulsive behaviour can the unpleasant psychological state be temporarily abolished. It is a hallmark of obsessive/compulsive phenomena that there is *resistance* to the obsessions and compulsions. Intense anxiety and depression are often occasioned by the purposeless thoughts and activities, and characteristically there is a severe disturbance in the ability to lead a normal

life. It is the extent of this disability, the degree of resistance and the bizarre inappropriateness of the thought content and the 'compelled' activity which clearly distinguish the condition from the innocent rituals of childhood – the avoiding of cracks in the pavement etc., and the recurring songs 'on the brain', the 'silly' desire to shout in church or the theatre which many of us from time to time experience.

Common compulsions involve cleanliness and washing rituals. The patient may have to wash his hands constantly, or clean the house for hours, perhaps a specific number of times. He may fear contamination by germs, going to ludicrous lengths to reduce the chance of contact with them. Checking, counting and ritualistic behaviour of all kinds may be seen in obsessive/compulsive illness.

Depressive illness very often co-exists with this condition and anxiety is often a prominent feature. Obsessive behaviour is also seen in schizophrenia and some organic states. In schizophrenia, in contrast to obsessive/compulsive states, insight into the ridiculousness of the thoughts and behaviour is usually absent.

Symptoms/Signs	Description	Diagnosis from M.S.E etc.
Obsessional Ideas	The patient becomes involved in often circular thought processes from which, despite the desire to do so, he seems unable to escape. He finds it unbearable to give up the obsessional ruminations until he has 'got to the bottom' of a *(cont.)*	*M.S.E. 'Obsessive/Compulsive Phenomena':* 'Do you ever have unpleasant and distressing thoughts?' 'Do you ever find that you seem to be compelled to keep thinking about something when you don't want to?'

Symptoms/Signs	Description	Diagnosis from M.S.E etc.
	problem, whose nature is usually such that it defies solution. Thus he may be obsessed with the meaning of life or the nature of infinity and other such philosophical conundrums. Such thought processes can result in a state of chronic doubt, the patient being unsure of everything from metaphysics to whether or not he turned off the tap.	
	Sometimes obsessional ideas take the form of words or sentences, often obscene and disgusting which invade consciousness, or of vivid images, or bizarre and only half-believed 'convictions' that by thinking of a situation it can be made to happen in reality. Obsessional impulses, the invariably resisted impulse to harm oneself or others – a newborn child, for example – are particularly distressing.	
Compulsive Acts	Checking, counting, washing and cleaning rituals are indulged in to the detriment of the patient's life, against resistance, in order to relieve great tension. Such actions are recognised as serving no rational purpose but are frequently occasioned by obsessional fears e.g. of knives or infection, or by other obsessional thoughts.	*M.S.E. 'Obsessive/Compulsive Phenomena'*: 'Do you ever find yourself compelled to do things that you would rather not do?' 'Do you ever find yourself having to repeat things, or check things even though you know it is ridiculous?' Discover the full extent of the disability and how much effort and time are involved in the observance of compulsive rituals.

M.S.E. 'Mood':
Assess the degree of concurrent anxiety and
depression.

P.E.
Exclude organic disease.

Anorexia Nervosa

As our preoccupation with dieting – evidenced by the phenomenal success of diet books – increases, so inexorably does the incidence of the life-threatening disease anorexia nervosa. A typical case might be described as follows, although few patients will resemble exactly this hypothetical 'classical' example.

A rather unhappy, middle-class adolescent girl stung, perhaps, by a remark about her weight from an influential figure, or merely falling in with her school friends, decides to experiment with one of the new diets. She is a hard working, conscientious, rigid, perhaps obsessional personality, tending to be perfectionistic, introverted and ascetic. She begins to lose weight fast (25 per cent of her body weight or more), but she continues to diet. Terrified of putting on weight, she becomes obsessive in her single-minded pursuit of thinness. Her whole attitude towards food and eating becomes highly charged – and she is at once fascinated and repulsed by food. It becomes her sole preoccupation and her knowledge of calorific values, cooking and all aspects of nutrition achieves encyclopedic proportions.

Simultaneously, in response perhaps to parental worries, she becomes devious and cunning, hiding food that she pretends to have eaten, avoiding carbohydrates and seeking out unfattening foods such as salads and diet colas. She begins to exercise frenetically in an attempt to burn off weight, and her considerable energy is in startling contrast

to her increasingly emaciated appearance. She may start to use laxatives and diuretics, or she may make herself vomit after eating. In hospital before being weighed she may drink large quantities of water, or load herself secretly with heavy objects in an effort to persuade the doctors that she is putting on weight when in fact she is losing it. As she gets thinner, and sometimes before weight loss is significant, her periods cease. She becomes painfully thin but denies the truth, which is only too obvious to everyone else. She seems literally to perceive herself in a special way as her own image of her body becomes distorted.

She actually believes she is bigger than she is. Her natural asceticism becomes more marked and she is increasingly callous towards her worried parents. Manipulating their concern she begins to control the family unit, punishing the often over-protective, dominant mother and the tradition-ally distant father with her relentless determination to get thin. Interest in sex, perhaps never marked, is now non-existent as she appears to cling to the pre-pubertal state, wearing clothes appropriate to a much younger girl and possibly even talking in a child-like voice.

Despite her success at dieting she is not contented and is frequently depressed, fearing all the time that she will lose control of her eating. Indeed occasionally she may 'binge' on food, inducing vomiting immediately afterwards, an activity she finds peculiarly disgusting.

As she loses muscle bulk and wasting becomes severe she may show fine 'lanugo' hair on her face and trunk. Her heartrate slows and blood pressure drops and her resulting in cold, blue extremities. There are various hormonal changes involving plasma cortisol, thyroid, diuretic and sex hormones. She is often constipated.

As weight declines further it is clear that she is physically ill, but she denies her predicament, having no insight into the extreme irrationality of her behaviour and attitude. She is dehydrated and electrolyte disturbance is severe, carrying with it the risk of coma and death.

5 per cent of those suffering from this disease will die. A further 25 per cent will not improve. About 30 per cent recover completely and approximately 30 per cent recover partially. 1 per cent or more of those suffering from anorexia nervosa are male. Diagnosis is based on the quantity of the weight loss, amenorrhoea (the loss of periods), and the extraordinary psychological attitude and behaviour towards food and eating. Significant wasting and emaciation in a teenage girl should always lead to questions about periods and dieting, when the symptoms described in this account may be elicited.

The Organic States

These organic states are included in the review of psychiatric diagnostic techniques largely because of the prevalence of dementing illness. However they are physical illnesses with clear-cut pathology and despite primarily

physicians as by psychiatrists.

Senile Dementia

The word dementia means literally 'loss of mind' and in the large majority of cases it consists of a global, progressive and irreversible loss of primarily intellectual function in one of previously unimpaired intelligence owing to organic deterioration of the brain associated with the ageing process. It is extraordinarily common. 5 per cent of people over 65 suffer from some significant degree of this disorder and above 75 the proportion is very much greater. All of us who have aged parents or relatives should be practised at noticing the signs an symptoms of this condition, so that we will be in a better position to understand, and to make allowances for, those we love. This is important because the dementing process is often insidious in onset.

Apart from dementia associated with ageing, generalised athero-sclerosis – itself age-related – is a common cause of the disease. Classically the onset is more sudden and there is usually physical evidence of heart disease or hardening of the arteries. These common degenerative dementias are untreatable, but others caused by vitamin deficiencies, drugs and poisons, infections, head injuries and tumours may be amenable to medical intervention.

Symptoms/Signs	Description	Diagnosis from M.S.E etc.
Loss of Memory	Memory for recent events is often the first intellectual process to be affected. Memory for distant events is usually well preserved in the early stages.	*M.S.E. 'Cognitive State: Memory':* 'Can you repeat this name and address?' Test immediately and after five minutes. 'Can you repeat this seven figure number?' One should be able to remember six or seven numbers forwards and four or five in reverse. Get them to repeat the Babcock sentence. 'The one thing a nation needs in order to be rich and great is a large secure supply of wood.' Test memory for distant events. 'Can you tell me where you live?' 'What did you have for breakfast/lunch/dinner?' 'Do you remember the events on the day you came into hospital?' Ask for details. 'Can you tell me about anything significant that has been going on in the world recently?' Ask name of Monarch, Prime Minister, President of USA, names of six large cities in UK, capitals of large European countries, dates of last world war.
Disorientation	As short-term memory fades there may be progressive disorientation. The patient may not know where he is or the time of day. There is a tendency to get lost. Confusion seems to increase at night when he may take to wandering about, because of his inability to sleep.	*M.S.E. 'Cognitive State: Orientation':* Ask the patient his name, address, the day of the week, date, month, year, time of year, time of day, morning or afternoon. Ask if he knows where he is.

Loss of Intelligence	Intellectual function fails progressively and the patient may misunderstand events that go on around him, drawing false conclusions that may become frankly delusional. Delusions of persecution are particularly common. He becomes increasingly unable to perform tasks, which previously presented no problem for him and this provokes considerable anxiety. Sometimes this anxiety explodes in a catastrophic reaction.	*M.S.E. 'Cognitive State: Intelligence and General Information':* Test the power of abstract thinking by asking the meaning of well-known proverbs. Ask 'Can you explain the difference between a child and a dwarf?' Ask patient to perform various sequential actions. Get him to write or to read aloud. Make allowances for the person's educational attainments.
Loss of Interest, Energy, and Vitality	The patient begins to withdraw in on himself, becoming increasingly self-centred and losing interest in his family and hobbies.	*M.S.E. 'Appearance and Behaviour':* Find out how he spends his time. Ask an informant if there has been any noticeable change.
Mood Changes	Typically there is increased lability of mood with emotional incontinence. Irritability, anxiety and depression are prominent. Later on there may be emotional blunting, the patient appearing cold and indifferent.	*M.S.E. 'Mood':* Ask about any change in mood.

Symptoms/Signs cont	Description	Diagnosis from M.S.E. etc.
Personality and Behavioural Changes	Personality change is often marked. The previously clean and tidy person begins to neglect his appearance, the placid, kindly man may become querulous and irritable. Disinhibition may result in extraordinary and uncharacteristic behaviour. There may be overt sexual behaviour, and possibly exhibitionism in a person who was previously the model of decorum. Eating efficiently may become a problem and there tends to be food on the clothes.	*M.S.E. 'Appearance and Behaviour':* Note the state of personal hygiene. Look for food stains etc. Is there a smell of urine? Ask an informant if there has been a change in behaviour.
Incontinence of Urine, Faeces. Loss of Mobility	As the illness progresses the patient becomes increasingly weak and immobile, unable to dress himself, to negotiate the stairs. He may become a fire risk as he potters about aimlessly at night. He becomes incontinent of urine and tends to smell of it. Eventually he may become incontinent of faeces as well. He begins to fall about the house, tripping over things and may break bones. He takes to his bed where immobility renders him prone to bed sores and chest infections. He loses interest in food and drink and may lose weight, easily becoming dehydrated. There may be signs of vitamin deficiency.	*M.S.E. 'Appearance and Behaviour':* Discuss the situation with an informant. *P.E.* Perform a thorough physical examination, and obtain a full medical history. *P.I.* Investigate with Full Blood Count, Urea and Electrolytes, Liver Function Tests, Serology for Syphilis, Skull and Chest X-Ray and E.C.G., Urine Culture and Microscopy, and Thyroid Function Tests.

Delirium

This organic condition is often known as acute brain syndrome in contrast to the chronic brain syndromes represented by the dementias. Drug abuse, infections with high temperatures, hormonal and metabolic disorders, delirium. In its mild form, during an unpleasant fever for instance, most of us have experienced the cotton-wool light-headedness and difficulty in getting one's thoughts together that in severe form represents the delirious state.

Symptoms/Signs	Description	Diagnosis from M.S.E etc.
Clouding of Consciousness	This is the cardinal feature of delirium. It may show itself as a mild perplexity or a profound confusion. Often these symptoms develop quickly and then fluctuate, alternating with periods of relative lucidity.	*M.S.E. 'Cognitive State: Attention and Concentration':* Assess the general level of consciousness and awareness. Does the patient respond to stimulus and to what extent? Does he co-operate and establish good rapport with the examiner or does he have great difficulty in concentrating, seeming to misunderstand simple instructions and requests? Is the attention easily aroused and easily held or is there considerable distractibility? Ask him to say the days of the week or the months of the year backwards. Ask him to do 100–7 serially, or 22–3.
Disorientation, and Memory Impairment	Unable adequately to process incoming information because of the clouding of consciousness, the patient is often grossly disoriented for time and place. As part of the confusional process, memory is usually impaired to some extent.	*M.S.E. 'Cognitive State: Orientation':* Test orientation for time and place. *M.S.E. 'Cognitive State: Memory':* Test memory for recent personal events.

Symptoms/Signs cont	Description	Diagnosis from M.S.E etc.
Illusions and Visual Hallucinations	Commonly in delirium the patient makes inaccurate perceptions of his environment (*illusions*), mistaking the furniture for people etc. Vivid and bizarre visual hallucinations may occur. He has considerable difficulty with his thought processes and may experience frank delusions, which are characteristically disorganised and chaotic as opposed to the more structured delusions found in schizophrenia.	*M.S.E. 'Thought':* Are the thought processes confused and incoherent? Are there unusual experiences related to the environment? 'Have you seen anything frightening or peculiar?'
Over-Activity and Irritability	Apprehension and fear are common emotions in delirium and account to some extent for the often frenetic if semi-purposeless activity of the delirious state. Insomnia is common. Occasionally there is a decrease rather than an increase in psychomotor activity.	*M.S.E. 'Appearance and Behaviour':* Is there evidence of over-activity and restlessness against a background of confusion, apprehension and fear in a patient who looks ill?
Symptoms and Signs of Physical Illness	A physical cause for delirium can usually be found during the physical exam in conjunction with pathological and other investigations.	*P.H. 'Personal History':* Get details of Past Medical History. *P.H. 'Use of Drugs or Medicines':* Any evidence of alcohol, or other drug abuse? *P.E.* Perform a thorough physical examination and take a full medical history. *P.I.* Investigate as indicated by physical exam and medical history.